The
Fighting Handgun

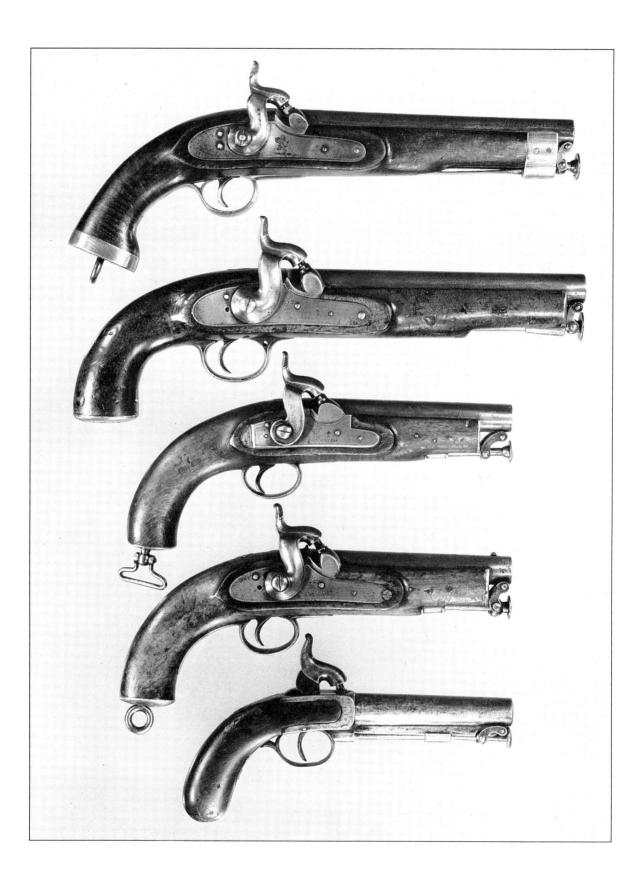

The Fighting Handgun

AN ILLUSTRATED HISTORY
FROM THE FLINTLOCK TO AUTOMATIC WEAPONS

Richard Law
and
Peter Brookesmith

ARMS AND
ARMOUR

ARMS & ARMOUR PRESS
An imprint of the Cassell Group
Wellington House, 125 Strand, London WC2R 0BB

Distributed in the USA by Sterling Publishing Co. Inc., 387 Park
Avenue South, New York, NY 10016-8810

British Library Cataloguing-in-Publication data:
A catalogue record for this book is available from the British
Library.

ISBN 1 85409 231 6

Edited and designed by Roger Chesneau/DAG Publications Ltd

Printed and bound in Great Britain

Title page photograph:
A selection of percussion pistols, all with captive ramrods.
Civilian carry pistols tended not to have a rammer at all, and
were reloaded by screwing the barrel off for easy access to the
chamber.

Contents

Preface

Most of the firearms reviewed in this book have been examined by the authors and in many cases used on the range. In most instances they were also photographed for us by Geoff Allen and can thus be identified from the picture credits.

Some notable exceptions include the French SACM M1935A, which has eluded us completely. Since we started on this project, there has not been one available for sale that we came across in the United Kingdom, either at auction or through the trade. The later MAB model D, conversely, has been much easier to obtain, numerous examples having been sold at auction in the last two years. Our reviews have thus included the MAB Model D, whereas our comments on the earlier pistol are necessarily sketchier because no example crossed our desks. There should be plenty of them about somewhere, yet they simply have not featured on the British market since 1992 or so. The only example we saw was in a museum, where staff are reluctant to allow pistols to be stripped and even less willing for them to be fired.

Other service pistols have been easier to obtain. Colt M1911 and A1 pistols are common enough, and military examples have recently been imported from Vietnam. Soviet Tokarev pistols likewise have been plentiful in Britain; Makarovs have not, so we have not, for example, been able to bring in the current variant made at Radom in Poland.

The earlier Radom pistol, which dates from 1935, has seen wider circulation in the UK, a few turning up at auction each year, and examples in museum collections include one in New Scotland Yard's Black Museum which was used by Günther Podola to murder Detective-Sergeant Raymond Purdy in 1959, and a pre-war example carried by Christine Granville throughout the war. She worked on escape lines, helping men from Poland to get to the Balkans, eventually fled to Egypt and was recruited by Britain's Special Operations Executive (SOE), who retrained her and parachuted her into France to work with F Section for most of the remainder of the war. Although we have had several of these pistols through our hands at various times, we did not have one available when completing this book.

Incidentally, almost all the firearms murders of London's Metropolitan Police officers since 1945 in which the firearm has been recovered were perpetrated with ex-military handguns. Britain's policy towards war souvenirs was that returning servicemen were not allowed to keep them—a short-sighted policy in our view as it meant that instead of including those weapons in the licensing system they were smuggled in and have been used in various crimes, including murder.

Many of the older firearms are available in reproduction form, and in most cases it was a recently produced example that we test-fired; in some instances, such as the London Colt Navy and the Wogdon duellers, we test-fired the originals. Old black powder weapons will not be harmed by use with black powder, provided they are properly cleaned afterwards. The main risk of damage to antiques, assuming that the barrel is still in good condition, is to the springs, which can give up eventually and may be hard to replace.

We were warned not to use black powder substitute in original firearms, which have iron barrels instead of the steel used for modern reproductions. Pyrodex is said to corrode old iron barrels and be harder to clean off. We are also aware of another problem attributed to black powder substitute, which is that, in storage, the water content (everything has a water content, even photocopier paper) can be reduced by evaporation, resulting in the grains shrinking and a greater charge then being measured by volume. All in all, a good-quality, genuine black powder seems to be the best bet, even though in Britain an explosives licence is required for its possession, in addition to any licence required for the firearm.

The market is changing, seemingly all the time. Walther's polymer P99, for example, appeared at the IWA—Germany's equivalent of the American SHOT Show—in March 1996 and a review example had not reached *Handgunner* magazine as this book went to press. We have still not had a Smith & Wesson Sigma to review (probably because of tardiness by their UK agents), and we have not seen a Glock to review for more than ten years.

Nomenclature

Some pistol designs have more than one name. For example, the Polish service pistol is known as either the VIS-35 or the Radom, and to Germans as the P 35(p). The British commonly called their service rifle an Enfield or a Lee Enfield, whilst Americans used to refer to the Mauser actioned P14 (in .303) and P17 (in .30-'06) as Enfields. In the commercial market, the Israeli IMI 9mm pistol is marketed in Europe as the Jericho, while in America it is the Baby Eagle.

We have tried to use the common names throughout, but, working and dealing with English firearms dealers as we have, it is the case that we have used English commercial names throughout also.

Acknowledgements

Recently made firearms that we have reviewed came to us via the UK *Handgunner* magazine, of which Richard Law is an associate editor, and we are grateful to Jan Stevenson and to those companies which supplied firearms to the magazine for review. Any apparent omissions from the current range of firearms reviewed will have been caused by their not being available to the authors during the preparation of this book. The photographs, except where individually credited otherwise, were taken by Geoff Allen.

We are both more than grateful to Anthony Law, who read the manuscript and sorted out our spelling and sentences for us, and Peter Brookesmith would like to thank Elizabeth Law for putting up with him while the project came together.

**Richard Law and
Peter Brookesmith**

From Cannon to Hand Gonne

The fighting handgun has always been a short-range weapon, used primarily for self defence on the battlefield or by civilians who want to go about their affairs without being hindered by footpads, highwaymen or, more recently, muggers. From this basic concept, other uses have developed for handguns, such as duelling and target-shooting. But throughout history the basic purpose of the fighting handgun has remained constant.

In this book we trace that history, setting the major milestones in handgun development in their historical and social context. We introduce firearms with anecdotes to show how they were used by their original owners, and we review their performance today—for it is still possible to acquire, and shoot, many of the weapons referred to in this book. Most of the twentieth century's fighting handguns can be had for quite modest prices. Those of earlier centuries are inevitably harder to find and are therefore more expensive, but they can still be seen in private collections and museums, or one can buy and use working reproductions of them.

Firearms have exerted a tremendous influence on the history of most countries. By understanding both the power and the limitations of firearms, one learns to understand that history a little better. For example . . .

Texas and the Six-Shooter

The revolver, and especially Samuel Colt's revolver, vies with the Winchester repeating rifle for the title of 'the gun that won the American West'. One may regret the fact today but, in the 1830s and 1840s the major obstacle to the pioneers spreading out from the eastern forests across the Great Plains was the American Indian. The Texas Comanche brave was a brilliant horseman, used to hunting and fighting from horseback. Armed for defence with a rawhide shield, and for the attack a 14ft spear, a bow and perhaps 50 flint- or steel-tipped arrows, he could ride 300 yards and shoot twenty arrows in the time it took a frontiersman to reload his rifle. The Texas Rangers, whose task it was from 1836 onwards to 'pacify' the land and hold the new Republic's border against Mexican incursions, first carried two horse pistols and a rifle—single-shot, muzzle-loading weapons. So feeble was this firepower compared with the Comanches' that it was not unusual for Rangers to ride thoroughbred racehorses—speed being the better part of valour in the circumstances.

According to legend, in 1830, when he was just sixteen years old, Colt whittled his first model of a revolver from wood, while serving before the mast on a voyage from Boston to Calcutta. By 1838 he had patents in the United Kingdom and the United States, and had organized a factory in New Jersey. By 1840 his invention had found its way into the hands of the Texas Rangers.

On 27 May 1844 Captain John C. Hays, with Captain Samuel H. Walker and thirteen Rangers, on patrol out of San Antonio, found themselves confronted by about 70 Comanches at Pedernales in Kendall County. Using their new six-shooters for the first time in anger, the Rangers killed more than 30 Indians in close fighting—so close that Walker was run through with a spear in the mêlée. Not long after this, Hays and another patrol were surrounded by Comanches at Nueces canyon. The Comanches swept around them on both sides, loosing arrows, while the Rangers took cover behind their horses. The Texans' usual tactics in this situation had been to leap into the saddle and flee once they had fired the one shot in their muzzle-loading rifles. The Rangers duly fired and remounted—and then went on to the offensive, Colts blazing.

'Never was a band of Indians more surprised than at this charge,' recalled one veteran. 'In vain the Comanches tried to turn their horses and make a stand, but such was the wild confusion of running horses, popping pistols and yelling Rangers that they abandoned the idea of a rally and sought safety in flight.' And a Comanche chief who was at Nueces said years later that he 'never wanted to fight Jack Hays and his Rangers again, [for] they had a shot for every finger on the hand'. In that battle he had 'lost half his warriors, who died for a hundred miles along the trail toward Devil's River'.

The Colt, in the words of two Texan officers, was 'the only weapon which enabled the experienced frontiersman to defeat the mounted Indian in his own peculiar mode of warfare'. The Texans, however, were the only major body of fighters who were impressed with the new-fangled device. The US Army failed to see its advantages, it was too expensive for most private citizens, and most frontiersmen were still working their way through timber, fighting Indian warriors on foot. Colt went bankrupt in 1842. In 1845 the Republic of Texas joined the Union. That same year the Texas Rangers joined a Union Army under General Zachary Taylor to defeat the Mexicans (who still laid claim to Texas), and showed the virtues of the Colt revolver in mounted warfare. Colt was hauled out of penury and given a contract to produce 1,000 weapons for $28,000. Modifi-

Top: The smoke from the smouldering match can get in your eyes while you aim.

Above: Smoke from both the vent and the muzzle obscures the view of the target. On this occasion it took four attempts to fire the gun—no fun at all if there were a hostile enemy bearing down.

cations suggested by Ranger Captain Samuel H. Walker—among them that the revolver should be heavy enough to be effective as a club when empty—produced an improved weapon that Colt named the 'Walker pistol'. Colt lost $3,000 on the deal, but the Texans made his guns world-famous. Their time had truly come.

The Treaty of Guadalupe Hidalgo in 1848 concluded the war and left the United States with a vast new tract of land that encompassed what is now California, Arizona, New Mexico, Nevada, Utah and parts of Colorado and Wyoming. All these events combined to create significant consequences for both American history and the development of the fighting handgun. Thereafter, as Walter Prescott Webb, the grand historian of the Great Plains, wrote, 'Those who went into the West went on horseback with six-shooters in their belts . . . Whatever sins the six-shooter may have to answer for, it stands as the first mechanical adaptation made by the American people when they emerged from the timber and met a new set of needs in the open country of the Great Plains. It enabled the white man to fight the Plains Indian on horseback.'

The Plains Indians, in due course, were to acquire repeating rifles which, perfectly suited to their superlative abilities as fighting horsemen, put them once more on equal terms with the desecrators of their hunting grounds and sacred places—but that is another story. And the six-shooter, for all its effectiveness, was still essentially a defensive weapon.

The Genesis of Fire-Power

When the sixteen-year-old sailor Samuel Colt began whittling a model for his first revolver from wood, the handgun was already a sophisticated and deadly weapon with over three centuries of development behind it. And, beyond that, it had taken more than 250 years from the first appearance of guns in thirteenth-century Europe for a practical fighting handgun to emerge—in the form of the wheel lock. This mechanism, as we shall see, was an enormous advance over earlier systems: it made the handgun a practical proposition, and made possible the building of easily portable firearms, capable of being concealed, for self-defence on the battlefield and on the street or highway.

In Saxony, in eastern Germany, cavalry tactics were developed around this new weapon. The earlier matchlock continued to serve military musketeers until it was finally superseded by the flintlock after the English Civil War (1642–49). Even then it remained in service and common use for succeeding centuries, fi-

nally passing into history in the twentieth century. However, the matchlock system was never of much use on a handgun; it was the wheel-lock, followed by the flintlock, ignition systems, and the tactics that developed to take advantage of their performance, from which the modern fighting handgun developed.

There could be no firearms without a propellant to send a bullet on its way, so the history of firearms necessarily begins with the development of a suitable propellent—gunpowder. This low-level explosive was not sufficiently earth-shattering at the time for anyone either to lay claim to its invention or to make a record of the achievement. Gunpowder itself—a mixture of saltpetre (potassium nitrate), sulphur and charcoal—was a development of earlier pyrotechnic substances that had been known about and used for centuries. The English Franciscan monk Roger Bacon described a mixture of 29.4 per cent sulphur, 29.4 per cent carbon and 41.2 per cent saltpetre in the year 1249, without saying what use it had.

As with many inventions, gunpowder was first used as a novelty—sparks, bangs, flashes and smoke. Anybody who has been close to gunpowder when it has been set off would have no trouble understanding its power as an explosive, and when used in ground charges its potential for launching a projectile becomes apparent: put a charge of gunpowder in a hole, cover it with a rock, light the fuse and see how high the rock travels. It is that simple.

Nobody knows when the idea of containing the charge in a pipe or tube in order to give control and direction to the projectile came along, but from the first clear reference in Western literature to gunpowder as an explosive in 1260 it was only a matter of time before experiments led to the development of the first guns. Within two generations the basic principles of using gunpowder and a pipe to launch a projectile became widely known. By 1326 guns were in fairly widespread use in European armies, but they were hefty, primitive artillery pieces, not sidearms or personal weapons of any kind.

They were still little more than crude, noisy and alarming, but the fact they were being experimented with so widely suggests that they had some effect. That effect may have been largely psychological—bolstering the confidence of armies with guns and shattering the morale of those who had to face them. Even so, if victory could be secured by routing the enemy through sheer terror, it was still a victory.

To put these early weapons in perspective, guns were in use in Europe some 100 years before Henry V of England fought his way through France to Calais via Agincourt in 1415. Guns would not have been practical arms in Henry's army, because they were just too cumbersome for the mobile fighting force he commanded (although there is some evidence that he had used them previously in the campaign, at the siege of Harfleur). Henry V was protected at Agincourt by archers, whose range would not be matched by firearms until the appearance of the American Colonial rifle of the 1700s. Nobody had a firearm capable of exceeding the archer's rate of fire before the invention of the early breechloaders just before the American Civil War (1861–55).

The French could conceivably have used cannon at Agincourt to prevent Henry's advance, as they held a static position blocking his route. There is no evidence one way or the other that they did or did not; without any evidence one would suspect that they had no guns, because the French battle plan was one of attack. If they had had artillery, they would have wanted the British to close to their range and would have fought a defensive battle.

Seventy years later, in 1485, guns seem to have been used at the battle of Bosworth, in which Henry Tudor's army defeated and killed Richard III. What appear to be stone round shot have been found on the battlefield. The choice of this oversized ammunition stopped guns developing into something more than terror weapons for some time. Medieval siege engines threw stone projectiles, and the earliest guns seem to have been designed for the same ammunition. This necessarily limited the guns themselves to being quite large, in order to cope with the size of the stones used. The guns were also somewhat fragile, for the amount of powder needed to lob rocks was considerable, and the required blast was often beyond the capacity of the metallurgy of the time. Guns often burst, and heavy stones could easily shatter, too. It was not until someone realised that a small projectile, launched with considerable force, would be more effective than a large, fragile, slow-moving rock, that any progress could be made—although, in turn, that could happen only when stronger guns could be built.

Stone-lobbing guns served well enough in medieval siege warfare, in which catapults had been used to lob rocks to smash castle walls. The cannon would do the same job, and had two advantages: it would last longer (unless it blew up), and it involved less physical effort to operate. The medieval catapult was made from green wood, for suppleness, and was normally built at the site of the siege, used there and then left to rot afterwards—for once the wood dried out the device lost its flexibility. The cannon could be prepared in advance and moved from operation to operation as required. However, guns of all types and sizes were to some degree at the mercy of the weather until an enclosed ignition system, impervious to wind and rain, was developed. This would be the key to the development of the firearm from the gun, and the eventual evolution of the fighting handgun.

Curious Ancestors
Progress in firearms development has always involved the propellant first. The gunpowder used for fireworks and pyrotechnics is made to a different formula from that used as the propellant in guns. Pyrotechnics use more sul-

phur to create a slower-burning, less explosive mixture. The formula for guns and explosives uses more charcoal—the fuel—to give the necessary force to propel missiles out of a barrel. The sulphur gets the mixture burning, and the saltpetre provides oxygen to sustain the flames. The efficiency of gunpowder has always been dictated by the quality of the charcoal, and the speed at which the mixture burns is controlled by the size of the gunpowder grains.

Below: Largest to smallest: original English dueller by Wogdon, circa 1810; original London Colt 1851 Navy; Beaumont Adams percussion 54-bore revolver; .450in Boxer War Department conversion of a Beaumont Adams; .455in Webley Mark V; .455in Eley Webley automatic pistol; 7.62mm Tokarev TT33 pistol; 9mm Makarov pistol.

The crucial part that propellants have played in the evolution of firearms has also meant that the fighting handguns we know today are not, as might be expected, thoroughbred descendants of other handguns. While all personal weapons have a touch of the cannon in their ancestry, handguns can boast both machine guns and rifles among their recent forebears. This is precisely because the powders developed for one configuration of weapon then inspired inventors to create ammunition around which, in turn, designers would create a suitable gun. The Smith & Wesson .44 Magnum revolver made famous by Clint Eastwood in the film *Dirty Harry* was built to accommodate a previously invented cartridge—a bright idea that in fact proved deeply uninteresting to most handgunners. So scarce was .44 Magnum hardware in 1971, when the

film was made, that Eastwood actually had to be content with a .41 Magnum with which to 'make his day'.

Early guns evolved slowly, improved by people whose names and exploits have not been passed down to us. By the middle of the fourteenth century in Europe it would have been possible to distinguish the ancestors of artillery from the ancestors of muskets, although no root for the fighting handgun had yet emerged. The basic ingredients were there— the gun barrel, the propellant and the projectile. What changed next was the method of ignition. The earliest guns were fired by way of a red hot iron pushed into the touch-hole to ignite the powder. This served defensive heavy guns well enough, but denied any prospect of mobility with smaller weapons.

By the end of the fourteenth century a mobile ignition system had come into use. This was the slow match—a piece of cord soaked or boiled in a solution of saltpetre, then dried. When lit, it would smoulder steadily and could be made ready to ignite the charge simply by blowing on the lighted end to clear the ash. This again served well enough for heavy guns used either for fixed defence or as siege attack weapons, but it was the development that first made a portable gun into a practical proposition.

The matchlock was a simple device: a burning match was clamped to a riveted arm called a 'serpentine' (from its snake-like form) that, by operating a simple mechanism, dropped the lighted match into a primer pan of powder, which then ignited the main charge. The matchlock weapon was still a cumbersome item and, despite spreading through Europe, India, eastern Asia and into Japan over some 500 years, was never refined very much. Typically over 5ft long, weighing in excess of 16lb and usually fired from a rest, the matchlock musket became a standard infantry weapon in Europe in the fifteenth and sixteenth centuries, gradually edging out the more efficient Welsh longbows and Continental crossbows.

Apart from their novelty value, matchlock muskets had the advantage of freeing gunners from static defensive positions where braziers could keep the irons hot to fire guns off. Guns were made smaller and lighter for mobility, and were now built to take lead ball ammunition. The use of lead for missiles was nothing new. The ancient Greeks had used lead projectiles in their slings to take advantage of the metal's heavy weight in comparison to the size of the shot. Lead offered the same advantage to musketeers. It was soft enough not to damage the bore, easy to cast because of its low melting point and, having been cast, did not shrink on cooling. It would be centuries before there was any need to improve on lead as the ammunition for small arms and, even today, lead remains an essential component in bullets.

The mobility of the smaller and lighter match-fired guns did lead to experiments with handguns, but nothing practical emerged. Artillery gained some limited mobility on wheeled carriages, and matchlock muskets began to challenge the supremacy of archers on the medieval battlefield. Not that the matchlock musket offered any improvement over archery—far from it. The English archer at his zenith in the fifteenth century was capable of firing an arrow some 300 yards with reasonable accuracy, and could do so some ten times a minute when the need arose. The musketeer, on the other hand, could make no better than two shots a minute, was more at the mercy of inclement weather, and could not shoot accurately over more than 100 yards. The matchlock lacked accuracy on three counts. The first two were the slow lock time and because of the smooth bore. However, the major problem with firing a matchlock is that the match on its serpentine has a long arc of travel. And the musket has to be kept aimed at the target while the serpentine moves. If the target is any distance away, one has to aim high, and doing that obscures the target with the barrel.

Enter the Spin Doctors

All the early muzzle-loaders were smoothbored; rifling came in about 1500 as a solution to the problems of range and accuracy that are endemic in smoothbored weapons. Rifling is simply the spiral grooving of a barrel. This imparts a spin to the projectile, which gives it stability in flight, in exactly the same way as a toy spinning-top is stabilized; as a result the projectile stays nose-on in flight. Rifling has another advantage: it allows an elongated bullet to be used. Whereas even a spinning ball loses speed quickly, because of air resistance, a cylindrical bullet with a streamlined nose creates an even flow of air around it as it spins. Accuracy as well as speed are dramatically improved.

Rifling was not an accidental discovery. The principle had already been used to stabilise crossbow bolts and the archer's arrows, whose angled flights (the vanes at the rear) made them spin in flight. Even the Ancient Greeks used to impart a spin to their javelins as they threw them. Cutting spiral grooves into the inside of a barrel to spin a tight-fitting bullet was the simple and obvious way to make a more accurate gun. The trouble was, a tight-fitting ball was not practical for military purposes because of the time it took to load. For over 300 years, the rifle was used solely for target-shooting and for hunting deer and wild boar.

So the military, more interested in high volumes of fire, kept with their smoothbore muskets. Because black gunpowder leaves sooty deposits in the barrel, the musket ball was made a little smaller than the diameter of the bore; otherwise, reloading a dirty musket would become impossible. This allowance for the fouling further compromised accuracy, as the musket ball effectively bounces randomly along the barrel and, when it leaves the muzzle, is biased away from its last contact with the bore. Moreover, the musket ball is spherical: when fired, it reaches maximum speed at the muzzle and thereafter begins to slow down and drop as wind resistance and gravity act on it. There comes a point, generally after about 100 yards, when wind resistance, acting unevenly on the musket ball, causes it to veer off line.

Sticking to Their Guns

Given these various disadvantages, there must have been some good reason why medieval armies persisted in using muskets. The basic answer, apart from the psychological benefit of flash and bang, has to do with the amount of practice needed with bows and with guns in order to use them reasonably well. While an archer at Agincourt in 1415 could achieve ten good hits a minute at up to 300 yards, developing the necessary skill required a lot of practice. The trajectory of an arrow is curved like a rainbow, so even at short ranges archery involves aiming high and dropping the arrow on to the target. The drop for a longbow at 200 yards is over 30ft, so to make his arrow travel that distance the archer must shoot still higher to compensate. Maximum range is achieved at around 30 degrees above level. To be proficient with a longbow, one has to be able to estimate both distance and the firing angle accurately, and that calls for a lot of practice.

Practice with longbows was compulsory on Sundays in medieval England for yeomen, although the observation of this law declined as time went by and guns became more common. Muskets had a shorter range and a much slower rate of fire, but they were much simpler to learn to shoot accurately because the bullet drop was less than an arrow's drop at similar distances. At 100 yards, the drop would be less than 2ft, so anyone in range could be aimed at, and still hit, albeit lower than the musketeer might have hoped.

The matchlock gave troops some mobility, and lead ammunition allowed gunmakers to reduce the size of their products, but the weapons were far from being handguns as we know them. Nor were they long arms designed to be fired from the shoulder. They were 'hand gonnes': the stock extension rested on the firer's cheek. All that varied was the barrel length—shorter ones (to save weight and give faster handing) for mounted troops, longer ones for infantry. All this by and large passed the civilian market by. Gentlemen carried swords and hunted with crossbows. Yeomen were armed with longbows, with which they had to practise, and carried a dagger. In military service they might also carry a sword and buckler—a small shield—for defence.

The missing ingredient at this point in history was a more reliable and portable ignition system and, as the fifteenth century came to an end, one emerged—the wheel-lock.

ONE

Of Peace and Honour

People made fire the hard way until they found that a piece of flintstone struck against steel made sparks that would set a suitable material alight. For centuries before matches were invented, people carried a tinder box, containing flint, steel and tinder, from which to make fire. Tinder is no more than a dry material that will smoulder when the sparks hit it—usually charred cotton rag or dried moss. The material had only to get hot enough to light a candle, which would maintain the flame for other purposes.

Leonardo da Vinci's notebooks of the early 1500s include what may have been an attempt to mechanise the tinder box, but it seems that it was in Germany at about the same time that a working wheel-lock mechanism first appeared. Although tinder boxes used flint to make the sparks, any other stone will do, as long as it sparks easily when struck. The wheel-lock is a steel wheel on a clockwork spring, which is wound up with a key. The stone is in contact with the wheel. When the trigger is pulled, the spring unwinds and the wheel spins rapidly, showering sparks into a pan to ignite the priming powder, which then sets off the main charge in the chamber. Flint does not work well in this system because it tends to shatter against the wheel. So the stone associated with the wheel-lock mechanism is iron pyrites, often called 'fools' gold'. It works better than flint in a wheel-lock as it is softer.

But flint is more common and so cheaper to obtain. Wheel-lock guns as first developed were, as one might expect with a new invention, for the top of the market, and were bought by the rich as a self-indulgence. But the wheel-lock did put practical firearms

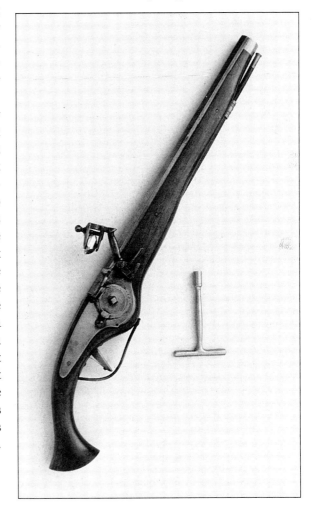

Right: Wheel-lock pistol, with the key that was required to wind it up before firing.

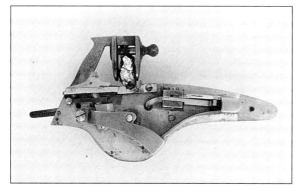

Top: Wheel-lock pistol. The wheel is external to the lock on this example, and can be seen in the bottom of the priming pan. The cock, containing a piece of pyrites, can be lowered on to the sliding pan cover after priming powder has been put in the pan. Once the mechanism is wound up, the firearm is then portable, requiring only the pan cover to be slid forward and the trigger pulled for a shot to be fired.
Above: Detached from the gun, the wheel-lock's springs can be seen on the inside of the lock plate.

within reach of the gentry for the first time, and made shooting fashionable. The first wheel-lock guns were produced with hunting and the pastime of target-shooting in mind. Surviving examples are often very ornate, as befitted their intended market. Self-defence came later, and warfare last as a use for the new invention. A mechanical weapon made entirely by hand, with hand tools, it still represented a considerable advance on the match-lock. The wheel-lock was always ready for ac-

tion, and did not depend on a hot iron or a burning cord to make it fire. Truly portable for the first time, handguns now appeared in a refined form for the aristocracy. Demand for them was fuelled primarily by social reasons.

Britain and Europe in the sixteenth century formed the Old World. Communications were gradually improving as roads and ports, neglected since the Roman Empire collapsed, were restored and improved. International trade brought advances in shipbuilding and cargo-handling, and the profits from such activities persuaded people with money to invest in overseas business ventures. Columbus had led the way to a New World that reputedly contained fabulous riches. Exploiting those resources involved travelling. On land, at the time of the Crusades, travelling meant walking or riding a horse. But as roads developed to let businessmen get to the ports and cities where their fortunes could be put to work, the gentry took to riding in carriages to get about.

A man mounts his horse from the left so that he does not get entangled with the sword hanging on his left side. As carriages became the fashionable way to travel, so swords gradually gave way to pistols—guns designed to be used with one hand, without being supported at the shoulder. People riding in a carriage would rather have a smaller, more portable weapon than a sword. Crossbows made sense for self-defence in the circumstances, but they were very bulky. The demand for a portable weapon stimulated the development of suitably compact wheel-lock guns, and then other mechanical ignition systems, to make personal firearms both practical and widespread.

Defending Life and Virtue
For the traveller, a brace of pistols on his person, a blunderbuss in the hands of his coachman and a sword in his luggage (as long as the fashion for wearing them continued) were probably sufficient insurance for most eventualities. Then, as now, a man who was ready,

THE WHEEL-LOCK AT WAR

Wheel-lock firearms remained very much a tool of the gentry, simply because of their cost. But in Saxony the government equipped the cavalry with them, and tactics for the use of firearms appeared for the first time on the battlefield. The Reiters (troopers) of the German Emperor Charles V (1519–55) made good use of their wheel-lock pistols by forming up into ranks sixteen deep and charging the enemy. As each rank came within range it would fire its pistols, each man carrying two of them, and then wheel to right or left as required. Each succeeding rank would do the same, while the retiring ranks would reload as they rode to the rear. The idea was that by the time the last rank had charged and fired on the enemy, the first rank would be ready to charge again, so maintaining a more or less continuous fire upon the enemy.

willing and able to defend himself and his property would be passed over by criminals in favour of a softer target.

A firearm offers an additional benefit in any encounter, which was recognised right from the start and holds true to this day. It is remote control. A gentleman equipped with pistols can outreach a thug armed with a knife or club. As firearms became more common among travellers, highway robbery went into decline until the technology available to villains caught up, which it usually did by becoming cheaper.

Despite their expense, wheel-lock pistols enjoyed considerable success in the sixteenth and seventeenth centuries among those who could afford them, and signalled the start of the decline in sword-carrying among the most affluent. A gentleman would probably have looked a little out of place without a sword in 1745, and similarly rather out of place with one thirty years later. Fashion always carries some influence, and if the fashion for wearing a sword was waning, something had to be carried in its place. Handguns became smaller and daintier in order to suit polite society and its dress codes.

In the process, they brought about another social revolution. Women could now arm themselves with these handy but perfectly effective weapons, and could venture out without need of the protection of a man and his sword. The function of any firearm carried for self-defence is merely to encourage others to mind their own business. A lady needs a firearm to encourage gentlemen to remain gentlemen and villains to remain at a respectful distance.

As the sixteenth century progressed, European society became more mobile, sociable and civilised. This turned the wheel further: more roads were improved, good ones became better, and carriages, ships and ports improved. As these means of communication became more efficient, they encouraged more travel, created more business and generated more wealth. The traffic in goods was matched by

Right: The early wheel-lock pistol is about as long as a modern sawn-off shotgun, and about as clumsy. Nevertheless, on the range, reasonable scores can be obtained—as long as the scoring rings are big enough.

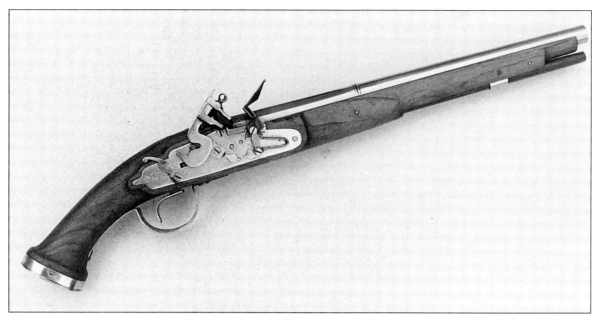

trade in ideas, and ideas about firearms were no exception.

Once the problem of mechanical ignition had been solved, other minds began to address the matter and come up with what they thought were better solutions. The next new development in handguns was a forerunner of what we now call the flintlock. First seen in the Low Countries, it initially represented a more utilitarian ignition system—a mechanical tinder box that also fired a weapon, and used the cheaper and more readily available flint instead of fools' gold.

The firing spring was compressed by cocking the hammer, which contained a piece of flint in a pair of jaws. When the trigger was pulled, the hammer flew forwards to impact the flint on a steel, showering sparks into priming powder beneath. The idea caught on quickly: most European countries had local variations on this theme by the end of the sixteenth century.

We now call these earliest flintlock mechanisms 'snaphaunce' locks, from the original *schnap-haan* (pecking-hen). In the British version, the 'cock' (hammer) with a flake of flint

HOARY DEFENCE

In 1515 an interesting court case recorded for posterity a defence to a wounding charge. The defence was, 'I didn't know it was loaded!' The plea has been used many times since throughout history by people who tested whether a firearm was loaded or not by pulling the trigger. This has been a safety problem more or less since triggers were invented.

In the words of the *Chronica Neuer Geschicten*, 'In the year of our Lord 1515 on the day of the Three Holy Kings [Epiphany, i.e. 6 January], there was a certain young citizen of Augsburg in Constance who invited a certain handsome whore. And when she was with him in a little room, he took up a loaded gun

in his hand, the lock of which functioned in a certain way that when used, it ignited itself and so discharged the piece. Accordingly he trifled with the gun and he shot the whore through her chin, so that the ball passed out through her neck.'

This incident cost the citizen, one Laux Pfister, the whore's medical bill of 37 florins, compensation to her of 40 florins and a pension (presumably in compensation for her reduced beauty) of 20 florins a year, plus court costs. Both the gentleman concerned and the writer were clearly surprised that the pistol could go off in the circumstances—without being lit first!

Left: Indian reproduction, made by the Bombay Gun Company, of an English doglock pistol of circa 1610.
Right: This close-up of the lock on a reproduction English doglock pistol shows the dog catch holding the hammer at half cock. This early safety catch has to be taken off before firing.

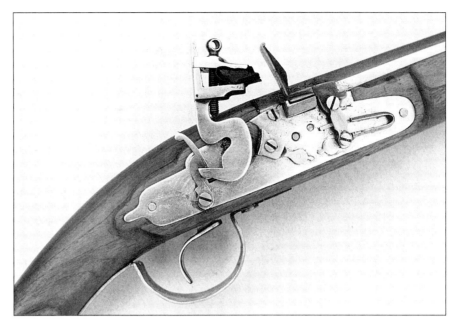

in its jaws struck a hinged steel plate above the priming pan to shower sparks for ignition, while the sliding pan cover was moved out of the way by the movement of the cock.

In Spain another version evolved. The pan cover and steel were confined into an L-shaped piece, simplifying the design. In about 1600 the French combined the one-piece steel and pan cover with an improvement to the internal mechanism of the lock. This was the perfected form, known as the French lock. The flintlock continued to be made in this form for over 200 years.

John Bull's Doglock

Early in the seventeenth century, English makers developed a unique version of the French lock. This snaphaunce mechanism became known in Britain as the 'doglock', and it had possibly the first mechanical safety catch ever on a firearm. The dog catch, which appears on the lock plate behind the hammer, slips on to the hammer when it is at half-cock to prevent it slipping off the sear. Without it, the firearm could 'go off at half-cock'.

This typically English invention dealt with the possibility that the hammer might be shaken off the half-cock notch. For the hammer to be fully forward, where the spring is most at ease, the frizzen plate is also forward and the pan open to the elements. Apart from being undesirable when the pistol is loaded, this also meant that the pistol could not be primed.

Once primed, the pistol has to be carried at half- or full-cock. The English 'safety' dog-catch made the weapon safer at half-cock than its European counterparts, although no half-cocked firearm was completely safe. There is a modern equivalent of the dog-catch—in better quality shotguns, which have a safety sear to catch the hammer if it is shaken off its sear, as may happen if the gun is dropped.

Curiously, the doglock lasted only a few decades in Britain. The English Civil War (1642–48) drove the king and his supporters into exile for some eighteen years. After the restoration of the monarchy in 1660, the doglock fell into disuse. The French form was used instead, presumably because so many Royalists had spent so many years in France. When they came home, they wanted French-style locks on their guns. That such a fundamental change occurred at all shows two things: how few people could afford modern firearms at the time, and how influential they were.

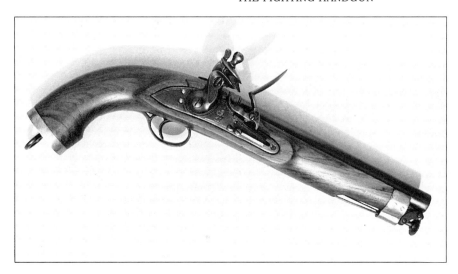

Left: Lancer flintlock pistol of around 1795. Note the sturdy lanyard ring on the base of the grip, and the captive ramrod.
Right: A Scottish all-metal flintlock pistol by John Campbell of Doune, circa 1745. The Scots favoured metal stocks on their pistols, seeming to like using them as clubs as well as firearms. (Sothebys)

What we now distinguish as the flintlock had arrived. What sets a flintlock apart from its ancestors is that the springs are inside the lock plate, leaving just the priming pan, with its combined pan cover, 'frizzen' or steel, and the hammer or cock on the outside. The earliest surviving guns on this pattern are French and date from the early seventeenth century.

When the English Civil War between king and Parliament (led by Oliver Cromwell) started in 1642, most troops were still armed with matchlocks. Officers and gentlemen might have had a wheel-lock or doglock pistol or two about them. But, as the war wore on, Cromwell's New Model Army started to sport the first military flintlock shoulder weapons. Another century would pass before the flintlock was in universal use as the military and civilian firelock. By 1750 the wheel-lock, the older doglock snaphaunce and the matchlock had all been replaced by the flintlock.

This is not to say that individuals were no longer using the older weapons. Although a system may no longer be manufactured, it remains in use for many years afterwards: that is certainly the case with firearms. One reason why so few old firearms have survived into the late twentieth century is that they were used until they wore out and then they were thrown away. Once flintlock technology was established, the new lock could be fitted to older matchlock weapons. Worn-out long arms were often cut down to finish their working lives as pistols. Only those that, once superseded, were put away before being used to destruction have passed down to us as antiques. Most of those survivors that fetch high prices now were expensive when new, and the most sought-after antique firearms are often of good quality. Some are very ornately decorated; others have the utilitarian simplicity that suits their function—and none more so than duelling pistols.

Law, Honour and Duelling

Until very recently in Europe, the defence of a man's honour and that of his family, and the protection of his property, were mainly his personal responsibility. A man of means could gather about him retainers, and in feudal times these men-at-arms could be called upon by the monarch to defend the realm in time of war. For the rest of the time their function was to preserve the peace, safety and wealth of their master. In the fifteenth and sixteenth centuries, as medieval chivalry and crusades gave way to the widening horizons of explorers and the commercial exploitation of newly discovered areas of the globe, the law took more of a hold on daily life.

The 'common law'—one law for all the people—developed as Parliament and sovereign

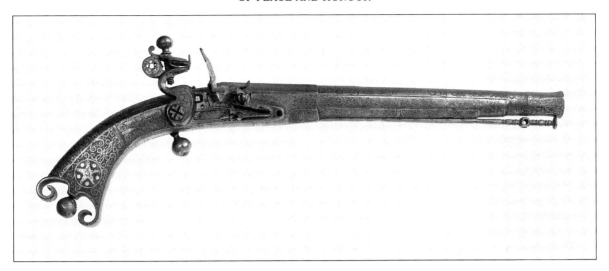

passed laws to regulate society and appointed persons to see that those laws were obeyed. These had nothing to do with public safety: most medieval laws were designed to ensure that the Crown received a share of any wealth generated by the king's subjects. Nothing much has changed on that score. Tax collectors were a fact of medieval life, just as they are now and just as they were when Jesus of Nazareth recruited one to his band of disciples. The responsibility for public safety was left to the county sheriffs, whose duty was to keep the roads safe and free from banditry. Then, as now, it was a case of looking for culprits after a criminal act was committed. Then, but much less so now, the travelling citizen was expected to look after himself during the actual attack.

For defending his carriage a gentleman's brace of pistols would do nicely; and for defending his honour the same pistols would do just as well. For, once a practical fighting handgun had emerged, there was naturally a tendency to use it for duels as well as for self-defence. The previous duelling weapon of choice was the sword. A sword, like a bow, called for considerable practice if best use was to be made of it. As a man got older, his skill with the sword would begin to decline along with his health, strength, and agility. A very experienced older swordsman would therefore always be at some disadvantage if confronted by a younger opponent. The appeal of the pistol as an alternative weapon in such cases is clear enough.

The growing preference for pistols was also a matter of fashion. From the mid-eighteenth century, carrying swords became a thing of the past, and duelling with pistols became more common. In 1745, at the time of the second Jacobite uprising—that of 'Bonnie Prince Charlie'—it was normal for a gentleman to have his sword buckled on; by the time the American War of Independence started in 1776 it was not. The duel became a flintlock affair and lasted into the nineteenth century, before it fell into disrepute as a way of solving personal disputes and was replaced by laws and lawyers.

Duels occurred when the courts were unlikely or unable to offer a remedy. From about 1650 until about 1750, European society was fairly stable. Most people lived at the level to which they were born, and had to spend their lives maintaining their position in society. It was difficult to improve one's position in society except by outstanding talent and possibly by marriage, but comparatively simple to lose it. Maintaining one's place in society—particularly high society—demanded that one maintain one's honour, and honour could not be guaranteed without fighting for it in certain circumstances. Duelling thus inevitably became a companion to the rule of law.

Broadly speaking, the courts dealt with common-law crimes such as murder and robbery as well as civil matters such as debt. Duelling regulated the behaviour that the law did not. This included sexual matters—a man would have to challenge his wife's adulterer if he caught him, or any man he caught *in flagrante delicto* with an unmarried daughter. Duelling was also the response to anyone who was deliberately insulting. It could also be the solution to comparatively simple matters like cheating at cards when there was not enough evidence to take the miscreant to law.

A man who found himself called out could try apologising, and that might be the end of the matter if there had been a misunderstanding. It might very well be the case that financial compensation could be offered to the offended party, but sometimes blood is thicker than money. It might be enough to turn up at the time and place appointed for the duel. If that did not work, firing first and into the air ('deloping') effectively gave the duel to the insulted party and satisfied his honour, although he could still take his shot if he wished and the deloper would have to stand his ground, hoping to hear the shot without pain.

Comedy and Tragedy

There were occasional moments of farce. One such, although it had a gory ending, occurred in May 1808 in Paris. One Monsieur de Grandpré discovered the startlingly named Mademoiselle Tirevit, a dancer, tenderly administering favours upon the no less aptly named Monsieur de Pique that he considered should have been bestowed upon his own person (she was, after all, de Grandpré's mistress) and naturally demanded satisfaction. Announcing themselves to be of elevated mind, the pair took to the air in hot air balloons, which ascended to some 2,000ft above Paris, whereupon the antagonists began to defend their good names with blunderbusses. De Pique fired first, to no effect. De Grandpré discharged his weapon, and holed his opponent's balloon. The contraption fell rapidly from the sky, crashed into a rooftop and splattered Monsieur de Pique and his hapless pilot across the tiles.

Two years earlier England had witnessed a no less ludicrous scene, although without affording such an opportunity for delightful puns. The Member of Parliament for Evesham, Mr Humphrey Howarth, when called to the field of honour by Lord Barrymore, was much concerned that pieces of his clothing might be driven into the wound should he be hit. He had good cause for concern: he had served as a surgeon in the East India Company's private army and had seen the infections that could result—and, no doubt, being a doctor, had no wish to put himself at the mercy of others of his profession. At the appointed time and place, therefore, Howarth disrobed himself entirely. Lord Barrymore, on witnessing this spectacle, declared that it was too ridiculous to take on an opponent who was in his natural state, and departed. Whether from outrage or mirth history does not record, but the pair never met again.

One matter of honour was not an occasion at all, but a series of them stretching over nineteen years. Joseph Conrad based a story on it, which was filmed in the 1980s. In 1795, one notorious duellist, a Captain Dupont—probably a psychopath, in today's jargon—serving in Napoleon's army, was refused entry to a dinner given by his commanding general. The general's unfortunate messenger, a Lieutenant Fournier, promptly received a challenge. Neither ever quite defeated the other in any of their many meetings, or at least not sufficiently for the mad Dupont to stop hounding Fournier. Their last duel, in 1814, took place in a wood, with each party armed with a pair of horse pistols. Dupont hit on a surreal ruse: poking a pistol from one side of a tree and his hat from the other. Fournier fired both his pieces, harming nothing and no one, and was then confronted by the smirking Dupont, who let him go with the warning that Fournier's life remained forever in his hands. Dupont abandoned his one-man vendetta when he discovered other pleasures on getting married.

Satisfying the Demand

As the fashion for carrying swords declined, so appeared the first dedicated duelling pistols—smooth-bored, without sights, perfectly balanced and with 'hair' or 'set' triggers. These guns need a heavy charge of powder to shoot accurately, which they will certainly do. With a calibre of around .50in, they are also deadly at the duelling range of twenty paces. Modern trials show that light loads invariably cause the ball to fly erratically at quite short range, which may, by accident or design, have been a way of satisfying honour without dying at the hands of what passed in those days for a doctor. It is certainly interesting that the powder measures supplied with these pistols were

often smaller than needed for a truly accurate shot.

In the early days sights were not provided on duelling pistols as taking a deliberate aim was disallowed—and any infraction of duelling etiquette was likely to result in a charge of murder. A snap shot had to be taken while swinging the muzzle across one's opponent. We found that starting muzzle-down and firing while swinging up was the most effective, giving a low strike on the target each time: chopping down from a gun-up position inhibited an instinctive shot because the firearm obstructed the view of the target until it had passed the point at which one should have fired.

'Oiks' could not fight duels because they had no 'place' to defend, so duelling was confined

Below: 16-bore overcoat pocket pistol by the London maker Durs Egg. A quality pistol for a gentleman, and probably one of a pair, or at least one of a brace.

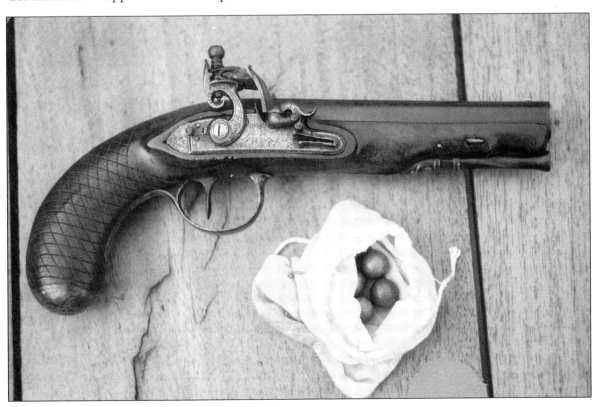

to the higher strata of society. Thus the money was there for any gunmaker who could refine the fairly slow-firing and cumbersome military and travellers' pistols of the era. In the second half of the eighteenth century gunmakers put enormous effort into making duelling pistols that fired as quickly and accurately as possible. The quick, snap shot from the smooth-bored barrel, giving a fair chance of a hit to the firer, and a fair chance of a miss for the target, was the order of the day.

The flintlock mechanism went through a continual process of improvement during the nearly 200 years that it remained the principal ignition system on handguns. From the earliest flintlocks in the early 1600s it improved steadily as metallurgy improved, springs became more efficient and lock times became faster. Early refinements included a swivel link between mainspring and tumbler, and a roller bearing for the pan's feather spring. 'Following through'—keeping the sights aligned *after* the cock has been released and the shot fired—is vital to accuracy with a flintlock pistol, and a 'hair' or 'set' trigger that releases the cock at the slightest pressure is ideal for this. It lets the shooter concentrate on maintaining the aim and forget about the mechanics of letting off the shot.

An Example by Barton

We tested a duelling pistol made by Barton, who was a late partner of Robert Wogdon, London's most renowned duelling-pistol maker. It had all the refinements and superb craftsmanship that made these pistols famous, including a set trigger and excellent sights. Made before the weapons became interchangeable with target arms, it was a transitional piece—half-stocked, and sporting the lighter barrel and better balance of the pure duelling pistol, with a single set trigger and a safety catch that secured the lock at half-cock.

A large roller is fitted to the pan's feather spring, and it works against a distinct hump on the pan's cover arm to give a very strong

(and hence reliable) over-the-centre action. A long, curved neck between the pivot and the pan cover lifts the cover quickly away once the flint strikes the steel.

This piece was meant for serious work: the weather could not be allowed to interfere in a matter of honour, and the pan itself is separated from the rest of the lock by channels designed to take away any raindrops falling on to the face of the steel. The pan cover has a raised lip, too, to stop water entry, and it is very precisely fitted to the barrel for further waterproofing.

The Barton's trigger was set so light that it released at the slightest touch. Using Elephant powder, with FFFFg for the primer and FFFg for the main charge, the shot seemed to go off instantaneously. There was none of the perceptible delay often found in less refined flintlocks between touching the trigger and the charge firing. With a suitable charge, the piece could easily, and repeatedly, hole a playing card at twenty paces. Such pistols show how much could be achieved even within the technology available to their makers.

Defending Honour Becomes Disreputable

The development of the dedicated duelling pistol around 1780 was followed by the evolution of further specialised types of handgun. The overcoat pocket pistol appeared, for example, and around 1810 this was followed by the heavy-barrelled duelling target pistol. (The rules had altered by then, and a deliberate aim was allowed.)

Prior to the appearance of the dedicated duelling pistol, most flintlock handguns were of the 'horse pistol' type, with a large grip, often raked back (making them look like cut-down muskets), generally of quite large bore (more than .60in) and usually without sights. It was rare, as it remains today, to use a pistol at any great distance. Target-shooting at galleries became popular once the technology to deliver a bullet accurately became commonplace in firearms. Rifling a barrel for accuracy,

A SHOT AT SHAKESPEARE

Early hand gonnes had a reputation for failing. William Shakespeare lived during the reign of Queen Elizabeth I and would have known veterans of the Navy who fought the Spanish Armada in 1588. He would have known that even by that date the wheeled guns used on ships were not particularly effective.

The problem was that it is easy to underestimate distances over water. Most of the exchanges of fire during the running battle up the English Channel were at longer distances than the English guns could effectively shoot over. The Spanish fared even worse: underwater archaeology off western Ireland, where some Spanish ships were wrecked, has revealed evidence about the Spanish guns, including one with the bore so far off centre that it would have been dangerous to fire.

Spanish cannon balls were water-cooled, which weakened them so much that they may have shattered on being fired. Some Spanish guns were on large wheeled field mounts, which would be unsuitable for use on ships—they tend to jump when fired, rather than roll back as do the small-wheeled can-non. The guns of the English fleet outclassed the Spanish Armada and prevented the Spanish invasion plans from succeeding.

Shakespeare may have alluded to this historic lack of reliability in guns and hand gonnes in *Macbeth* (Act V, Scene IV), when Malcolm says, 'Cousins, I hope the days are near at hand when chambers will be safe.' Malcolm could be saying that it would be nice if everyone could sleep safe in their beds, but Macbeth had not terrorised people outside his immediate control. One scholarly interpretation suggests that he is referring to the dubious qualities of the early hand gonnes, some of which were breech-loaded.

It is a shaky interpretation, relying as it does on the assumption that Shakespeare's knowledge of history was sufficiently scrambled for him to be placing the earliest hand gonnes in the eleventh rather than the thirteenth century. The question really, as the line is a throwaway introductory remark, is what sense it would have made to his audience, and to that nobody knows the answer.

a technique that had been around from the late fifteenth century for target and sporting rifles, was not used in pistols until the nineteenth century. Externally, target pistols looked quite like duelling pistols, and Continental, if not British, duelling rules allowed rifled barrels anyway.

The wars with France that occupied Britain for more than two generations from the mid-eighteenth century had a profound effect on society. The need in the armed forces for natural leaders became widely understood. Men of ability and courage soon outstripped the supply of gentlemen officers, and men from the ranks on land and at sea were promoted to officer ranks to fill the gaps and to prosecute the war against France to the best of their ability. Derided by genteel society as 'temporary gentlemen', these men served Britain's military interests in the front line, many making their fortunes in the process, from prize money and rewards.

When the war ended in 1815 with victory over Napoleon at the Battle of Waterloo, these men were at a loose end. No longer needed in military service, some drifted off into the far-flung corners of the British Empire or the New World in search of adventure and new riches. And some settled in London, earning a living as social parasites. Men who have been in battle have little to fear from those who have not, and it became a simple matter to call out real gentlemen in a duel and accept a payment in lieu of going through with it. Some people just like fighting, and, with duelling legal, there were, in the post-war period, altogether too many duels over trivial matters. Society in the end put a stop to it, thus paving the way for two major developments—the extension of the judicial system and, in 1829, the first policemen to feed defendants into that system.

Duelling, for all its faults, had served to keep society polite and civilised. History can judge whether the current system of police and lawyers is any more effective or not. It was at this point in history that the next step in firearms development was made: the percussion cap appeared.

TWO

Shooting Rain or Shine

The flintlock system, efficient though it was, was susceptible to the weather. It was difficult to prime the pan with loose powder in any kind of wind, and obviously the powder would get wet if it was raining. Neither of these problems mattered as much in a duel or in warfare as one might think. A duel could be postponed, and warfare is as much about manoeuvring as it is about shooting. Artillery has been the main cause of casualties in wars between manoeuvring armies since the invention of effective artillery in the Middle Ages.

Individual weapons have their place on the battlefield, but the positioning of the men who have them is critical—so much so that a battle can be won or lost by the tactics used. Consider briefly Texas's war of independence against Mexico. In February 1836 fewer than 200 soldiers and volunteers defended the Alamo mission at San Antonio, Texas. They were besieged for thirteen days by the Mexican dictator General López de Santa Anna, with a force of 3,000 men. The Texans were well-equipped with light artillery and individual weapons. The overwhelming majority would have had rifles rather than muskets. Rifled arms were developed initially for hunting and in America were necessary because smoothbore guns just did not have the range to take game—or fend off the native Indians— at the distances involved. In the fledgeling United States virtually all shooting was over

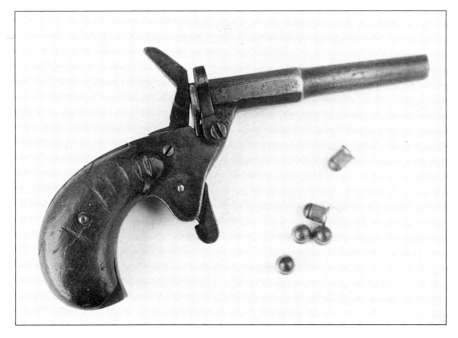

Left: Flobert's bulleted breech cap was developed in 1845, and pistols that fired them continued in production for at least the rest of the nineteenth century. This one dates from the beginning of the twentieth century and was made in Belgium. The Flobert BB caps are modern.
Above right: Colt Walker of 1847. Reproductions like this one are faithful to the original and great fun to try out.

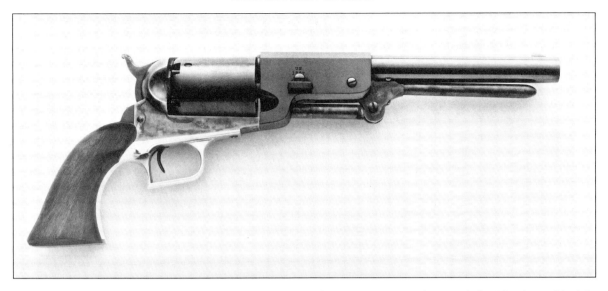

longer ranges than was customary in Europe, whether for the pot or in self-defence.

The Texans, with their artillery and rifled arms, gave Santa Anna a casualty list estimated at more than 1,600 men, a ratio of more than eight to one in a no-holds-barred, no-quarter, set-piece series of assaults. The Mexican troops were armed with smoothbore muskets, as was every army at the time. Like any muzzle-loader, the musket is difficult to reload on the move, and Santa Anna's infantrymen were reduced to the role of pikemen. With fixed bayonets they pressed forward, supported by their own artillery, until by sheer weight of numbers they overcame the Texans' ability to shoot them down. When the Mexicans breached the walls on 6 March, the battle became a straightforward hand-to-hand affair as Mexican infantrymen fought against rifles, swords and pistols with their bayonets. The surviving Texans broke off the fight and retreated into the long barracks. The Mexicans brought their artillery up and fired into the barracks until resistance ended. None of the defenders survived.

After that, Santa Anna moved east towards the coast and was met on 21 April at the San Jacinto river by General Sam Houston's army, which numbered about 600 men, most of them volunteers outraged by the massacre at the Alamo. Houston observed the Mexicans' habit of taking a siesta, and struck in the middle of the day. When the battle was over, some 500 of Santa Anna's 1,400-strong contingent had been killed in exchange for Texan losses of sixteen dead and 24 wounded. Santa Anna was captured at San Jacinto and obliged to acknowledge, in writing, the independence of Texas. He had won one battle at horrific cost and lost another—and Texas—because he treated bands of shrewd and unforgiving frontier sharpshooters as if they were elements of a European army. The British had made the same mistake with the rebellious American colonists 60 years before and they were to make it again in southern Africa, fighting the Boers at the turn of the nineteenth century. Tactics make a significant difference to the butcher's bill.

Defeat for Scotch Mist

Away from the slaughter of war, the one kind of weapon that indisputably needed a weather-proof ignition system was the hunting piece. The Reverend Alexander Forsyth was a hunter with a more persistent weather problem than most. Living in Scotland in the early nineteenth century, Forsyth was a keen fowler. Wildfowling on the foreshore is very much a winter sport, and with winter comes snow and

Above: American Transitional revolver. The side hammer was cheaper to manufacture than central hammer systems.

rain. Any moisture in the pans and even the best flintlock fowling pieces would fail to ignite, and were difficult to reload in windy or wet conditions. Worse, in fine weather, Forsyth noted, ducks would see the flash of the priming powder and dive out of the way of the shot. All this was especially frustrating when out fowling, as the chances of more than a couple of shots each dawn and dusk was (and still is) remote. What Forsyth needed was an ignition system that did not flash visibly and that would let him to use his gun in anything the inclement Scottish winter could throw at it.

Forsyth was an accomplished amateur chemist. His solution was a small amount of fulminate of mercury, a metallic salt that detonates when struck. Fulminating (detonating) salts had been discovered in about the mid-seventeenth century, and chemists had been experimenting with them from that time on.

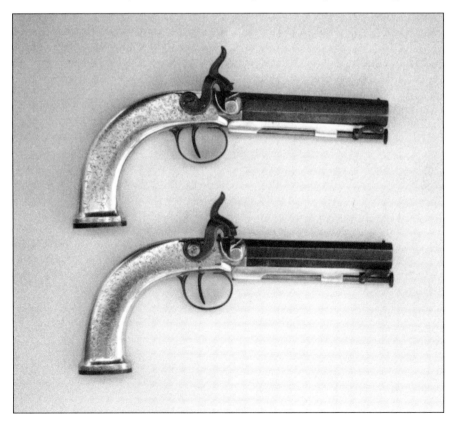

Left: A pair of silver-handled German overcoat pocket pistols with captive rammers. These are early nineteenth century pistols, probably belonging to the last generation before cartridge weapons took over. **Right:** Percussion target pistol in .45 calibre. After duelling was outlawed in Europe, pistol makers turned out some very good quality target pistols in cased pairs.

Several had departed this life prematurely and unexpectedly as a result. Fulminates are sensitive, and detonate fiercely on receiving a blow. Some experimenters had tried using them as a main charge in a gun, with disastrous results. Black powder burns very rapidly, like the mixture of petrol and air in an internal combustion engine, whereas a high explosive such as a fulminate goes off instantly. A bullet, like a piston, needs a period of pressure to get moving and then to accelerate. A detonation creates instant pressure, allows no time for the bullet to overcome its own inertia, and sets up a shock wave that travels at around 4,000m/sec. Loaded with fulminate, a gun's firing chamber turns into a small bomb and, needless to say, any barrel made will fail dramatically under such stress.

Knowing this, Forsyth set about using fulminate (of mercury in his case) to ignite the main charge of black powder. He first tried applying some as a paste in the open pan of his flintlock. When the paste dried it was waterproof, which he hoped would give him faster ignition and better reliability in wet weather. But he found that the flame produced by the fulminate lasted for a very brief time. It would heat the black powder to its ignition temperature of 350°C only if it was directed right into the middle of the charge.

To be sure the powder ignited every time the fulminate exploded, Forsyth devised his 'scent bottle' lock, so called because it was shaped like the lady's scent bottle of the time. Forsyth's solution was to put a small amount of fulminate of mercury into a container (the 'scent bottle') over the touch-hole. Swivelling the scent bottle upside down and then back upright dropped a measure of fulminate on the anvil ready to be struck by the piston when the hammer dropped.

The scent bottle might hold enough for as many as twenty shots—roughly what you would expect from a good flint before needing

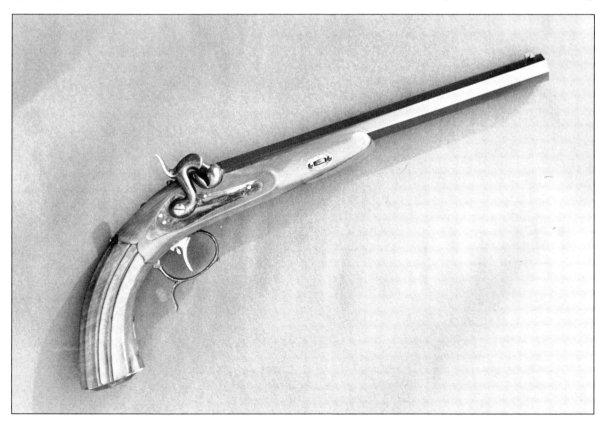

to adjust, sharpen or replace it—and plenty for Forsyth's beloved fowling. The system was to all intents and purposes waterproof so, as long as the shooter could keep his powder dry for the main charges, he was assured that his gun would not let him down in wet weather.

Forsyth patented his new lock in 1805 and set off for London to see if the military might be interested in his invention. At first they were, but when a new Governor-General came to the Ordnance Workshop at the Tower, he ordered experiments to stop and Forsyth to remove his 'rubbish'. No doubt he spent the rest of his life denying this down at his Club after the world's armies began tooling up with percussion ignition arms 30 years later. Forsyth could have been instrumental in the British Army getting there first, but . . .

Capping It All

Forsyth's lock was adopted for hunting guns. But it was imperfect—and expensive. Before long, the gun trade was busy putting pinches of fulminate composition (which included sulphur—the resulting flame worked better) into all manner of receptacles—tubes, paper wafers, pills—but best of all was the copper cap. This was to have several claimants for its invention. A man named Shaw was a strong contender, but possibly it just developed from one of many ideas being pursued. A dab of

composition was placed in a small thimble, and this was placed on a short tube or 'nipple' (our ancestors had a nice sense of humour) already screwed into the barrel. A vent led to the firing chamber. A 'hammer', which replaced the flintlock's cock, struck the inverted thimble, and the flame from the detonation shot down the vent to ignite the main charge. Simple and effective, this copper thimble or 'cap' was to revolutionise arms design.

Flintlock sporting arms or pistols in Britain were being replaced by the new system from 1820, and by 1830 the copper cap had superseded flint on the civilian market. The colonial market and military continued with flintlock until the 1840s. There was good reason for this. A flintlock gun owner could keep his weapon operational virtually anywhere in the world with very limited supplies. Flints might only give twenty good ignitions, but could be sharpened to give twenty more repeatedly. A man who had the knack could get 100 strikes from a single flint, and could easily carry a hundred of them. The military knew and trusted the flintlock, and were not going to change from a proven system until they knew the percussion lock had reached its final form.

Gunpowder could be made locally in most places, although some batches would not be as good as others—the quality depends on the quality of the charcoal more than anything

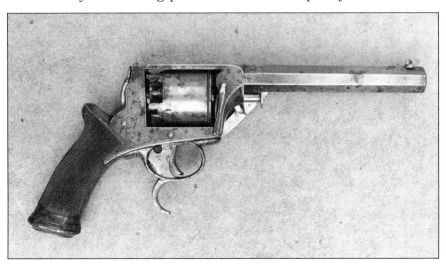

Left: Tranter self-cocking percussion revolver. Faithful to the British preference for not thumbing the hammer back, this revolver was cocked by the trigger extension seen below the trigger guard and fired by the shorter trigger seen within the guard.
Right: Tranter at the peak of its recoil. A target shooter's grip allows the muzzle to climb quite sharply.

GETTING A BEAD

The earliest firearms had no sights on them at all: the shooter simply looked along the barrel and fired when he could see the intended target, partly obscured by the end of the barrel. No one knows when the idea of a front sight came along or when one was first used, but pin front sights began to appear on firearms, long and short, during the flintlock era by about 1690.

Front sights were common enough by the time of the American War of Independence (1776–81) on smoothbored guns, where they also served as a bayonet lug, and rear sights had begun to appear by then on rifles. Neither rear sights nor rifling were permitted on duelling pistols in Britain when pistols were first becoming accepted as an alternative to swords for matters of honour, although they were allowed in Europe. Rear sights started to appear on pistols as they came into general use, and rear sights were allowed on duellers by around 1785.

Sam Colt fitted front sights to his revolvers and had a clever, practical idea for the rear sight. The hammer spur on Colt revolvers obscures the line of sight when not cocked, which acts as a useful reminder to thumb back the hammer if one wants to hit one's target. When it is cocked, a notch on the nose of the hammer forms the rear sight. Adams put a notch in the rear of the frame, to be copied later by Colt for their single action revolver in 1873.

Both front and rear sights were universal on automatic pistols from the start, although Browning used a full-length gutter along his M1910 pocket pistol to serve as both the rear sight and a protector for the front sight ,so that it would not snag on the pocket lining. Most auto pistol sights were quite narrow, and some followed the rifle format, which required the top of the front sight bead to be aligned with the bottom of the rear sight notch.

As a general rule, V-notched rear sights are intended to be used in this way, while the top of the front sight should be aligned to the top of square bottomed rear sights. As using sights became more fundamental to pistol shooting, and more particularly as two-handed shooting techniques became more common, rear sights became wider.

By the 1980s sights were being picked out in white by manufacturers, and the end of the 1980s saw tritium inserts for cats'-eyes 'glow-in-the-dark' sights. Then lasers and aimpoints (optical sights that show a red dot, which is 'placed' on the target) came along and tried to make iron sights on handguns obsolete.

else. Low-grade powder would do for artillery, and the very best for priming. Lead was easy to melt and cast. Everyone who had a gun would have had his own mould for ammunition, and way out in the wilds recovered ammunition could be melted down and re-used.

Copper caps could not. Although they take up a lot less room than flints, the supply is finite and, once it is used up, the weapon is useless except as a club. For these reasons, the British military did not take up a caplock weapon until 1842. It was the last large, smoothbore military musket to enter British service. British civilians, of course, took on the new system more readily, as re-supply was not much of a problem in the shires. Road communications were good, canals and railways were developing, the industrial revolution was well under way and prices were falling in real terms. Britain was at peace with Europe and America, leaving her free to take over much of the Third World on the way to ruling the greatest empire the world had seen since Roman times.

Percussion target pistols and military fighting handguns appeared, and news of the system spread. At the Alamo, Colonel Jim Bowie was armed with a flintlock rifle, if the one attributed to him and now preserved in the Texas Rangers Hall of Fame Museum in Waco, Texas, was indeed his. The arguments against percussion caps would have made sense to him, Texas being well beyond the communications infrastructure that had developed at that time in the United States. He would have preferred to have sharpened his flints rather than risk running out of caps, although he would have been familiar with caplock weapons. By 1836 the system had been around long enough to have become established for hunting, if not for war.

On the other side of the American continent, in the year that Jim Bowie died in the Alamo's hospital, another great player in the history of firearms stepped into the limelight—Samuel Colt.

From Colt to Pepperbox—and Back

Colt was working on a repeating pistol. The idea was nothing new, in the sense that it had been done before. But revolving flintlocks were extremely cumbersome and expensive. Colt wanted to make a repeating handgun that was a practical tool. He came up with the weapon that history knows as the Patterson Colt. This was a five-shot, single-action revolver with a folding trigger, and its chambers were primed with percussion caps. It worked, but it was an intricate weapon of 110 component parts. Expensive to make, it achieved some notoriety in Texas and it had novelty value, but the real need for Colt's revolver had not yet arisen.

The essential idea remained to tantalise, however. In England gunmakers experimented with a repeating mechanism that revolved a cluster of four, five or six barrels around a central axis. These 'pepperbox' revolvers achieved considerable popularity and success in Britain during the 1830s because they were made with an eye to concealed carrying. Surviving examples are usually no bigger than a gentleman's overcoat pocket pistol, and no heavier. But, with several shots to dispose of,

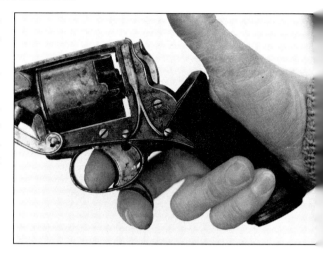

Above: Tranter mechanism in close-up.

admittedly of relatively small calibre, they represented a considerable advance on the single-shot flintlock for the gentleman who wished to remain untroubled by unsavoury types while going about his business. A brace of pepperboxes, one for each pocket to balance him up, provided the gentleman with up to twelve shots with which to discourage others from foul play.

In America the problem was different. There were Indians, Mexicans, outlaws, and the need for accuracy at long ranges. It did not matter whether a firearm was carried openly or concealed: either way it was likely that it would have to be used. In 1836 the newly independent Republic of Texas formed its own police force, the Texas Rangers, not so much to maintain law and order as to establish the notion that evil-doing would not be tolerated and then enforce it—with the gun and the rope, and no courtroom costs. Such enforcement called for sufficient firepower to get everyone's attention and, knowing of Colt's repeaters, Colonel Walker of the Rangers sought Colt out and discussed a new model firearm with him.

This collaboration produced the improved Colt Walker revolver in 1847. This 12in long, 4lb monster was a .44in six-shooter. Like the Patterson, the powder was loaded loose into the front of each cylinder and retained by a tight-fitting lead ball seated over it. At the rear of each chamber was a percussion nipple screwed in over the touch-hole, and a copper cap was seated on each nipple. This gave the owner six shots that were as reliable as the copper primers. Two guns would be better, but the first order was for 1,000 weapons for the Texas Rangers to use in the Mexican War of 1846–48.

The war brought the pistols renown in the hands of the Texas Rangers. Samuel Colt was a success and never looked back. He produced more designs, smaller pocket revolvers, large

Below: 1851 Adams revolver, of the kind that Robert Adams displayed at the Great Exhibition in London in 1851. The ramrod is a later addition, and is seen folded over the trigger guard. It swivels on the screw on the front of the frame to seat the ball in the chamber, and was probably added to the gun by Adams after he had seen Colt's 1851 revolver with integral rammer at the Great Exhibition.

military revolving pistols. If Colt originated nothing else, he pioneered successful mass production.

The Adams Revolver

Meanwhile the British trade had not been idle. Revolving arms with stationary barrels had been made occasionally since matchlock days. The trouble was that, until the percussion cap came along, arranging a satisfactory ignition system was a difficult matter. Once the cap appeared, and the pepperbox became popular, it was only a matter of time before someone tried once more to cut down the bulk with a stationary barrel and a rotating breech.

The earliest of these single-barrel pepperboxes is now known as the transitional revolver. It is a historic milestone between the multi-barrelled pepperbox and the later Colt and Adams revolvers. Each chamber of the cylinder breech had to align and lock up accurately with the barrel, of course. On the tran-

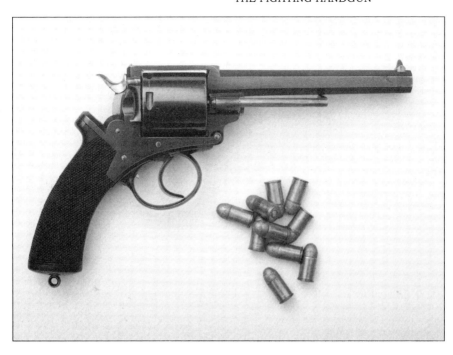

Left: John Adams revolver of 1867 in .450 Boxer. Operating single- or double-action, these revolvers served British officers well throughout the Empire, although the ammunition was underpowered for some of the feats required of it.

Below right: The John Adams still groups nicely, despite its age. The condition of the bore is important to shooters, and the finish to collectors. This revolver is A1 in both departments.

THE GREAT EXHIBITION OF 1851

Queen Victoria's Royal Consort, Prince Albert Edward, is credited with the idea for the Great Exhibition of 1851. Its full title was 'The Great Exhibition of the Works of Industry of All Nations'. The intention was to showcase British manufacturing expertise and the goods produced, but as the project developed it became a world exhibition, with exhibitors from all over Europe and America wishing to take part.

In the days before television and still photography, it was difficult to communicate ideas and inventions to potential customers without their having the opportunity to see the products at first hand. All that could be obtained otherwise were artists' impressions in magazines, newspapers and catalogues.

The Industrial Revolution, which started during Britain's wars with France (1793–1815), had changed the face of Britain, and of its society. The population was increasing rapidly, and the demand for labour was increasing faster than the population, despite the automation of industry. The 'Luddites' had tried to reverse the trend to mechanisation: between 1811 and 1816 they had systematically attacked and destroyed machinery in Britain's industrial heartlands in a bid to preserve traditional jobs, mostly in the weaving and clothmaking industries.

After 1815 Britain was at peace with the world, and concentrated on building her Empire. The massive expansion of overseas interests and the wealth that those interests generated had funded the further development of industry. The Industrial Revolution led to an expansion of the towns and cities. By 1851 more than half Britain's population lived in the major urban conurbations.

The exhibition took place in the Crystal Palace. Built of some 4,500 tons of ironwork and more than 300,000 panes of glass, the palace covered nineteen acres of Hyde Park and was packed with 14,000 displays of British, European and American industrial prowess. Officially opened by Queen Victoria on 1 May 1851, the Exhibition was host to more than six million visitors before it closed on 11 October.

Steam power was used to operate a huge variety of machines, and it was steam engines, mobile and static, that formed the centrepiece of the Exhibition.

The Exhibition made a profit of £186,000, some of which was used to buy land in Kensington on which the national museums (Science, Geology, Victoria & Albert, Natural History) were built, and the remaining fund—the Royal Commission for the 1851 Exhibition—continues to invest money in the arts and sciences.

The Crystal Palace was dismantled after the Exhibition and rebuilt at Sydenham in south London, where fire destroyed it in 1936. The south London site is now a sports ground.

sitionals, this was achieved by the hammer falling on to the cap. Colt, however, invented a lock-up of his own. Another man with the same idea was a London gunmaker named Robert Adams.

Adams developed his excellent design from the pepperbox, and both Colt's and Adams' revolvers were introduced to the British and Europeans at the Great Exhibition in London in 1851, starting a battle for the market share between the two that Adams would eventually win in Britain and its Empire, while Colt was to reign supreme in the USA.

The fundamental difference between the Colt and the Adams is that all Colt's products were single-action—the hammer had to be cocked, an action that at the same time engaged a lever to turn the cylinder. The trigger had to be pulled for the shot, then the hammer cocked

again. This system reflects the fact that Americans generally had to shoot over quite long ranges and needed greater accuracy from their pistols than the English. Adams's revolver was 'trigger-cocked'—what we would call double-action only. Pulling the trigger rotated the cylinder and raised and dropped the hammer. This allowed faster shooting, with less accuracy (without more training and practice) than could be achieved with a Colt. Both systems had their place. Colt's products had a significant influence on the British gun trade and on the military, if only because Colt gave away so many examples of his work to people in high places.

At first Colt won hands-down on marketing and on his ability to deliver in quantity on time. The Adams was a hand-finished product and, although both were available to officers going off to the Crimea three years later, Colt filled the official orders. However, it transpired that the Adams' high rate of fire in a mêlée was more useful than first thought. The Colt was the more popular arm at the beginning of the Crimean War in 1854, but by the time of the Indian Mutiny of 1856–58 the Adams had become the more popular pistol.

Improved by an effective rammer for seating the bullet (matching that of the Colt), the Beaumont-Adams revolver appeared in 1856. And it featured a world's first: a lock that could be fired both double-action like the 1851 Adams or hand-cocked like the Colt for greater precision at long distances. The new lock mechanism was the invention of Lieutenant Frederick Beaumont of the Royal Engineers.

Actually, tests at Woolwich showed that the two rival designs were equally accurate, thanks to the superbly smooth lock of the Adams. Other improvements were a longer cylinder to accommodate a heavier powder charge, and the provision of a satisfactory lever ramrod with which to seat the combustible cased cartridges used. Adams' first model was intended for use with a felt-wadded bullet, thumb-seated when loading, and had no ramrod. The

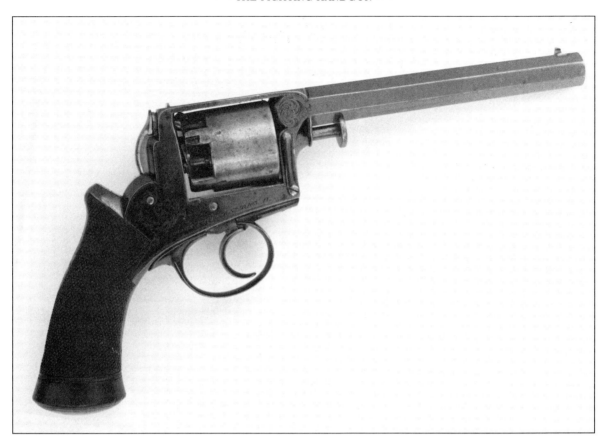

Colt, on the other hand, featured an excellent loading ramrod in its design and used a tightly fitting ball that would not shake loose when carried in the holster, a defect for which the early Adams was criticised.

Superior to the Colt revolver of its time in many ways, the Beaumont-Adams remained in service in one form or another until 1880, when the Owen Jones-Enfield revolver was adopted as a replacement. The Adams then faded into history, relegated to the further

Above: Adams 1851 revolver, right side view.

reaches of the Empire from which very, very few of them would ever return. It had begun the development of the classic British revolver of later years. However, long before this, even as Colt was enjoying his first success with his 1847 pistol, a new development in France was already gearing up to render his cap-and-ball revolvers obsolete. The self-contained cartridge was making its debut in Paris.

THREE

All in One

Two Frenchmen were working independently on self-contained ammunition during the percussion era. Casimir Lefaucheaux developed a breech-loading shotgun that used an all-in-one metal cartridge. It first appeared in 1836—the same year as the percussion-fired Patterson Colt. Lefaucheaux's double-barrelled shotgun is the ancestor of those in use today.

The term *le Système Lefaucheaux* is as familiar to the European shooter and collector as 'rimfire'. It means, quite simply, the 'pinfire' system that Lefaucheaux patented in 1835. It achieved widespread popularity and was the starting point of both the metallic cartridge industry and the breech-loader as we know it today.

Born in 1800 in the village of Bonnetakle in the Sarthe district of France, the young Casimir was apprenticed to a local gunsmith. From Sarthe he went to Paris, and became interested in the remarkable hinged-barrel breech-loader being produced there by Samuel Pauly, the first one to use a completely self-contained cartridge. Pauly's gun appeared in 1812, only seven years after the invention of percussion ignition by Forsyth. This had become public knowledge after being patented in 1808.

Both shoulder arms and pistols were made for this cartridge ammunition, which utilised an external cup in its base that was packed with fulminate. The arm embodied all the features necessary for a successful breech-loader and was years ahead of its time.

It was a modest success. Pauly himself moved on to other ventures, but his shop in Paris continued to produce his unique guns. In 1826 Lefaucheaux took over the management of the shop. He strove to improve the Pauly gun and rectify its fragile primer and inefficient gas seal. His efforts brought forth

Right: Reproduction S&W Schofield revolver. Jesse James carried a .44 calibre Schofield in a shoulder rig, which one day he reputedly took off after removing his jacket in the presence of his friend Bob Ford—who drew the gun and shot James dead. Original Schofields are now scarce, and reproductions for shooting are a worthwhile buy.

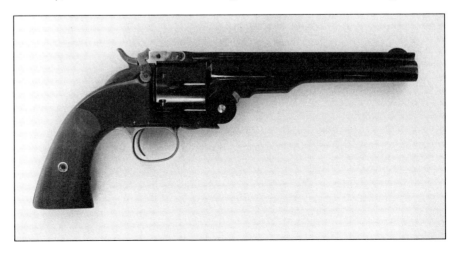

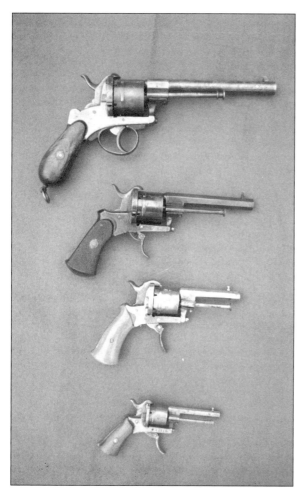

Left: Pinfire revolvers of diminishing sizes, from a 12mm military revolver (top) down to a 5mm pocket at the bottom.
Right, upper: Loading a pinfire revolver. Instead of having a primer in the base, pinfire ammunition has a pin on the rim which strikes a primer cap mounted sideways inside the case. The pin has to be located in a slot on the chamber when loading.
Right, lower: A pocket-size pinfire revolver with folding trigger. Colonel Colt used a folding trigger on his Patterson in 1836, and a century later some makers still favoured this form of trigger.

Although Lefaucheaux seems to have been mainly interested in long arms, he did go on to adapt his system to a pepperbox revolver, which he duly patented in 1845. Like the shotgun, this, too, took a paper-cased cartridge. Its significance is often overlooked outside France.

In 1845 the Americans had yet to appreciate the value of Colt's new percussion revolver, while the British were oblivious to even that advance. All this was to change with the Great Exhibition of 1851 in Britain, where the world's finest examples of engineering and technology were brought together under one glass roof. Both Colt's and Lefaucheaux's arms were exhibited, bringing them to the attention of a wider market thirsty for new ideas. Lefaucheaux exhibited both his double-barrelled sporting gun and his breech-loading pepperbox, but Colt's revolver attracted so much interest that the pinfire revolver was overlooked. Even Colt did not appear to have foreseen its possibilities. But one or two British gunmakers, Joseph Lang especially, immediately grasped the advance that Lefaucheaux's sporting gun represented and set about improving on it. Before long it began to oust the tried and tested percussion muzzle-loader. After some initial reluctance, the British sportsman was beginning to equip himself with the pinfire gun by 1857 or thereabouts.

A British gentleman's revolver, though, should he require one, would have been a per-

the early form of the drop-barrel sporting gun still in use today and its self-contained, metal-based and paper-cased cartridge. This was the first cartridge of modern type.

At first the emphasis was on perfecting a breech-loading sporting gun and improving the cartridge upon which its success ultimately relied. Lefaucheaux's initial double-barrelled shotgun set a pattern, and pinfire shotguns were usually double-barrelled. Some singles were made, with the pin offset so as not to obscure the line of sight, but surviving examples are scarce. As with other guns of the day, most pinfire shotguns were used until they were worn out and thrown away. The cartridges continued to be available for more than a century. In the United Kingdom, Eley finally stopped making them in 1968.

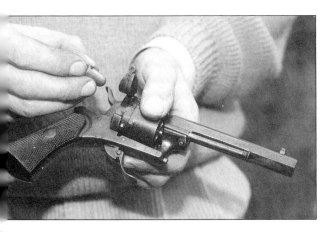

recognised the adaptability of the pinfire cartridge to such an arm. His father had patented a metal-cased version of his cartridge in 1843, and Eugene proceeded to design a revolver for it, which he patented in April 1854. It was destined to become one of the most widely used military sidearms in Europe.

The Pinfire Revolver

Eugene Lefaucheaux's original drawing shows the familiar outlines of the .36in-calibre Colt 1851 Navy revolver (the Navy was the Royal Navy, which ordered 4,000 in March 1854). It was never manufactured in this form, but the initial patent had the effect of preventing competitors from converting percussion revolvers to pinfire while Eugene was finalising the design of the revolver he intended to manufacture. Twelve days after the registration of his French patent, further drawings were registered in England and this time they showed the configuration of what was to become the Model 1854 military revolver.

Following trials by the French Navy, this revolver was adopted by them in 1856. It was a six-chambered, single-action arm of 10.7mm calibre and was the first metallic cartridge revolver to be used by a military power. It had a simple rod ejector on the right-hand side of the frame, and a loading gate was fitted to the recoil shield on the same side. The influence of Colt's percussion revolver can be plainly seen in the open top frame, but instead of the cross-wedge and frame-mounted locating pins that fastened Colt's barrel to the frame, the front portion of the cylinder arbour is threaded and the barrel screwed into place. Rotation in use is prevented by a locking screw at the bottom of the barrel lug.

The Spanish Army and Italian Navy ordered the pistol in 1858 and the Danish Navy in 1861, and by 1865 the Norwegian Navy and Swedish Army had taken it too. Both the Union and Confederate forces in the American Civil War used it, Union purchases alone totalling some 12,000 pistols. Despite that, the

cussion muzzle-loader. The heyday of the percussion revolver lasted from its sudden acclaim with the appearance of the American Colt and British Adams revolvers at the Great Exhibition until the mid 1860s. Meanwhile the French were far ahead of the game: by 1857 the French Navy had adopted a pinfire revolver designed by Casimir Lefaucheaux's son Eugene.

Eugene Lefaucheaux had taken over his father's business at 87 Rue Vivienne in Paris after Casimir's death in 1852. He had worked his apprenticeship in his father's shop from an early age and was only twenty years old when he assumed control of the concern. He proved to be more than capable of continuing and improving the business. He had seen Colt's revolver at the Great Exhibition and had

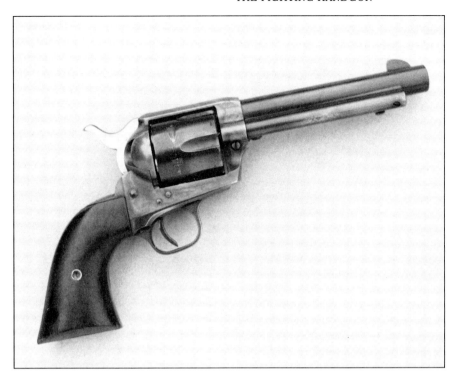

Left: The classic Colt Single-Action Army design. The first group had 7^1/$_2$in barrels for the army, followed by 5^1/$_2$in barrels for civilians. In 1884 lawman and expert pistol shot Bat Masterson wrote to Colts to ask for his new revolvers to have the barrels finished to the same length as the ejector rod shroud—and the 4^3/$_4$in was born. The Single-Action Army has been in almost continuous production for over 100 years. This model, in .357in and with a 5^1/$_2$in barrel, was built in 1964.

system still failed to catch on in the United States.

When Lefaucheaux secured British Patent 955 of 1854 for his breech-loading revolver, Rollin White was precluded from obtaining protection for his famous bored-through revolver cylinder in England. Had Lefaucheaux patented his 1854 revolver in the United States at the same time as he did in England and France, the American monopoly on the bored-through cylinder, breech-loading revolver would have belonged to Lefaucheaux rather than to Smith & Wesson, who used the Rollin White patent protection from 1854 to 1869.

The following year a double-action Lefaucheaux revolver was patented. Eugene Lefaucheaux obviously had his eyes on lucrative government contracts, but the financial stability that came from the popularity of his Model 1854 allowed him to expand into the civilian market. Here, too, he was hugely successful, and before long the other arms makers of Liége and St Etienne were producing variants of the Lefaucheaux revolver. In 1862 Lefaucheaux contributed yet another refine-

ment when he patented a folding trigger. This became hugely popular and was typical of the smaller-calibre civilian pinfires, which ranged in size from 5mm to 15mm. Although the tiny 5mm pinfire was very weak in power, its 18-grain bullet being propelled by just 3 grains of powder, it nevertheless remained extremely popular until the turn of the century, its very small size making them attractive to ladies and others who wanted an easily concealed firearm. The quality of these 5mm revolvers ranges from poor to excellent, and they are considered quite collectable today, especially the better-made examples.

It is a common belief that all pinfire revolvers are of low quality. The truth is that they come in all grades, from cheap pocket revolvers to good military and civilian sidearms. The pinfire enjoyed a much longer period of popularity on the Continent than it did in Britain, and some really fine quality revolvers on the Lefaucheaux system were produced—particularly while the British and Americans were fiddling about with percussion revolvers and rimfire arms.

Pinfire for Collectors

The 7mm and 9mm arms were more practical and, again, were extremely popular for a long time. Nevertheless, examples in good condition are becoming increasingly difficult to find. In recent years the value of all pinfire arms has rocketed. For a long time they were no more than collectors' curios. The pinfire revolver was largely ignored by collectors because its ammunition was long unavailable, but now reproduction pinfire cases can be had in all the popular calibres except the almost miniature 5mm. The keen hand-loader can once again try his luck with these revolvers in comparative safety, provided that only black powder is used in the cartridges.

The construction of these reproduction cases is ingenious. To avoid the need to use a base wad as in the original cartridge, the base of the reproduction item is left about 0.2in thick and a hole is bored in the internal face to make a reverse primer pocket inside. There is no flash hole, of course, since the cap or primer is internal, and on the sample 12mm case we measured the thickness of the brass at the base of the primer pocket or cap chamber was 0.088in. When the cartridge is fired its base is supported by the revolver's recoil shield. These new cases have more than adequate strength for any charge of black powder that could be crammed into them.

As in the original ammunition, ignition is provided by an ordinary percussion cap, placed sideways in the cap chamber in the base of the case and detonated by the projecting pin. The pin holds the cap in place until the powder charge is poured in, whereupon the cap is fixed firmly in position by the powder—which is itself packed down well by the seated bullet. A little experimentation with various caps did reveal one slight problem, however. The pins supplied with the cases are lengths of welding rod, neatly cut to length. However, their ends are cut square. While reproduction pinfire cases in a 12-bore sporting gun had been perfectly satisfactory, the lighter blow of the revolver's hammer would not detonate any of the caps we tried out. This problem occurred only with 9mm and 12mm cases. The 7mm uses a smaller diameter wire pin, and the more concentrated blow this delivered to the cap was sufficient to detonate it reliably.

The answer was quite simple: reduce the area of the pin nose to increase the force of the blow it delivered. Original pins seem to have been cut at the business end at an angle, almost a point, to overcome just this difficulty. It was easy to alter the pins of the new cases to the same form.

The smaller pinfire revolvers generally lacked a rear sight, which was considered unnecessary in an age when the revolver was purely a close-quarters defensive arm. But the 9mm pocket revolver proved to be quite capable of producing perfectly acceptable groups at 20 yards, which was surprising considering its lack of a rear sight.

Right: This Colt revolver was converted to .44 rimfire by Mason, probably around 1867—certainly before Colts got their Single-Action Army on to the market in 1873

It functioned smoothly and had a very crisp trigger pull, albeit a little on the heavy side. Its grip proved to be very comfortable indeed, filling the hand surprisingly well. The little finger was curled round underneath it to provide a firm and stable hold from shot to shot. The double-action pull felt smooth and was reasonably light. The revolver proved to be a good deal more pleasant to shoot than some of the British .380in pocket revolvers of equivalent vintage.

The 12mm Model 1858 Navy revolver had a rear sight on the hammer nose, as did the 1851 Colt revolver. The grip filled the hand well, in spite of its rather skinny appearance, and the revolver seemed to be a practical and very usable arm. The ramrod lacks the refinement of Colt's. It sits on the right of the frame with nothing to stop it rocking back to bind the cylinder except a slight enlargement at its rear end. Despite these minor defects, it anticipated Colt's 1873 Single-Action Army metal-cartridge revolver by fifteen years, and served the various European armed forces who adopted it well enough for a generation. Pinfire revolvers were widely manufactured in France and Belgium until the Second World War, along with both rimfire and centrefire variants. The centrefire cartridge was the ultimate survivor as an ignition system, but the competition took many decades before a clear winner emerged.

The First Rimfire Cartridges

The other French innovator, Flobert, fitted a lead ball into a slightly enlarged copper cap that contained more fulminate than usual in 1845. This 'bulleted breech cap', which had a small rim to facilitate extraction, was the forerunner of .22in rimfire ammunition. It survives to this day, still manufactured in various calibres including 5.5mm, 6mm, and 9mm rimfire.

The modern Flobert is intended to be low-powered indoor ammunition. Fired from a modern .22in rifle, the 5.5mm Flobert bulleted cap generates about 16ft/lb of energy—a lit-

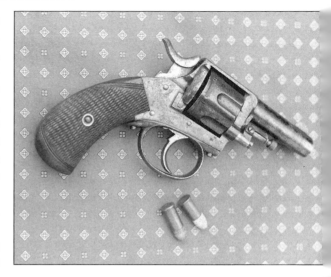

Left, top: European pocket bulldog revolver in .320in, a round that was never loaded in nitro. These little revolvers turn up in various states of preservation, but none has been used for many decades—the ammunition ceased to be made at the start of the Second World War.
Left, centre: A .320in Bulldog revolver, of German manufacture in the late nineteenth century. The cartridges are even scarcer than the revolvers.
Left, bottom: The loaded .320in revolver in an adult hand to give an idea of scale.
Below right: Black powder revolvers are smokier to shoot with than the later nitro cartridges.

tle more than a high-powered airgun. This ammunition effectively converts a rifle into the equivalent of a good airgun for indoor practice or pest control, being powerful enough to shoot pigeons roosting in a barn but (usually) too weak to make holes in the roof!

Flobert's original pistols for his cartridge were intended for low-powered indoor shooting but naturally became associated with self-defence as they were so small and light that they could easily be carried in a pocket. The little guns designed to fire breech caps were very popular throughout Europe and can still be seen, modestly priced, at arms fairs and auctions.

These single-shot pistols are single-action. The hammer has to be cocked to enable the breech face to be swung clear for loading. Apart from live-firing guns, this design was also produced as a blank firer with a blocked barrel and a vent in the top of the chamber.

A third variant has the same vent, as in blank firers, but also has a bored-through barrel, which is too small for a bullet to pass through. This variant was probably intended for lighting a dynamite fuse: the black-powder blank would be capable of lighting such a fuse inserted into the barrel. The top vent would be necessary to prevent the barrel bulging while the forward vent was blocked. Although this is a plausible explanation of this variant, we have seen no historical evidence to support it.

The Bored-Through Cylinder Arrives

These two Frenchmen's ideas came together for Americans in 1855. Rollin White developed and patented a revolver gun that incorporated a bored-through cylinder. White got a patent on that development because, although Lefaucheaux had been producing revolvers with bored-through cylinders for some time, he had not patented the idea in the United States, and there is no evidence to suggest that Rollin White was aware of the Frenchman's work. White offered his product to Samuel Colt, who apparently did not spot the significance of the bored-through cylinder and rejected the project.

Horace Smith (1808–93) and Daniel B. Wesson (1825–1906) had formed a partnership and originally worked with Tyler Henry on the Volcanic rifle. They parted with Henry

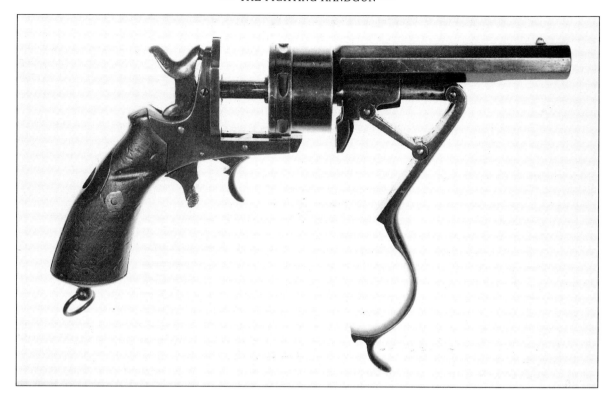

and started to develop a revolver with an eye to the expiry of Colt's master patent. (Tyler Henry moved on to work with Winchester, and by 1860 the first 'Henry' repeating rifle was the result.)

Smith & Wesson naturally became aware of Flobert's rimfire bulleted caps, but apparently not of Lefaucheaux's large-calibre pinfire revolver being developed at the same time. They inevitably found out about Rollin White's bored-through cylinder patent, and secured exclusive rights to it on exceptionally advantageous terms. Smith & Wesson's first revolver was a diminutive .22in rimfire pocket weapon, which appeared in 1855. Remington followed with various cap-and-ball revolvers. Their larger models utilised a solid frame, with a readily detached cylinder like the English Adams; speed-loading with both could easily be achieved simply by dropping out the empty cylinder and replacing it with a pre-charged one. The axis pin-and-wedge arrangement used by Colt, on the other hand, meant that the pistol had to be 'broken'—and the barrel

removed—to expose the cylinder for reloading or to change it.

These developments led to the production of firearms that were available to Americans for the War between the States (1861–65). It was in fact mostly a cap-and-ball affair where fighting handguns were concerned. Breech-loading single-shot rifles were developed, and repeating rifles made their first appearance in the form of the Henry in 1860 and the Spencer in 1863.

Pinfire never caught on in the USA. The natural reluctance to depend on proprietary ammunition over adaptable products like loose powder, lead and flint held sway west of civilisation for decades. Easterners experimented, of course, but pinfire ammunition was expensive, and the alternative rimfire ammunition produced for Smith & Wesson firearms was all low-powered and short-range.

Tyler Henry developed a .44in rimfire cartridge for his 1860 repeating rifle, and Christopher Spencer likewise used a .52in rimfire cartridge for his repeating rifle. Centrefire ammunition was a later development and, like the bored-through cylinder, was invented on both sides of the Atlantic at about the same time by men with the same military background.

Berdan, Boxer and Centrefire

In the United States, Colonel Hiram Berdan retired from the Ordnance Department in 1864 to develop a rifle and ammunition. His contribution to history was a centrefire cartridge— a brass cap similar to the copper cap used on revolvers was inserted into a pocket in the base of a drawn brass cartridge. The primer pocket was made with an anvil inside it to perform the same function as the nipple on a revolver— it steadied the primer for it to be struck by the hammer. Richard Jordan Gatling (1818–1903) had used a primitive version of this system for his first machine gun in 1861. He simply fitted percussion nipples and caps to the closed base of a metal tube, which contained the powder and was sealed at the other end by the bullet. His second gun used rimfire ammunition. It was not until the 1870s that he made guns that took centrefire ammunition.

Berdan's development was adopted by the Russians as the 1871 rifle, and a production line to produce the weapons was purchased from Greenwood Batley in Yorkshire. The Berdan primer was widely accepted in Europe and is still in use. Colonel Berdan's rival claimant for inventing the centrefire cartridge was Colonel Edward M. Boxer (1819–98) in Britain. Boxer made a number of improvements to artillery shells in the 1850s, but his name lives on for the Boxer primer he developed for the Snider rifle ammunition.

Britain had adopted a .577in muzzle-loading rifled musket in 1853. This weapon represented a considerable technical advance over the smoothbore 1842 model—it was accurate out to half a mile. The ammunition came in the form of a paper cartridge, which contained the bullet and powder. The twisted paper end of the cartridge had to be torn or bitten off so that the powder could be poured down the barrel. Then the bullet, still inside the paper, could be seated at the muzzle and driven down the bore. The paper cleaned the barrel as it went down, and the grease on it kept any fouling in the bore soft.

This rifle served Britain well in the Crimean War, but was also partly blamed for the Indian Mutiny of 1857. The paper was greased with lamb fat, but rumour had it that either pig fat or beef fat had been used. The story outraged Moslems and Hindus in the British

Above left: Galand revolver, showing patent extractor. Until quite recently British officers could purchase their own revolvers and were free to choose what to buy. The Galand is quick for extracting the empties, but a bit more fiddly than the Webley to load.
Right: Revolver, Adams, Breechloading, Mark 1, as the British Army put it.

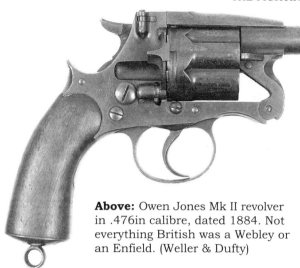

Above: Owen Jones Mk II revolver in .476in calibre, dated 1884. Not everything British was a Webley or an Enfield. (Weller & Dufty)

Indian Army. Moslems regard pigs as unclean and refused to bite the ammunition for that reason; for Hindus, the cow is sacred. After the Mutiny, Britain looked for a military rifle with a breech-loading system. The one that was adopted was a conversion of the Enfield rifle musket. This involved making a swing-out breech block at the breech end and chambering the first part of the barrel for a cartridge. Boxer's primer was developed for this cartridge and it was adopted in 1866.

The difference between the Boxer and Berdan cartridges is that in the Boxer the anvil is part of the primer unit; in the Berdan, the anvil is part of the cartridge case. Both systems are still in use. Boxer primers are almost universal on shotgun cartridges and in ammunition where there is a market for loading at home. Berdan-primed military ammunition is still quite common, and Berdan brass can be converted to Boxer, but not the other way around.

Cartridge revolvers did not appear for years after rifles taking Berdan and Boxer ammunition because various relevant patents affecting pistol manufacture were still valid, and those who controlled them were rivals. All the principles were known, but they did not finally come together until the Rollin White patent expired. Then the cartridge revolver came of age in the United States with the Colt 1873

Single-Action Army revolver. Sam Colt did not live to see it; he died in 1862.

The Colt 1873 Single-Action Army revolver brought together the best aspects of pistol and ammunition development to that date. The revolver retained Colt's single-action mechanism, but was built on a solid frame for a centrefire cartridge. The first models were built in .45in calibre with 7.5in barrels for the US Army and 5.5in barrels for civilians. Bat Masterson wrote to the factory in 1884 asking for his barrels to be finished shorter, to the length of the ejector rod shroud—creating the 4.75in barrel and a style that was to become famous. A decade later, the screw that retained the axis pin was replaced with a spring-loaded rod so that the cylinder could be dismounted from the frame without tools.

Apart from becoming available in new calibres, this design has developed no further in a century, and it is still made by Colt and a variety of sycophantic manufacturers in various parts of the world. The Single-Action Army quickly established a positive reputation in both military and civilian circles. Those who could afford them switched from cap and ball to cartridge revolvers. The murder of Wild Bill Hickock in 1876 is attributed to an early single-action revolver—22,000 had been made by the start of that year. In 1881, single-actions were used on both sides in the gunfight at the OK Corral.

In Britain, locks and systems continued to develop while the Americans stuck with their single-actions. The first solid-frame cartridge revolver made by Webley appeared in 1867—the 'Royal Irish Constabulary' model. British makers offered their revolvers briefly with both cartridge and percussion cylinders before moving over to cartridge revolvers altogether. Gunmakers throughout Europe offered centre, rim and pinfire handguns.

The quality and efficiency of the fighting handguns of the later nineteenth century were superb and can still be enjoyed today. Many firearms made in that era survive in good enough condition still to be used. It is a fact of life that most firearms, regardless of what they were made for and by whom they are owned, spend most of their time in storage. A well-made, adequately maintained firearm will remain in firing order for well over a century.

Keep Your Distance

Colt's legacy of single-action revolvers remained the benchmark to which other manufacturers had to try to measure up. They were designed for military and police use, to be fired one-handed, leaving the other hand free for the reins of the horse. They were accurate enough for longer-range shooting when necessary and could be fired fast at short range in an emergency.

The distance over which gunfights took place is mostly a matter of speculation. Duellers who started back to back and took ten paces each would be around twenty yards apart when they turned to fire. At the gunfight at the OK Corral in 1881, Wyatt Earp and his cronies were close enough to their opponents at the start of the

fight for Ike Clanton, who was unarmed, to be able to try physically restraining Wyatt from shooting as the fight started.

The distance across a room would limit any indoor gunfight to a few feet, while the distance across the street of a frontier town could easily be 30 yards. Accurate shooting with one of Colt's percussion revolvers is quite possible at 50 yards. Depending on the weather and the skill of the shooter, hits on a man-sized target at 100 yards are possible, but cannot be guaranteed for every shot.

Fitting a shoulder stock to a firearm immediately increases the relative accuracy over distance. As we noted, a good shot, firing an 1873 Single-Action Army revolver, should be able to hit a man-sized target reliably at 50 yards. But an average shot, using a Winchester 1873 carbine and the same ammunition as the revolver, should achieve a better score at 100 yards. That is the difference a shoulder stock and a longer sight radius makes.

Early police agencies like the Texas Rangers were staffed by men who knew both the power and the limitations of their weapons. While it may be possible to shoot a man at 100 yards with a handgun, it would be very much harder to do it if he were moving later-

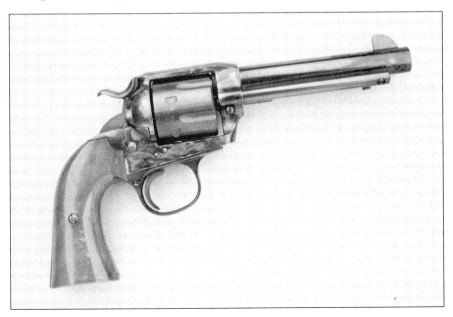

Left: Reproduction of the Colt Bisley model. This one is chambered for the .357 Magnum round, and thus cannot compete with originals in UK competitions for 'Classic' pistols as it is not 'in the spirit of the original'.

ally at the time. By not approaching his adversary directly, a peace officer could remain fairly safe under fire, while saving his ammunition until he was sure of a good shot. Gunfighting skill is, to that extent, a question of knowing the limitations of one's weapon, and having the nerve to apply that knowledge in practice.

The fighting handgun comes into its own at very short range. It is generally reckoned that most gunfights with pistols, like that at the OK Corral, take place at a range of seven yards or closer. Few rooms are more than 21 feet long and, even in the open, armed antagonists tend to get close enough to trade insults, but without closing to knife-fighting or fist-fighting distances, before resorting to gunplay.

Pistols For an Empire

Soldiers of the British Empire faced a variety of enemies in the latter part of the nineteenth century. On the North-West Frontier of India, and in Africa, the fighting handguns carried by officers were usually used against attacking tribesmen whose weaponry would not have been unfamiliar to Alexander the Great. That officers carried handguns reflects their function on the battlefield: they kept their hands free to direct their men until the enemy came close enough to use contact weapons. Only then would the officers use their handguns for immediate, close-range self defence.

At the battle of Rorke's Drift in January 1879, the officer commanding, Lieutenant (later Colonel) John Rouse Merriot Chard, used his revolver to good effect as the Zulus attacked. He also had occasion to use his sword and a rifle during the twenty hours of fighting. Chard's part in the action won him the Victoria Cross.

The fact that handguns tended to be used at shorter ranges favoured the double-action revolver—one whose trigger both cocked and fired the weapon. At very short ranges this proved no disadvantage. Colt's 1886 Lightning revolver is a case in point. Other American

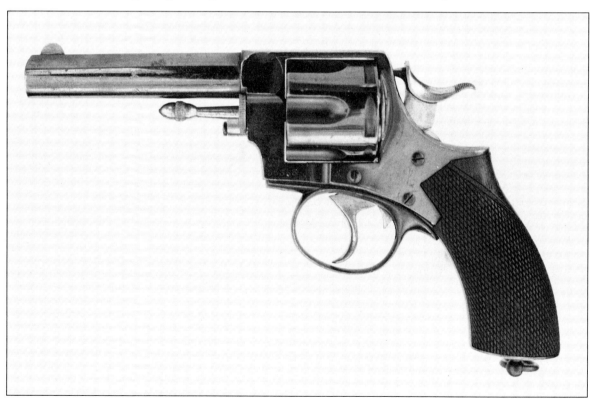

Below left: Webley Royal Irish Constabulary (RIC) pattern revolver, introduced in 1867, in .476. If Sherlock Holmes had been a real-life character, this is the sort of revolver he would have carried in his overcoat pocket—although he may have preferred one of the shorter-barrelled models.
Right: Classic 'bird's head' form of the Webley .455in revolver, No 1 Mk I. Having served in India, Dr Watson would have carried one of these.

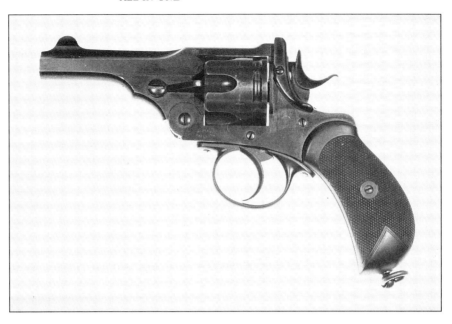

manufacturers followed suit, and at the end of the nineteenth century the US Army adopted a revolver that offered both single- and double-action—catching up at last with the British and European armies, who had been using double-action revolvers since the days of the Beaumont-Adams.

The Beaumont-Adams served the British Army and the Royal Navy well. But the adoption of a service rifle that took a metal-cased centrefire cartridge—Snider's conversion and the .577 coiled-brass case cartridge developed for it by Colonel Boxer at Woolwich Arsenal—meant that the search was on for a cartridge revolver to replace the cap and ball.

The first to be adopted was a breech-loading conversion of the Beaumont Adams, approved on 26 November 1868. The government conversion replaced the percussion cylinder with a new one bored through to accept the centrefire cartridge, with a reshaped hammer nose striking through the original frame aperture. The loading ramrod was removed and a rod ejector assembly fitted to the other side of the frame. This was a simple sliding rod with a right angled 'foot' that was grasped when using the ejector. A hinged loading gate at the rear of the frame, which was relieved

slightly to allow the cartridge rims to pass, completed the arrangement.

The conversion was devised by Robert Adams' cousin John, and carried out by the Adams Patent Small Arms Company (APSA). Initially at least, the converted revolvers were issued to the Royal Navy, the British Army adopting in addition a breech-loading revolver manufactured by John Adams. In fact two models of John Adams' breech-loading revolver were made, the 1867 and 1872; the difference between them was an improved rod ejector on the later version. The three different .450 revolvers adopted for service use were given the designations Mk I, Mk II and Mk III. The converted percussion revolver was the Mk I.

More Than Meets the Eye

Although altering the Beaumont Adams to a breech-loader appears, on the surface, to have been a straightforward operation, the conversion involved a considerable amount of work. The hammer nose aperture in the breech face had to be reduced in diameter (otherwise the cartridge cap would have protruded upon firing), and, as the replacement cylinder was bored through, the cylinder ratchet and pawl also had to be altered.

A plate was dovetailed into the rear of the frame's cylinder aperture to form a breech face, and to this was attached the loading gate. Below this, the frame was milled to a depth of approximately 1mm and a width of 17.5mm. An L-shaped plate was then let into the frame below this, extending along the cylinder aperture floor. The reason for this appears to be that the pawl slot in the frame had to be lengthened and the cylinder locking spur of the trigger brought forward slightly. A new pawl was used, its nose angled in towards the cylinder axis slightly to clear the mouths of the bored-through chambers. The cylinder ratchet diameter was also smaller than the original, for the same reason.

For a .442in rimfire commercial conversion that we examined, a similar procedure had been adopted, but the frame had not been milled away for the cylinder ratchet because in this case the ratchet had been cut into the rear face of the new cylinder. On comparing the government and private conversions, one is left with the impression that John Adams' method must have been easier to machine and possibly the more durable.

The front of the frame was also considerably altered, not only to accommodate the ejector assembly but also to accept a new cylinder arbour release—a change from the original winged screw on the right side of the frame lug to a very neat and convenient spring-loaded button. After conversion the revolver was completely refinished, and then renumbered. The example featured here was given the new number 978, and marked with the acceptance date of 9.69 (September 1869).

While the conversion of government Adams percussion revolvers to breech-loading was being considered, the matter of a suitable cartridge for it was also being given some attention. The one eventually used, the 'Cartridge, Small Arm, Boxer, for Deane and Adams Converted Revolver Pistol', to give it its full title, was derived from the .577 cartridge developed by Colonel Boxer.

Boxer did not originate the 'central fire' (centrefire) cartridge. His design was developed from that invented by the French gunsmith Clement Pottet some twenty years earlier and introduced into Britain and improved by the London gunmaker George Daw in about 1860.

Daw's cartridge was a paper tube construction—the forerunner of modern shotgun cartridges. It was successful enough in sporting guns, but its susceptibility to swelling when damp made it unsuited to military use. Boxer substituted a rolled, sheet-brass body for the paper and incorporated improvements to the primer anvil and cartridge base. His .577 Boxer cartridge for the Snider-Enfield rifle was adopted in 1866.

Boxer revolver cases were simply constructed. The case body was an elongated version of the base cup used with the coiled-brass rifle case. This was riveted to an iron base disc—lacquered to prevent rusting—and an internal base wad by a primer cup similar to the modern 'battery cup' shotgun primer. The powder charge was 13 grains of fine powder behind a 225-grain, round-nose, hollow-base bullet, which was lubricated with beeswax. In 1877 the base disc was replaced with one of hard brass, as the soft iron was prone to buckling during the riveting operation, and distorted ones could stop the cylinder rotating.

Shooting the Converted Adams

The conversion of Beaumont Adams revolvers to breech-loaders seems to have been successful, if laborious. The Royal Navy used them until 1880 and beyond. Some 7,000 Beaumont Adams revolvers were available for conversion, although possibly the actual number converted was no higher than 5,000 or so. Commercial arms were also converted by APSA. It was certainly a sound conversion, but how well did it shoot?

The Beaumont lock gives a very easy trigger-cocking (double-action) pull, and the single-action let-off is beautifully crisp and light. Contemporary sources remark, however, that

Above left: Webley
.455in revolver. This is
the Mk V variant.
Above right: .476in Enfield,
the first attempt by the British
government factory at producing
a service revolver for the Army.

converted revolvers shot high at the shorter ranges. The reason was thought (rightly) to be the increased distance travelled by the bullet before it entered the barrel. While the load column length of the percussion cylinder and .450 cartridge were the same, that column was placed significantly further back in the cylinder when in a cartridge.

The consequence was that the bullet had an extra inch or so to travel prior to emerging from the muzzle, which had climbed up more in recoil before the bullet emerged. A similar problem was encountered with the Mks II and III revolvers manufactured by John Adams, for the same reason. Why he did not alter his production machinery to shorten the cylinder recess of his design is not certain (presumably cost was the major factor), but with the converted Beaumont-Adams he was stuck with the long cylinder.

Rim diameter on the .450 Boxer case is just 0.04in or so larger than the case head, resulting in a very narrow rim. The chamber mouth on the Mk I Adams was recessed, and a wider rim than the .450 will not fit. Given the rod ejection system of these revolvers, all the rim had to do was stop the cartridge falling into the chamber.

The percussion Adams grip is very comfortable, possibly beating the 1851 Colt Navy's 'handle' for convenience, as its shape ensures that the hand can be placed consistently. The example we tried grouped about 20in high at 20 yards, using .450in Fiocci brass and 230-grain lead .45in bullets. Given the view of the British Army of Victoria's time that a revolver was for fast shooting at short range in emergencies, and that at other times officers were supposed to concentrate on directing their men, the incorrect sighting of the converted Adams was probably not considered important. It was excused at the time by claiming that by sighting the revolver to shoot high, one could aim low and keep one's adversary in full view the whole time—an opinion endorsed, for rather different reasons, by Massad F. Ayoob, who today advises police officers to aim low so that a suspect's hands can always be seen.

The extra free travel of the bullet was also reputed to increase its penetration: the bullet from the converted revolver was said to penetrate one inch further into wood. Nevertheless, a taller foresight was fitted to the Mks II and III revolvers—but they fouled the issue holster so the regimental armourers filed them down again!

Above: Webley-Pryse type revolver in .455in to a pattern made for the British Army, and nickel plated—which was a common requirement for weapons that were to be used in India and the tropics. This example is marked 'John Rigby & Co. London & Dublin' on the barrel, and there is some doubt whether the Rigby guns were made by Webley or by Francotte in Belgium. This gun bears no proof mark. This is not unusual, as military weapons are exempt from civilian proof, but its absence lends weight to the notion that this piece was made in England, as the Belgians would have proofed it prior to export. A negative review of this model in *The Field* magazine in 1878 led to a robust response from John Rigby & Co, defending the quality of their products.

The Webley Emerges

The converted Beaumont Adams continued in service alongside the later John Adams revolvers, and, apart from complaints about the stopping ability of the .450 Boxer cartridge when attacked by some of the heftier mammals of the Third World, it appears to have given satisfactory service. The appearance of simultaneous extraction and automatic ejection on new designs during the 1870s resulted in the 'manual extraction' revolver becoming obsolescent. In 1880 the Owen Jones-Enfield revolver was adopted as a replacement for the Adams. A few years later, in 1887, the British settled for the Webley revolver. The Mk I was the joint finalist in a closely run race. The eventual loser was a Smith & Wesson top-break revolver. S&W went on from this defeat to develop their military and police series of solid-frame revolvers with swing-out cylinders, but the British stuck with the robust Webley top-break, automatically ejecting revolvers for many years thereafter.

All these cartridge revolvers were configured for centrefire cartridges loaded with black powder and a lead bullet. The pivotal development of the first nitro powders, in the 1890s, had little immediate impact upon revolver designs. The Webley series continued with the Mk II (1894), Mk III (1897) and Mk IV (1899). It was 1913 before the nitro-proved Mk V was adopted, the only change from the Mk IV being a slightly enlarged cylinder diameter.

Mks I to IV look the same in photographs. The differences are minor and are primarily the result of changes in production methods. The Mk I frame was expensively milled from solid metal; this rapidly gave way to the Mk I* in which the shield was a separate piece. The Mk II had an enlarged hammer, reputedly to make cocking the piece easier for cavalrymen wearing gloves. The Mk III had changes to the cylinder release, axis mechanism and the action; the Mk IV is little different from the Mk III apart from the hammer spur shrinking from the earlier cavalry type. All were proved for black powder ammunition, as were most other revolvers of the period.

Time was marching on, however. The development of nitro 'smokeless' powders in the latter part of the nineteenth century paved the way for the development of automatic weapons.

FOUR

The Smokeless Revolution

A Swiss chemist, Christian Frederick Schonbein, developed the first 'smokeless' explosive in 1846. Known as guncotton, it was literally cotton wadding steeped in a volatile mixture of nitric and sulphuric acids.

It was not suitable as a propellent—it burned too fast—but a Prussian army captain, Johann Friedrich Eduard Schultze, managed to develop a fast-burning powder based on it.

This was still too volatile to be suitable to propel rifle ammunition, although it was eventually used in shotgun shells. Another chemist, Austrian Frederick Volkmann, found that treating nitrocellulose with a mixture of alco-

Below: 1897 plans for the Bergmann pistol, which was subsequently marginalised by better designs.

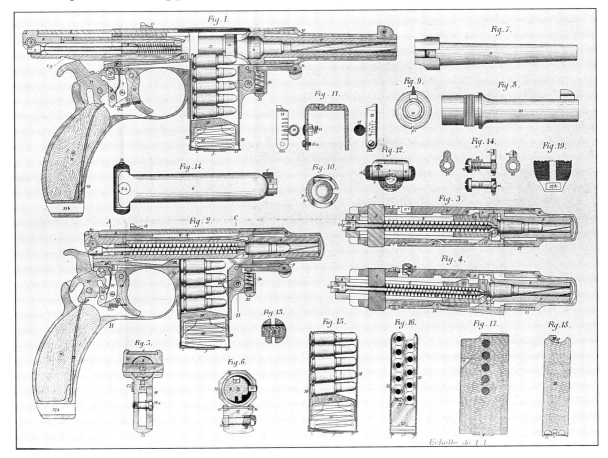

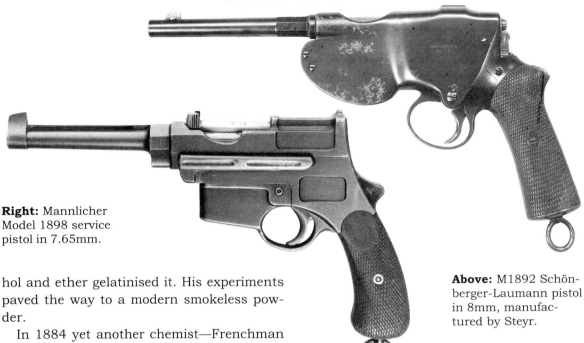

Right: Mannlicher Model 1898 service pistol in 7.65mm.

Above: M1892 Schönberger-Laumann pistol in 8mm, manufactured by Steyr.

hol and ether gelatinised it. His experiments paved the way to a modern smokeless powder.

In 1884 yet another chemist—Frenchman Paul Vieille—contributed to the development of a smokeless propellent compound. His product was a non-porous, slow-burning nitro-cellulose powder. It impressed the French government sufficiently for them to adopt it as the propellent for their 8mm Lebel repeating rifle in 1886. The French were by no means the first to adopt a repeating rifle for military service, but they were the first to adopt one with smokeless ammunition.

Such a development naturally stimulated people in other countries to do their own research, and the following thirty years to 1914 saw a gradual change to ammunition that used

BRASS AND ENERGY

Percussion revolvers have quite long cylinders, the rear part of which is made up of a solid breech face through which the nipple is screwed. When Rollin White first bored through the cylinder, making room for a cartridge to be loaded from the rear, it was found that the size of cartridge necessary to hold the same amount of powder and the ball was not nearly as long as the old cylinder.

The commonest self-contained revolver cartridge in this early breech-loading era was the .450in Boxer, which looks quite pathetic in the long cylinder of an Adams. We tried photographing it from the front, but the bullets are seated so far back that they were invisible in the prints.

In practice, however, it turned out that putting the same amount of powder behind the same-size bullet in a self-contained cartridge gave less velocity than

putting the powder and ball loose in a percussion revolver. The reason for this appears to be that some of the pressure generated when the cartridge is fired is used up in expanding the brass case—forming it to the chamber—before any of it is used to propel the bullet forwards.

Shotgunners found the same, and the amount of powder was actually increased by 50 per cent to achieve the desired results. In Adams' revolvers, the ammunition was improved from .450in (which, although underpowered, remained popular for pocket revolvers for many decades) to .476in. Then it was found that a lighter bullet would do just as well, and the .455in calibre became standard for the British Army. When cordite became used as a propellant in the Mk 2 case, the amount of space required was even less than it had been on the old .450in cartridge.

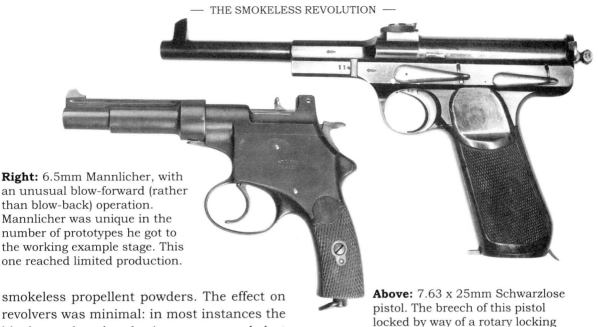

Right: 6.5mm Mannlicher, with an unusual blow-forward (rather than blow-back) operation. Mannlicher was unique in the number of prototypes he got to the working example stage. This one reached limited production.

Above: 7.63 x 25mm Schwarzlose pistol. The breech of this pistol locked by way of a rotary locking system, a method to be echoed in the 1980s by the Colt All American 2000.

smokeless propellent powders. The effect on revolvers was minimal: in most instances the black powder chamberings were used, but nitro-based powders were loaded instead of black. The difference was in the volume of propellant required per round. The Smith & Wesson .38in Special cartridge was originally a black powder loading, and the case was designed to hold enough black powder to accelerate the bullet to an acceptable velocity. The change to nitro powder left a lot of redundant space in the cartridge case. Nothing could be done about that without changing the case and making existing revolvers obsolete for lack of ammunition.

To this day the .38 Special round continues to have more stale air by volume in each cartridge case than it does propellent powder. In 1935 the .357in Magnum round was developed, based on the .38 Special cartridge but with a slightly longer case. The .357 load would have fitted into the shorter .38 Special case quite cheerfully. The case was made bigger so that excessively powerful ammunition could not be chambered into older, unsuitable firearms.

By the mid-1920s the choice of ammunition was wide. Mantons of Calcutta, chosen as an example because we had access to their 1926/7 catalogue, offered .455in revolver ammunition loaded with either black powder or nitro. The .320in cartridge, for pocket revolvers, was available in black powder only, and 7.63mm for Mauser pistols was offered in nitro only.

The new nitro powders, incidentally, seem to have had a curious effect on shooters' housekeeping. When all firearms used black powder ammunition, owners knew to clean their weapons after use as the residue from firing was highly corrosive, especially when it got damp. There was no great secret to cleaning. Cold water would rinse off the residue, aided by a little elbow grease and sometimes soap. Boiling water was used to heat the metal up to chase any remaining water off the metal parts, and natural duck oil made an excellent lubricant and preservative.

The arrival of nitro powders seems to have discouraged such efficient cleaning habits. Although the nitro residues are less damaging to firearms than were black powder residues, for many years the priming compounds were corrosive, so using cartridges loaded with smokeless powders did not reduce damage to guns. But it seems that a lot of people thought it did.

Left: Military Model M1897 Bergmann-Bayard pistol.
Below right: Mars 9mm pistol made by Webley. Unfortunate bottle-necked ammunition contributed to the failure of this design.

Early breech-loaders are often seen now with barrels like coal mines, which diminishes the opportunities for today's gun reviewers to assess the accuracy of these weapons. The content of ammunition has also changed, so some loads that were common a century ago are not now available unless made up by hand, and using modern loads will affect accuracy also.

Making the Most of Recoil

The development of nitro powders began the development of automatic pistols. The idea of using the recoil generated by firing one round to work the mechanics of the weapon and automatically load the next round had been understood, in theory, for some time.

Sir Hiram Maxim developed his tripod-mounted machine gun in the 1880s for military black-powder ammunition. The Maxim gun was recoil-operated in the sense that it was the rearward pressure generated by a round being fired that cycled the action. There had been machine guns before, notably Richard Jordan Gatling's multi-barrelled system, but that did not use the recoil for anything. The Gatling gun was a series of barrels, each being mechanically loaded, fired, unloaded and reloaded as the barrels rotated on their common axis.

The stumbling block at the time to any further development of the practical fighting handgun was that black powder ammunition is bulky and, broadly speaking, unsuited to pistol development. The availability of nitro powders stimulated the development of modestly proportioned ammunition, around which the pistol smiths of the period could realize their theories. That thinking was taking place in Germany.

Hugo Borchardt had emigrated with his parents from Germany to America as a teenager, and his name is associated with various American companies for whom he worked between 1872 and 1882, including Colt, Sharps and Winchester. He developed a single-shot, falling-block rifle that was marketed as the Model 1878 and became known as the Sharps-Borchardt. While at Winchester he worked on a solid-frame revolver with a swing-out cylinder. Like many of his other designs, it never reached production; the prototypes were consigned to Winchester's museum.

After a spell in Budapest working for Rudolph Frommer, Borchardt went to Berlin. There he struck a deal with Ludwig Löwe, who manufactured the Borchardt pistol after it was patented in September 1893. Crucial to making Borchardt's theory work was a suitable cartridge, and for his firearm a new cartridge was specially developed.

Borchardt's pistol used a toggle-lock mechanism that owed much to Hiram Maxim's machine gun design. The toggle lock worked like an elbow joint. It locked in the straight position for firing, after which barrel and toggle recoiled a short distance until the rear end of the toggle was cammed downwards, allowing the joint to break upwards to enable the empty case to be ejected. As the mechanism closed, a fresh round was stripped from the magazine and fed into the chamber.

Maxim's machine gun in British service used a bottle-necked cartridge, the .577/450in developed in 1872 for the Martini Henry rifle. Borchardt's pistol used a miniaturised version of this, a 7.65mm jacketed bullet in a small, bottle-necked case. Lacking a rim in the traditional sense, the case had a cannelure for the extractor claw to catch in. 'Rimless' ammunition has followed this pattern ever since. The rim is, in effect, the same diameter as the rest of the case.

The rim on revolver ammunition stops the cartridge going too far into the breech, holding the base of the cartridge within striking distance of the firing pin. On the Borchardt, the cartridge was stopped from chambering too deeply by the shoulders of the bottle neck. On later cartridges the case mouth was used for this purpose.

The pistol itself looked cumbersome with the main spring housing at the rear of the frame, but actually balanced quite well. Some 3,000 were made between 1894 and 1899, most being supplied with a shoulder stock. After about 800 pistols had been completed, production was taken over by Deutsche Waffen und Munitions-Fabrik (DWM), a new company formed by Löwe, who completed the production run. Other figures were populating the automatic pistol stage by then, and perhaps DWM thought the Borchardt was being superseded. Great leap forward as it was, it was a cumbersome piece to carry, and too delicate a piece of engineering for the battlefield.

Mauser Storms the World

In 1896, the Borchardt was comprehensively eclipsed: the Mauser C/96 made its appearance. This pistol, too, used a bottle-necked cartridge, and was clip-loaded from above with an eye to attracting military interest.

Right: M1907 Danish Schoeboe 11.35mm blowback service pistol. This fired a cupro-nickel jacketed bullet, which had a wooden core and aluminium base plug, at 1,625ft/sec. This may sound impressive, but the bullet was extremely light, giving poor accuracy and equally poor penetration if it did hit something.

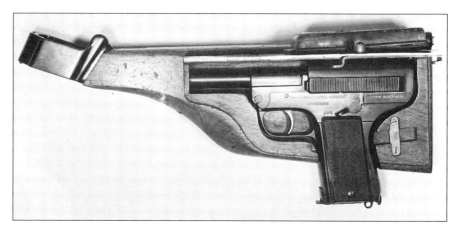

Although made by the million and universally known as the Mauser, the pistol was actually developed by Mauser's factory superintendent Herr Feederle and his two brothers. One of its remarkable features is its lack of bolts, screws or wedges: the Mauser fits together like a Chinese puzzle, and is almost as difficult to reassemble once taken down. The cartridge for this pistol was of 7.63mm calibre. The round can be regarded as the father of the modern 9mm, although it was superior to the early 9mm in its day, and is still highly regarded as a fast, flat shooting round.

The Soviet Union adopted a similar cartridge for its pistols prior to the Second World War, and that 7.62mm x 25mm is still the acid test of soft body armour. Some body armour will stop it, some manages to stop only bad batches of the ammunition, and with some one just has to hope that one is having a good day.

Mauser's C/96 pistol came with a wooden shoulder stock that also served as the holster. The rear sight was optimistically graduated to 1,000 metres. The small pistol grip provides enough to hang on to during firing, but is not quite long enough to clear the web of the hand from the mechanism. Shooting this pistol is actually easier with the stock fitted, provided one does not use the index finger of the strong hand for the trigger.

Shooting with the shoulder stock fitted, we found that trying to use the strong-hand in-

Left: Commercial Bayard pistol in .32 Auto—a lot of pistol for a small cartridge. **Right:** Military variant of the Bayard, with its holster, cleaning rod, stripper clips and spare magazine.

TOM HORN'S DILEMMA

It may have been a Borchardt pistol that first saved the life of a Wyoming law enforcement officer in 1903. The night before outlaw Tom Horn was due to hang for the murder of Willy Nickell, he successfully disarmed one of his guards, but Horn was unable to use the pistol to shoot his way out of trouble. He did not know how to release the safety catch.

From the day the safety catch was invented, this theme has repeated itself throughout the history of firearms. Virtually all revolvers will work if the hammer is cocked and then released by the trigger, but automatic pistols are not always so cooperative.

Some automatics can be fully loaded and need only a pull on the trigger to fire them. Some need the hammer to be cocked first, and/or the safety catch to be released. Most, but not all, need the slide to be racked at some point to chamber a round or to cock the hammer. The safety catch may still need to be released. Where is it? Which position locks the gun, and which releases the action? There are so many alternatives and variations on this theme that those unfamiliar with a particular pistol need time to work out how to get the weapon functioning.

This works to the advantage of a peace officer whose automatic pistol has been snatched or wrested from him. While the intricacies of his piece are being studied and misunderstood, he has the opportunity either to grab the weapon back, or to bring a back-up pistol into play.

Tom Horn's guard may have been the first lawman to be saved by the complexity of his own firearm, but he was by no means to be the last.

---

dex finger for firing the C/96 put the web of the hand against the angled metal above the pistol grip, as the hand is pushed upwards by the shoulder stock itself. It was easier to take a firm grip with the strong hand, and use the weak hand for the trigger. The weak hand has to be somewhere. It cannot support the Mauser under the barrel, as there is no wooden forend to act as a heat shield, so it may as well look after the trigger. Whether this was discovered by the C/96's original users is another question, because pistols and revolvers were universally designed for one-handed operation until past the middle of the twentieth century. When grabbing the pistol with both hands became more common, manufacturers responded by making allowances in their designs for shooters who used the new style.

Not when the C/96 Mauser was designed though. The grip is a strictly one-handed affair, and with ten shots in the integral magazine, a shoulder stock-cum-holster and a reputation for reliability, it quickly became the firearm of choice for those travelling to the further reaches of the globe.

Winston Goes to War

One such was Winston Churchill (1874–1965). His mother bought him a new C/96 pistol in 1898 to take on the British expedition to the Sudan, where he used it to good effect during the Battle of Omdurman on 2 September that year. It was not Churchill's first action: his baptism of fire had been in 1895. Then, on leave from the Army and acting as a correspondent for the London *Daily Graphic*, he accompanied the Spanish General Valdez on an expedition to quell an uprising by Cuban inhabitants who preferred the idea of home rule to the corrupt and inefficient regime put into Havana by the Madrid government.

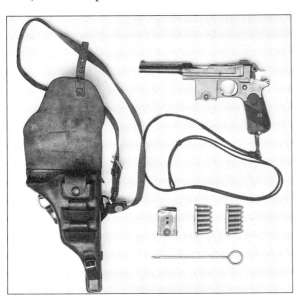

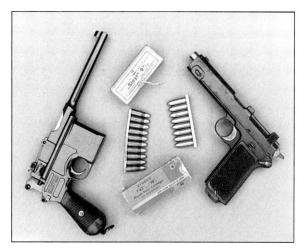

Top left: Mauser C/96 Broomhandle pistol (left, with 10-shot stripper of 7.63mm ammunition) and Steyr M1912 pistol with 8-shot stripper clip of 9mm Steyr ammunition. The ammunition boxes are commercial rather than military.
Top right: C/96 Mauser Broomhandle pistol, with its action locked open, and stripper clip ready for loading.
Above left: Author Richard Law found when firing the Mauser C/96 that this grip is much safer and stronger than a conventional one. All the fingers of the dominant hand are in front of the grip below the trigger guard, and the thumb is behind over the shoulder stock. The weak hand provides support while its index finger operates the trigger. Using a conventional 'rifle' hold, the shoulder stock pushes the dominant hand so far up the grip that the web of the hand is susceptible to damage when firing. Even with the hold pictured, care has to be taken to avoid hammer bite.
Above right: Mauser C/96 ready for loading with its stripper clip.

Transferring from the 4th Hussars to the 21st Lancers, in 1898 he joined Lord Kitchener's expedition to the Sudan, and took part in what turned out to be the last cavalry charge of the British Army. After the main Dervish attack was broken by artillery, the 21st Lancers chased what appeared to be spearmen, only to find that they were armed with rifles and fronting a larger force of men armed with edged weapons. Winston wrote:

'We passed through without any sort of shock. One man in my troop fell. He was cut to pieces. Five or six horses were wounded by back handers etc. but otherwise unscathed.

Then we emerged into a region of scattered men and personal combats. The troop broke up and disappeared. I pulled into a trot and rode up to individuals firing my pistol in their faces and killing several—3 for certain—2 doubtful—1 very doubtful.'

Of the 310 men who took part in that last charge, one officer was killed, four were wounded, and of the other ranks twenty were killed and 45 wounded, all in the space of two minutes. The regiment regrouped and defended their position with dismounted fire. Three Victoria Crosses were awarded in this action, but there was nothing for the ruthlessly ambitious Winston Churchill.

Auto Mania

The Mauser C/96 and the Borchardt are both mechanically recoil operated, which is to say that the barrel and slide or toggle assemblies recoil together on rails in the frame for a short distance while the pressure in the barrel is peaking. After that short travel, typically a quarter of an inch, the barrel stops and the breech unlocks. This form of operation is typical of most self-loading pistols intended for combat use, but there is another system, which it is essential to understand in order to study handguns—blowback.

Blowback operation is simple: the barrel is fixed and the breech face is held closed by the recoil spring, which on most designs either is located on a guide under the barrel or surrounds the barrel itself. When fired, the expanding gases blow the bullet out of the barrel, but also drive the cartridge case rearwards. The case thus acts as a piston, pushing the breech face rearwards until the ejector boot throws the case to one side. Then the recoil spring closes the slide again, carrying a fresh round from the magazine with it.

The blowback system is popularly used on pistols that have low-powered ammunition, such as those chambered for .22in rimfire cartridges. It also comes into its own, as we shall see, for sub-machine guns, where a heavy bolt

needs a powerful cartridge to shift it. An early variation of blowback was Ferdinand Ritter von Mannlicher's blow-*forward* mechanism of 1898, in which the breech is fixed to the frame, and the barrel assembly blows forward to clear the empty case and reload.

At the dawn of the smokeless powder era, though, the ambition of most pistol smiths was to get a working prototype—or, to put it more bluntly, to get a prototype working. Nobody did that better than von Mannlicher, who developed over 150 different weapons to the working prototype stage between 1875 and 1904. Most never went into production, but that should not detract from von Mannlicher's achievement as a prolific inventor who saw most of his projects through to working examples.

One of the reasons for the profusion of oddball designs in the twenty years before the First World War was that every designer was trying to crack much the same problems, and most of them seem to have designed their own ammunition as well as the firearms to fire them. The majority of von Mannlicher's pistol designs were built to fire cartridges he also designed. One such was his blow-forward pistol; later refined into a blowback system, it became the basis for the very successful M1912 Steyr.

An Era of Eclectics

It took some years for certain cartridges to become established and for others to fall by the wayside. During this time most designers found themselves taking one step back in order to take two forward—adapting their ammunition until it worked with the firearms they had designed and built. One such example is the 8mm Dormus pistol. Manufactured in Austria around 1894, this simple five-shot blowback was designed by Georg Ritter von Dormus. No ammunition appears to have survived.

Other automatic pistols and their cartridges appeared in rapid succession once nitro pow-

Automatic Pistols and Their Cartridges

Weapon	Ammunition chambered
1892 Schönberger Steyr	8mm Schönberger
1894 Bergmann	8mm Bergmann
1896 Bergmann No 5	9mm Bergmann
1900 FN Browning	7.65mm Browning
1902 Schouboe	11.35mm Schouboe
1902 Bergmann Simplex	8mm Simplex
1903 Bergmann Mars	9mm Bergmann
1905 Adler	7.25mm Adler
1907 Roth Steyr	8mm Roth Steyr Cartridge
1908 Bergmann-Bayard	9mm Bergmann-Bayard
1908 Luger P08	9mm Luger
1910 FN Browning	9mm Browning
1911 Colt M1911	.45in Automatic Colt (Pistol)

Right: Mauser *Schnellfeuer* ('Fastfire'), the fully automatic variant of the classic C/96 Broomhandle, with the Westinger patent change lever on the left side of the frame. Note also the commercial Mauser banner impressed on the stock. (Weller & Dufty)

ders were available. A brief checklist (see accompanying table) demonstrates how little of the ammunition at the time was interchangeable between the products of one designer and another, even when nominally of the same calibre. Thus we can see, from today's perspective, that the period from the development of nitro powders that were practical in the 1890s through to the outbreak of the First World War in 1914 saw an interesting variety of designs of both firearms and ammunition. Some were to survive in production for decades, and others disappeared virtually without trace.

The development of self-contained metallic ammunition in the mid-nineteenth century had allowed manufacturers to vary the size of their firearms much more than had been possible earlier. To get sufficient stopping power

Right: Browning Model 1903. The basic layout confirms it as an ancestor of both the classic M1910 and the later Browning Hi-Power.
Far right: 9mm Mauser model 1906 pistol. The by then traditional Broomhandle was preferred by the buying public.

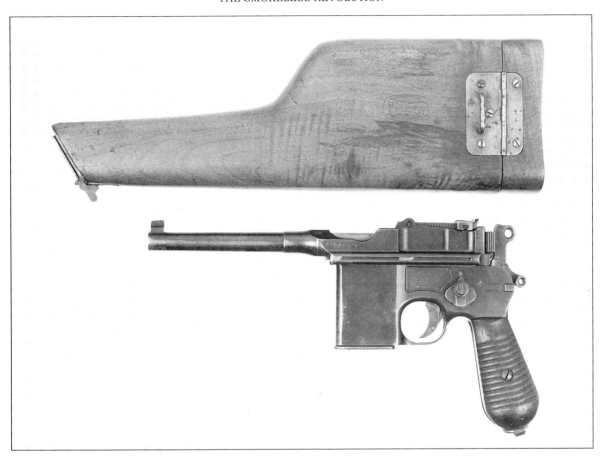

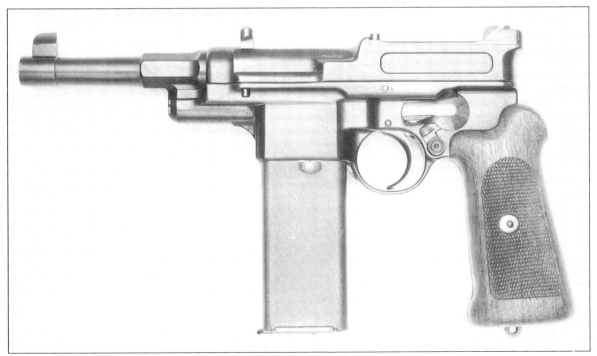

from a percussion pistol for military purposes required a ball diameter of between one-third and half an inch, with enough chamber depth to allow for sufficient powder and the seating of the percussion nipple behind it. The gradual change to self-contained ammunition reduced the required cylinder length.

At this point, British and US thinking seems to have diverged. The later nineteenth-century British revolvers were built around short-cased revolver ammunition—the .450in and the slightly longer-cased .455in and .476in—with .380in and .320in for the more compact de-

signs. The Americans stayed with the much longer-cased .45 Long Colt and .38 Special ammunition, in which much of the interior space of the cartridge case became redundant once smokeless powders were introduced.

Size Does Mean Something
For simple ergonomic reasons, all manufacturers of revolvers arrived at roughly the same overall sizes for military handguns and pocket models in the end, if by slightly different routes. Those who aspired to sell automatic pistols had to match those dimensions, de-

Left: Bayard .32 pocket pistol. Having the recoil spring over the barrel brings the bore (and the ejector port) about as low to the hand as it will get. The Bayard is in .32 Auto, although it has the compact dimensions of some .25in-calibre babies.
Right: Bayard .32 pocket pistol seen from its front.

Far left: Webley .32 auto pistol with the slide locked open against the empty magazine.
Left: .32 Webley automatic pistol and magazine. The safety catch on the left above the grip is in the 'fire' position.
Right: Model 1906 Browning in .45ACP. As can be seen, the M1911 was about to emerge from this chrysalis.

spite the possibilities offered by the new nitro-loaded ammunition. The Borchardt did not come out at a conventional size because of the space taken up by the mainspring housing, but it got around that by being offered with a shoulder stock. This turned it into a pistol carbine that would appeal to those for whom concealment of the weapon was irrelevant.

Mauser followed the Borchardt by providing a shoulder stock, which doubled as the holster for their C/96 pistol. For the next half-century, a shoulder stock figured in the thinking of firearms manufacturers as a way of selling automatic pistols to the military.

With or without a shoulder stock, neither the Borchardt nor the Mauser was adopted by any European army—not because these pistols lacked engineering refinement, but because they were long-barrelled, needed precise maintenance and were too awkward to operate with one hand in the heat of close-quarter combat. It was Georg Luger who understood that size and controllability were crucial in automatic handgun design just as they were in revolvers; and from that insight he produced one of the twentieth century's most distinctive battle pistols.

Luger had served in the Austro-Hungarian Army and understood the needs of soldiers. In 1875—and by then a civilian railway engineer—Luger met von Mannlicher and developed a rifle magazine with him. The experience kindled his enthusiasm for firearms design, and by 1896 he was working for Löwe at DWM, confronted with the task of turning

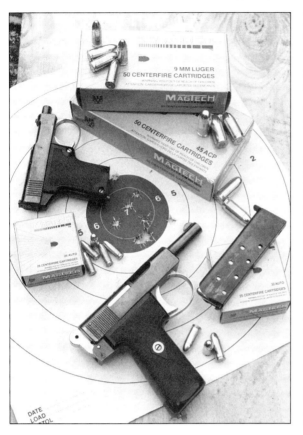

Borchardt's pistol into a practical combat weapon. His first attempt, after some revisions, became the first automatic pistol to be adopted into military service—the Borchardt-Luger 'Pistol, Ordonnanz 1900' taken by the Swiss Army on 4 May 1900. This chambered the bottle-necked 7.65mm Parabellum cartridge.

Georg Luger's development of the Borchardt design into a successful one-handed automatic pistol rivalled the work of John Moses Browning in the same period. Four years later Luger had refined the pistol even more, and it had been taken by the rapidly expanding German Navy as the Selbstladepistole 1904, or P04. Variants of essentially the same design became the German Army's 'Pistole 1908'.

These pistols were only part of the genius, however. Luger's other contribution to the history of firearms development was the cartridge they took—what is now the 9 x 19mm NATO cartridge. Known as 9mm Parabellum in Europe, and commonly as 9mm Luger in the United States, this is a descendant of the Mauser 7.63mm round. They share the same

SELF-LOADERS: CARE AND FEEDING

Magazine-fed rifles and pistols use three basic kinds of ammunition carrier. The three types are:

(a) A magazine into which the ammunition is loaded before the whole magazine is fitted to the firearm. It contains both the ammunition and the spring thatforces rounds to the top of the magazine to be loaded into the chamber. The advantage of this system is that several such magazines can be carried ready for quick reloading. The disadvantages are that troops may fire off their ammunition too quickly and the firearm is either useless or, lacking a suitable magazine for whatever reason, is reduced to being loaded by hand and only single-shot capacity. This system became virtually universal on military rifles developed after the Second World War.

(b) An integral charger clip into which the ammunition is loaded. The whole clip is then loaded into the firearm where the spring is already located to force rounds up for loading into the chamber. This system permits troops to carry a large number of rounds ready for immediate use, but again the

weapon becomes a single-shot system without the clips. The last successful design to incorporate this loading method was the American M1 Garand rifle.

(c) A charger clip into which the ammunition is loaded and from which it is thumbed into the magazine on the firearm. The charger clip is then discarded. This system permits the weapon to be loaded with loose rounds as well as from pre-loaded clips. The British Lee Enfield rifle series used this system.

The development of breech-loading rifles in the latter part of the nineteenth century led various armies to try out these options as alternatives to carrying loose rounds in a bag or bandolier to be loaded one at a time.

Mauser developed a rifle loaded by way of a clip that was discarded after the ammunition was thumb-loaded into the magazine. When he came to the C/96 pistol, he devised exactly the same system for loading. The 'rimless' ammunition was retained in the clip by the cannelures, and rested against a sprung floor plate.

Far left: A .32 and a .25 Webley displayed with a selection of Magtech ammunition. Modern ammunition is perfectly safe in these pistols, provided they have been maintained in good condition.
Right: Browning's classic M1910 pocket pistol was extended after the First World War to become the model 10/22. Note the slide extension and the take-down catch on it.

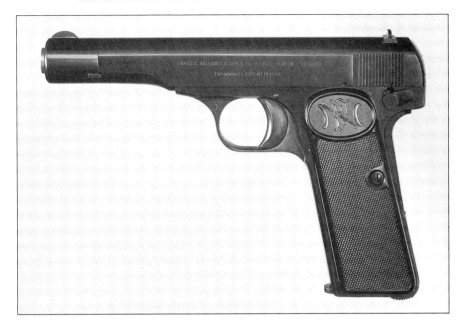

base size, but Mauser bottle-necked a longer case down to 7.63mm to simplify extraction, while Luger left it as a straight-sided case. This made no difference to its extractability, but it did produce a harder-hitting round than the 7.63mm, which had failed to impress the German military.

The ballistic effect was interesting, and is most obvious when one looks at the 9mm version of the Broomhandle Mauser. The tangent rear sight of the 7.63mm version is graduated to 1,000 metres, while the 9mm version, with otherwise exactly the same rear-sight bed, is graduated to just 500. (In truth, both distances are rather optimistic for a pistol, even one with a shoulder stock. Without an optical sight it is hard enough to see elephants at that distance unless they have been painted pink first.)

The Luger is somewhat vulnerable to fouling as the trigger linkage is exposed on the left side and the toggle breech is a very neat fit. The solution was the fully enclosing holster, which would keep the worst of dirt, dust and debris out of the mechanism. In the 1991 Gulf War, British troops had to use adhesive tape on their weapons for the same purpose; little has changed on the battlefield in that respect.

Revolver makers were on solid ground, offering six reliable shots from a pistol whose essential simplicity shrugged off mud and sand and kept on going. Nevertheless, it was late in the nineteenth century before American troops got a double-action revolver. Colt's Model 1889 Navy and 1892 Army weapons were ahead of rivals Smith & Wesson at the time, as the latter were still building break-action revolvers. The Colonel himself, who died in 1862, was fundamentally opposed to double-action handguns, saying that the necessary trigger pressure denied all accuracy. He may have been influenced by his brief period as a manufacturer in London, where his chief rival was Robert Adams. It was to be fifteen years after Colt's death before his company produced its first double-action models on a solid frame and, with the 1889 model, brought together the solid frame and swing-out cylinder that are virtually universal today.

No sooner had double-action revolvers been established with the American military than along came the first US services' trials of automatic pistols, and with them came one man whose name is more important in the development of automatic pistols than any other—John Moses Browning.

FIVE

Into the Great War

The first shot in the Great War was fired from a pistol. It was a shot that really did 'echo round the world', for the conflict it set in motion was not entirely resolved until 1945. Using a .32 Browning 'Old Model' 1900, a nationalist Serbian student named Gavrilo Princip assassinated the Austrian Archduke Ferdinand and his wife as they drove through Sarajevo on 28 June 1914. The Austro-Hungarian empire accused the Serbian government of hatching the plot, a charge that was probably untrue and was vehemently denied. On 28 July the Austrians declared war on Serbia. They had long regarded Serbia as a 'hornet's nest', but the private quarrel between the two nations was bound to drag in the rest of Europe. All the European nations were tied together in an intricate web of defensive alliances: an attack on any one of them would oblige one or more of the others to come to that country's aid.

Russia was the first to react, mobilising in support of Serbia along the borders of Austria and Germany. The Kaiser responded by declaring war on Russia and her ally, France, and promptly invaded Belgium. This brought Britain, a Belgian ally, into the war on 4 August. Turkey joined the German-Austrian side in November 1914, as did Bulgaria in 1915, while eighteen other nations joined the Allied side—Japan, Italy and Romania among them. The United States entered the war against Germany in April 1917.

The German armies reached the Marne in Belgium but were pushed back by the British Expeditionary Force and the French. Along the Western Front, the battle bogged down as both sides built huge static defensive lines that ran from Nieuport on the Belgian coast to Verdun in France and on to the Swiss border. For three and a half years neither side gained more than a few miles from the other, although prodigious quantities of blood and munitions were spent in periodic attempts at set-piece battles. As many as 100,000 men might perish in a single day's fighting. Neither poison gas, first used by the Germans, nor tanks, first used by the British in 1916, made any difference: the infantry continued vainly to die in droves on both sides. Apart from losses to artillery, many were victims of the first calculated tactical use of the machine gun.

On the Eastern Front, the Russians advanced into the Carpathians and into East Prussia, but this theatre, too, stagnated as the assault ground to a halt, and the Russians became entangled in a long defensive campaign. An Allied attempt to relieve the Russians by opening up a sea route through the Black Sea ended in disaster at Gallipoli. Disease and a hopeless position, combined with endless futile attempts by the invaders to advance much beyond the beach-head, helped the defending Turks to wipe out whole regiments of British, Australian and New Zealand troops between April 1915 and January 1916. Eventually, internal stresses took the Russian Empire out of the war, as the Czarist regime crumbled in the Bolshevik Revolution in October 1917.

The European colonies in Africa and territories in the Middle East also saw major campaigns, as the Allies wrested control (and resources) from Germany in sub-Saharan Africa and from the already enfeebled Ottoman Empire in the North. The fighting here was often 'hit-and-run', a guerrilla-style war across desert or jungle terrain that permitted few set battles.

Serbia, where the whole grim business had begun, first threw the invading Austrians back, but was overrun by a combined force of Germans, Austrian and Bulgarians during 1915–16. Only in September 1918 did an Allied expeditionary force break through the Bulgarian lines from Thessaloniki in Greece and advance towards the Austrian border. The Italian front, too, stabilised along the River Isonzo until October 1917. The Austrians pushed the line back then, but a year later the Italians had regained the lost ground and advanced to inflict a major defeat on their enemies at Vittorio Veneto.

By this time the Germans—thwarted on the battlefield—had unleashed unrestricted submarine warfare in the Atlantic in January 1917. Attacks on American shipping bringing food to Britain brought the United States into the war. The additional manpower helped stop a major German offensive in spring 1918, and the summer saw the Allies gaining ground along the Western Front. When the armistice was signed in November 1918 the Allies had recaptured nearly all the overrun French territory and eastern Belgium.

The Allied victory, however, especially as expressed in the vindictive clauses of the Treaty of Versailles, merely laid the foundations of enormous resentment in Germany and sowed the seeds of future conflict. Within

twenty years a still more bloodcurdling war, fuelled as it was by Adolf Hitler's demented and nihilistic vision, would engulf the world again. And the tools of war, not least the fighting handgun, continued to evolve.

The King's Handguns

Britain had kept with a revolver during the transition from black powder to cordite smokeless ammunition. The Adams revolvers briefly had some competition from a revolver designed by the military factory at Enfield, which had been set up in the 1850s along lines suggested by Colonel Colt. At the time Colt was regarded as the world's greatest authority on methods of mass production. It has been said of Samuel Colt that he never invented anything, except perhaps mass production—a dubious art that is often credited to another genius of marketing and self-promotion, Henry Ford.

The Enfield revolvers of the 1880s were short-lived, and in 1887 a Webley revolver was adopted. James Webley and his brother Phillip had set up in the 1830s and made various 'longspur' percussion revolvers from around 1853 onwards. Their solid-frame, gate-loaded centrefire 'bulldog' revolvers inspired a good few copyists and found their way into the

Right: The distinctive squarish shape of the Webley automatic pistol, with .455 Eley ammunition. Although a full-size pistol, it would fit in an overcoat pocket. One for each side would be better.

world's hotspots—including the battle at the Little Bighorn River in the hands of George Armstrong Custer, according to some accounts.

In 1867 the Royal Irish Constabulary (RIC) adopted one version of the bulldog, which was thereafter marketed as the RIC model. After developing a top-break revolver using the Pryse locking mechanism, Webley developed their own stirrup-latch .455in revolver—the one that the British Army adopted in 1887. The Webley No 1 Mk I was modified at various times through Mks II to V between 1894 and 1913. The various models reflect changes to ease manufacture and the advent of nitro ammunition. It was with this revolver that Britain entered the Great War of 1914–18.

Above: Webley Fosbery revolver, left side view with safety catch visible on grip.

As a historic curiosity, it should be said that, although the Webleys were fine revolvers, they were not universally taken by British officers on to the battlefield. The rule in the Army was simply that officers should carry a pistol that took the issue .455in ammunition. There was no firearm registration or licensing system in force at the time, and officers could, and did, if they wished, buy any .455 pistol that they preferred. The Army & Navy Stores catalogues of the era, which supplied the British gentry with everything from exotic blends of tea to mosquito nets by mail order, show a wide

Left: The Webley Fosbery self-cocking revolver of 1901. After each shot, the barrel, cylinder and standing breech all recoil on rails in the frame to recock the hammer. The zig-zag grooves on the cylinder serve to rotate it at the same time. Among the few revolvers fitted with a safety catch, these weapons are still sought after for target shooting and by collectors, and can fetch high prices.

Right: Prideaux loader used in conjunction with a Webley Fosbery, which in common with all the other Webley top-break revolvers automatically ejects the spent brass on opening. Having located the bullet noses in the chambers, a firm push on the back of the loader chambers the rounds.

range of reasonably priced, suitable hardware among the plethora of pocket pistols, shotguns and sporting rifles. No doubt the lack of bureaucratic interference encouraged many officers to practise with their own weapons in some quiet corner of their estates as well.

What British officers wore into battle changed as the reality sank in as to the kind of war they were fighting. In the early months an officer would go 'over the top' wearing a revolver on his right hip and a sword on his left. The sword was soon recognised as an encumbrance. By 1916 officers would as often as not be wearing a revolver but carry and use a rifle and bayonet, which were more practical accoutrements than a pistol in the battles as actually fought. The rifle's practical application went two ways: it was more useful as a weapon, and it made officers harder to distinguish from the other ranks, and so less likely to attract more than what they deemed to be their fair share of enemy fire. British officers

in various colonial insurrections after the Second World War learned the same lesson all over again. The man wearing the pistol was always the favourite target for guerrilla snipers, and he soon learned to purloin a rifle to take out on patrol.

The Webley Revolver at War

A further change to the service Webley, made in 1915, altered the outline completely, from the bird's-head grip to a square butt borrowed from the commercial Webley revolvers, and to a 6in barrel as standard. This Mk VI Webley is capable of superb accuracy in properly trained hands, and is a favourite in British 'Classic' pistol competitions today for that reason. The 'Classic' course of fire, like actual combat in the early twentieth century, calls for high-speed reloading without the benefit of a speedloader, and in this the Mk VI is faster to operate than its contemporary rivals with swing-out cylinders.

A fumble-proof, heavy-duty stirrup lock keeps the barrel-cylinder group in place, and when released drops them forward and simultaneously ejects the empty cases. With the cylinder entirely exposed, with no frame in the way and facing up, hand-loading single rounds can be very quick. In close-quarter fighting, as in modern competitions, this saves valuable seconds. Early forms of speedloader, such as the Prideaux, were commercially available during the Great War (and are now rarities), and with them the Webley can be reloaded almost as fast as a semi-auto. Another Mk VI accessory much sought by collectors is the detachable bayonet made for the revolver in the later years of the war. Desperate fighting called for desperate measures.

Shooting the Webley No 1 Mk VI today shows not only that it can be extremely accurate in practised hands (pre-Great War competitions were shot at up to 100 yards' range), but that it lacks the sting of a modern heavy-duty auto's recoil, despite its large calibre. This is partly because the hefty 265-grain bullet al-

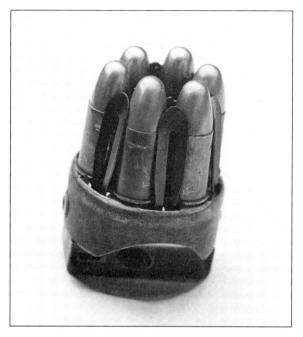

lifting the revolver sharply but not uncontrollably, even when shooting with one hand in the style of the period.

The No 1 Mk VI is by far the most common variant of the series—over 300,000 were issued—and it was widely used by British officers in the First World War, supplemented by various private purchases and contracts, including Colt New Service revolvers and, in the Royal Flying Corps, Colt M1911 pistols chambered for the .455in Eley Automatic cartridge.

An Opportunity Missed for Webley

The Eley Automatic round had been developed by Eley and Webley for a self-loading pistol that was adopted by the Royal Navy and Royal Marines in 1912 and later by the Royal Flying Corps, who had them alongside their Colts. Squarish and looking rather ugly in photographs, the piece is well balanced and shoots very well. But it did not interest the British Army, who took the view that the conditions in which infantry officers fought were likely to be too muddy for a weapon that would jam if fouled. The Webley & Scott .455 Mk I was briefly issued to the Royal Horse Artillery in Flanders during the Great War, and soon proved the point: revolvers rapidly replaced it.

most saunters to the target at 660ft/sec; nonmetheless, it is effective at up to 50 yards and at close quarters will stop most human targets, literally dead in their tracks. The round did occasionally have problems overcoming angry tribesmen under the influence of exotic potions and smoking mixtures, but they were not in the trenches of the Western Front. The Webley's recoil is rather like the Colt M1911's,

Above left: Prideaux speedloader loaded with .455 ammunition, ready for use with a Webley Fosbery or the military Mks I to VI Webleys, all of which have the same cylinder diameter.
Left: The Webley Fosbery revolver.
Above right: Cased and nickel-plated Webley RIC (Royal Irish Constabulary) revolver in .455. All Webleys were made to a quality rather than a price, but some are still nicer than others.

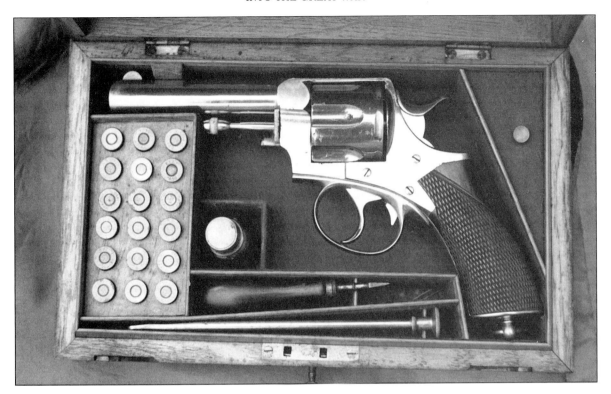

For all that, the 'Webley & Scott Pistol – Self-Loading .455 Mark I' was no mean piece of kit. Beautifully made and finely engineered, it showed a fresh approach at a time when John Browning's work was strongly influencing most other makers. Designed by William Whiting, it included several neat solutions to the problems that faced anyone wanting to produce a heavy-calibre military automatic—which means devising a workable breech lock (or, more accurately, a practical way to *unlock* the breech), and fitting a heavy-duty recoil spring and breech-locking mechanism into a pistol of manageable size.

Whiting kept the recoil spring down to sane dimensions by mounting a huge V-shaped spring, like that used on Webley's sidelock sporting arms but bigger, alongside the magazine, under the right grip. The spring worked a pivoted lever, and the lever worked the slide. To unlock the breech, instead of using Browning's swinging barrel or the idiosyncratic complexities of the Luger or Mauser systems, Whiting's barrel sank gracefully down in grooves in the frame as it recoiled, unlocking and releasing the slide as it went. The grooves were machined at 45 degrees, and matching ribs on the square-sectioned chamber section of the barrel fitted into them. The top of the chamber fitted the square ejection port in the top of the slide.

This simple, refined design has been called one of the finest machine-made pistols ever built. One of its cleverest features is the grip safety. All the lock mechanism is mounted in the safety lever and can only operate when the grip is squeezed in the hand. If the pistol is dropped cocked and loaded, and the hammer is jarred off the sear, it still will not fire. The lever spring is holding the whole lock frame out, and the hammer is angled so that it can drop only on to the rear of the slide.

The Webley Mk I auto was lost to sight for years, partly because of the limited military orders it attracted, and partly because there were not that many of these pistols about. The numbers were not improved by the British Admiralty, who, in 1939, told Webleys that there

Right: Webley No 1Mk VI revolver in .455in calibre—the most common British revolver from the Great War. This fully ordnance-marked example is dated 1918.

would be no further orders and then, a month later—after Webleys had scrapped their production line—asked for a quotation for a large order. Too late. The other reason for the Webley auto's obscurity was its cartridge. This unique 'rimless' round was designed to have all the knock-down power of the .455 revolver ammunition, and threw a 225-grain, spherical-nosed, jacketed bullet at around 750ft/sec. It was not available commercially for decades, but brass and bullets have both become available from specialist makers since the early 1990s.

Probably the largest-calibre self-loading pistol made until IMI produced their monstrous .50in-calibre Desert Eagle, the Webley Mk I is nonetheless amazingly gentle to the shooter. Recoil seems lighter and less sharp than the Colt M1911's, most likely because of the comfortable grip and wide backstrap, which let the pistol sit low in the hand. The trigger is crisp and quite light, while the sights are nearer

Left: This .455in revolver, made by Enfield in the 1920s, is in every respect identical to the Webley No 1 Mk VI revolver, made without the benefit of a licence or royalty agreement. The British government, acting in the name of the monarch, can get away with cavalier actions like this as the Crown cannot be sued.

modern target-shooting quality than traditional military squinters. The rear blade is even easily adjustable for windage. And, despite the British Army's gloomy reports, it does keep shooting. Royal Navy tests found it stronger and more reliable than the M1911. They showed only nine jams in 1,254 rounds fired—and those came only after 750 rounds had been put through the pistol without cleaning or oiling it. The loss of the Webley auto to wider military service was a sad and perhaps unnecessary thing, but the company made other self-loaders along the same lines in .38 ACP and 9mm that were adopted by London's Metropolitan Police and the colonial police services.

The Kaiser's Pistols

The Germans had also considered this potential problem when adopting the Luger pistol manufactured by DWM in 1908. Their solution was a wrap-around, virtually dustproof holster in which the pistol was carried. Three standard models were adopted for service, a 4in-barrel pistol for general service, a 6in model for the Navy and an 8in 'artillery' model which was issued with a shoulder stock attached to the holster for long-range use. Lugers with 4in and 6in barrels are also routinely encountered with the lug on the rear of the grip, with which to attach the stock.

Few if any pistols are better known than the Luger. The distinctive raked-back grip and toggle on top of the receiver make it easy to spot. It was a favourite souvenir of Allied troops in both world wars and has been made, with slight variations, for nearly 100 years by at least ten different manufacturers, who between them turned out more than three million weapons.

Comfortable to handle, if perhaps a little whippy to shoot, the Luger maintained its position throughout the war as Germany's front-line service pistol despite its tendency to jam if dirty, or if incorrectly reassembled after cleaning. On firing, the barrel and toggle lock recoil together briefly before the barrel stops and the toggle breaks. The empty case is ejected virtually straight up and slightly rearwards, making the firer's head one of the most likely placcs on which it will fall. The Luger is one of the good reasons why most firearms instructors now recommend a duck-billed cap as well as safety glasses and ear protection while shooting.

The Luger is widely sought after and collected. There are enough different models to

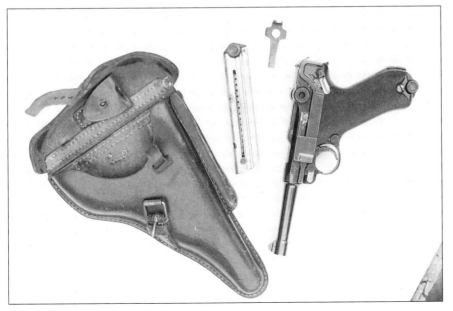

Left: P08 DWM 9mm Luger pistol, shown here with issue flap holster, spare magazine and the stripping tool, which lives in the small pouch inside the top flap. The safety catch is in the 'on' position.

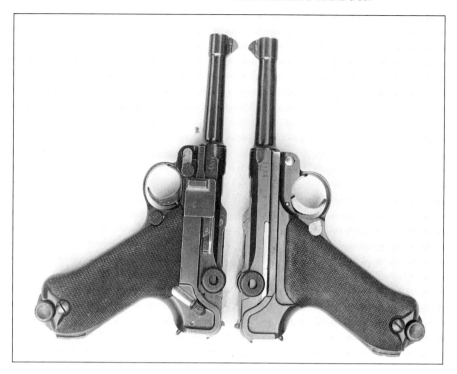

Left: A brace of DWM Luger pistols, showing left and right sides.
Below: 1913 Luger detail. The extractor, which is seen just below the date with the number '44' on it, is sitting flush with the breech block, indicating that the chamber is not loaded.

create interest at every level of purchasing power in the market. Marks on the pistols offer some clues as to their source. Military ones have the manufacturer's code or logo on the breech, with the year of manufacture. Later models may just have a manufacturer's code. Most Lugers seem to have four-digit numbers, and the last two digits are repeated on many of the small parts. One such part is the trigger action bar, visible on the left side of the pistol. If there is a number here, the pistol was captured before about 1917. Those remaining in German service after that were adapted so that they could be cocked with the safety catch on. The modification involved grinding off the piece with the serial number on it. Thus, those with the modification left German service later in the Great War or some time afterwards. Later production Lugers (the one we looked at to check this was dated 1938) were made with the modification and the serial number was stamped on the shortened trigger bar.

The Luger's extractor claw, which can be seen on top of the pistol and usually bears the last two digits of the serial number, also acts as an indicator that the piece is loaded. It is prominent when there is a round in the chamber and can be seen or felt to be so. It also has the word *geladen* ('loaded') stamped on its edge. When the chamber is empty, the extractor lies flush with the breech block. Production continues to this day in the USA, where stainless-steel Lugers are still being manufactured and marketed by Stoeger (see below for more about this intriguing handgun).

The Luger in an Emergency

One interesting aspect of the Luger's mechanism, which works with many of the old models as well as the new Stoeger variants, is that the pistol will function in a dismantled state. Once a round has been loaded into the chamber by the toggle lock, one can put the safety catch on and strip the pistol by easing back on the barrel and dropping the take-down lever. Now the side plate, which contains the trigger linkage, can be removed and the slide assembly rolls off the frame forwards. The barrel and slide assembly is now a single-shot pocket pistol, which can be fired by taking the safety catch off, gripping the toggle and pressing on the trigger bar. It is rather violent to shoot with, but the action does not attempt to open as the toggle is held shut.

We learned of this technique from an old soldier who had encountered a German officer armed in this way at the end of the Second World War. The German would have shot his way out of trouble, but, with only one round and confronted by six British soldiers, he gracefully surrendered instead.

However, the Luger should be checked before this variation is tried. Early-model Lugers cannot be stripped with the safety catch on. The design was officially modified in 1917, as noted earlier. The piece of metal in front of the safety catch was ground down. Only after modification can the toggle be worked to load the chamber and the pistol also be stripped with the safety catch on.

The Czar's Pistol

On the far side of the Great War battlefields, Germany was also fighting the Russians. The Czar's officers were armed with a Belgian revolver, designed by the Nagant brothers and adopted in 1895. This seven-shot, 7.62mm-calibre revolver has an unusual, elegantly tapered cartridge, in which the bullet is seated inside the case. The mouth of the case extends about $^3/_8$in past the bullet—much as the cardboard filter on a Russian cigarette has an empty space at the end. The reason for the taper on the brass is this. When the pistol is cocked, the whole cylinder is cammed forward and locks. The mouth of the brass case is pushed

Right: Luger artillery model, shown with the shoulder stock board to which the holster is attached on the other side, and the 32-round snail-drum magazine, which was also used on the MP18 sub-machine gun.

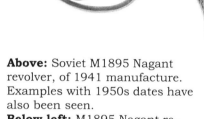

into the forcing cone and forms a gas seal between the cylinder and the barrel. When the pistol is cocked again (Russian officers had double-action models, other ranks single-action), the cylinder and tapered case retract from the barrel before turning and locking up again.

All revolvers lose some of their power through the cylinder gap, which is typically .006in wide. The Nagant design was intended to impede that escape of gas. Modern thinking is that the escape of gas is insufficient to worry about. It does not reduce the velocity significantly—the difference is about 15m/

Above: Soviet M1895 Nagant revolver, of 1941 manufacture. Examples with 1950s dates have also been seen.
Below left: M1895 Nagant revolver with commercial ammunition. This combination turned in excellent groups on the range.

sec—and it actually acts as a safety feature as, if the barrel is blocked for any reason, the gas has somewhere to vent.

This gap is also the reason why the report of a revolver shot cannot be moderated effectively, although silencers still appear on revolvers in Hollywood films giving the false impression that they can. The Nagant would probably accept a moderator, but we have not found anyone yet who has tried that.

Handguns in Other Armies

The French also went into the Great War with revolvers. They had adopted an 8mm revolver of their own military arsenal inspector's design in 1892. By 1915, however, the demand for handguns sent them to Spain for a supply of Gabilondi and Urresti's 'Ruby' pistol—a simple, 7.65mm blowback semi-automatic. The Italians started the war with their Bodeo revolver, adopted in 1889. They had also adopted the self-loading Glisenti Mo. 910, which was structurally so weak that it called for a specially loaded, underpowered 9mm round. That and the full-powered Parabellum round were

impossible to tell apart, and the Glisenti frequently came to pieces after firing a couple of rounds of Parabellum. As an immediate replacement, the Italians, too, bought the Spanish Ruby, but from 1915 took Beretta's Model 1915, another 7.65mm blowback. A variant was also made that took the Glisenti cartridge. It had a tougher recoil spring for the heavier load, but was still a blowback.

The armies of the Austro-Hungarian Empire had adopted a self-loading pistol in 1907—the 8mm Roth-Steyr, which fired from a locked breech. A long bolt is solid at the rear, and at the front is hollowed out to shroud the barrel.

Above:
M1910 Glisenti pistol for the Italian Army. This pistol took a cartridge that was dimensionally similar to the 9mm Parabellum but ballistically inferior. Glisenti pistols are not suited for use with modern 9mm Parabellum ammunition, but can be home-loaded for using modern components—carefully!

When fired, barrel and bolt recoil together, while the barrel turns through 90 degrees. The bolt cocks the hammer, then springs back to strip a cartridge into the breech and turn the barrel into its original position and lock it. This unusual piece was superseded by the 9mm Steyr-Hahn Model 1911, which also had a locked breech and rotating barrel. Both these pistols had integral magazines and were loaded from the top with an eight-round charger clip. The other Empire that was to vanish by the war's end, the Ottoman—today Turkey—went to war with a version of the Smith & Wesson Russian revolver, chambered for .44 rimfire and delivered in the 1870s.

Battlefield experience in the Great War persuaded nearly all the combatant nations that a change of handgun was necessary, and the period in between the wars saw every major

Left, upper: M1912 Steyr ready to fire. The pistol is a good handful, but the long barrel makes this a steady and accurate weapon to shoot.
Left, lower: M1912 Steyr, stripper clip at the ready. The ammunition is thumbed down into the integral magazine and the clip discarded.

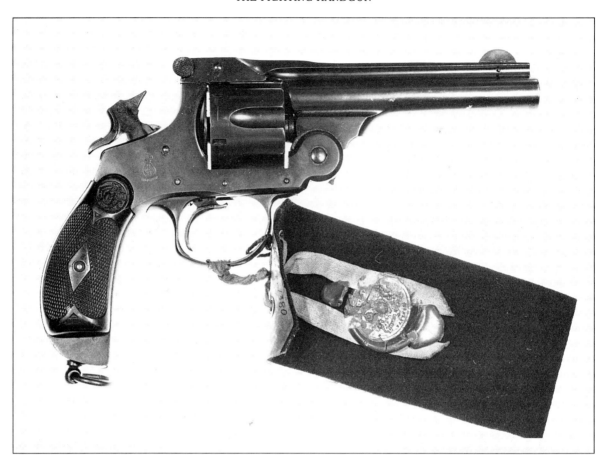

European power adopt a new fighting handgun for its armed forces. The exception among the great nations was the United States, who saw no call for change thanks to the work of one of the few true prodigies among small-arms designers.

The Genius of John Moses Browning

Born in 1855, Browning is said to have designed his first firearm before he left school and had his first patent awarded when he was only 24 years old. By the time he died in 1926, he had been credited with designs in every firearms department—automatic pistols and shotguns, machine guns and automatic rifles. Yet his name is directly associated with only some of his designs.

In handgun history, he was responsible for two basic types—a simple blowback mechanism for pocket pistols and the locked-breech military pistol. Both are significant to the history of twentieth-century firearms, and both were off the drawing board and in production before the First World War. The simple blowback mechanism first appeared on a pocket pistol in 1900 and inspired a host of copies from manufacturers all over the world.

The idea was simple enough, although, as we have seen, it was the development of nitro powders that made small automatic handguns a practical proposition. In simple blowback, the barrel is fixed to the frame, and the breech is held shut by the pressure of a recoil spring. On Browning's 1900 'Old Model' that spring is located in a guide above the barrel, but in later models he wrapped the recoil spring around the barrel, letting it double as the guide.

When the pistol is fired, the propellant burns and the gases that are produced push the bullet up the barrel. Simultaneously, they drive the cartridge case, like a tiny rocket, against the breech face. Since the breech is not locked, the slide is pushed back by the cartridge case to the full extent of its travel, at which point the case hits the ejector and is thrown sideways. The recoil spring then forces the slide to close, stripping another round of ammunition from the magazine on the way.

This system works very well for small, low-powered cartridges, several of which Browning had a hand in designing. His introductory cartridge, around which his first blowback pistol was designed, was evolved in 1897 and is known in Europe as the 7.65mm Browning and in the United States as the .32in ACP (Automatic Colt Pistol). Countless handguns have been designed around this cartridge apart from Browning's own Models 1900, 1910 and 1910/22. It became, in Europe at least, the most widely used police and military cartridge of the early twentieth century.

Most famous, perhaps, in the pocket pistol market was the 6.35mm Browning, which in the USA became known as the .25in ACP. This diminutive round became *the* pocket handgun cartridge, despite being ballistically inferior to the cheap .22in rimfire. That remark is often disputed as modern .25 is capable of higher velocities than the original ammunition. In any case, .25 offers two advantages over .22 rimfire for the modern shooter. It is a reloadable centrefire case, and the discerning shooter can tailor his loads to the pistol; an old firearm, like the 1906 Browning, deserves gentler treatment than a recently made 'Saturday night special', and that can be allowed for by the handloader. The other advantage of the .25 is that the noise and flash, particularly in the dark, grabs much more attention than the .22—which may be a consideration if one carries a firearm for the time-honoured reason of encouraging other people to leave one alone.

Next was the .380in or 9mm Short, which Browning developed in conjunction with Colt in 1908. The Browning Model 1910 pistol produced by FN in Herstal, Belgium, was manufactured in this calibre, along with a multitude of other police and military pistols. Most recent perhaps are Russian-made Makarov pistols, chambered for this cartridge for export to the United States. All three of these cartridges feature in the portfolios of most cartridge manufacturers, although the .380 is probably the most common, followed by .32 and then the .25. They have thus outlasted

Above left: A .455 Anitua Garate Y Cia revolver, made in Eibar, Spain, to a British contract. This is a sealed pattern example, to show that in every respect it matches the contract requirement. These pistols were of low quality and many were rejected on delivery.
Right: 1903 Browning-designed Colt in .38 auto. The clean lines of this pocket pistol still do not look very dated although the gun is approaching its 100th birthday.

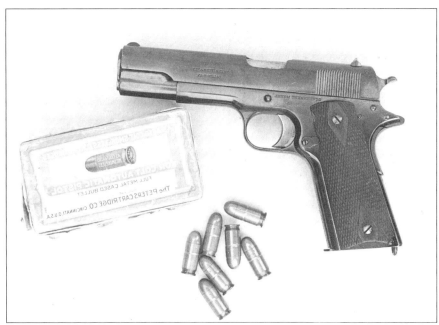

Left: .45 Colt M1911 pistol, with a commercial finish. Note the straight butt and distinctive plain diamonds left around the grip screws by the absence of checkering. **Below:** Classic .45 Colt M1911, over later custom Series 80 derivative.

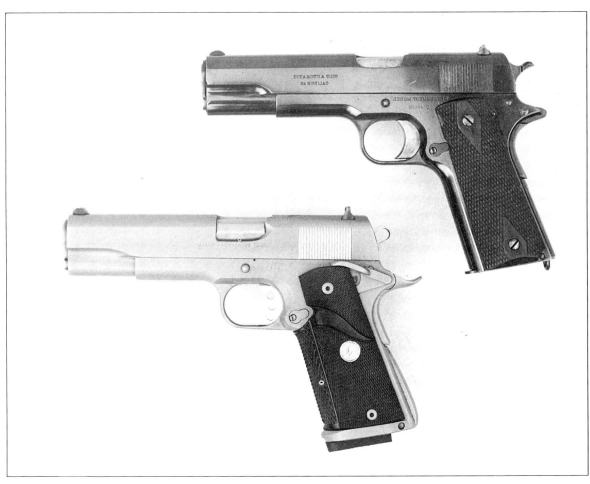

Right: A Colt M1911 pistol that has been customised for practical shooting. The trigger guard profile has been changed, the grip strap etched with grooves, commercial sights added and the value roughly halved in the process.

most of their contemporary competitors—such is the influence John Browning had on the firearms business.

An All-Time Great

Although his pocket pistols alone were successful enough in these three calibres to earn John Browning a permanent and distinguished place in handgun history, he also designed the locked-breech, swinging-link automatic pistol for Colt. This was adopted by the US Army in 1911 as the M1911, in preference to competing designs by George Luger and Savage—against the latter, the Colt underwent extensive tests. John Browning had designed the .45in ACP cartridge in conjunction with Colt as early as 1905, in the light of military experience during the Philippines campaign of 1899, which found the lighter .38in Long Colt round to be ineffective.

The debate over what makes the ideal man-stopping round is a long-running one, and no one who shoots pistols is likely to be unfamiliar with it. A bullet, directed at any target, will either penetrate it or bounce off, depending on the velocity of the bullet and the resistance of the target. Those that penetrate will carve a

track through flesh and bone. At the same time they create a displacement shock wave, which can damage tissue otherwise unaffected by the passage of the bullet.

The most effective knockdown comes from a bullet that is powerful enough to penetrate and at the same time delivers a substantial shock wave. The argument continues that a bullet that rips right through and carries on is taking with it energy that it has not dumped in the target. However, bullets that do not penetrate right through may not be powerful enough to deliver the knockdown strike that is sought from military ammunition.

British experience in the nineteenth century, the latter half of which was mostly taken up with fighting tribal groups in what is now the Third World, was that large, heavy, slow-moving bullets would knock down hefty tribesmen. Lighter, less powerful ammunition was sufficient for dealing with Europeans, such as those low-lifes one might encounter in Britain's cities, who might try to earn their living by violence towards a gentleman out walking alone.

Americans had their own wars with tribal Indians, and never complained about the .45in

Long Colt's ability to deal with hostile natives. The American trend in the latter years of the nineteenth century had been from .45in to .38in. But in the 1899 Philippines insurrection the .38 consistently failed to stop crazed, sword-swinging Moro tribesmen, and US forces there were hurriedly re-armed with .45 handguns. In tests conducted in 1904, the .45 seemed the most effective available round for combat, and the US Army specified the calibre for pistols offered for trials for a new combat handgun in 1907.

John Browning thus designed the locked-breech pistol that won this competition around the .45 ACP cartridge he had helped develop. The M1911 pistol has barrel and slide locked together when in battery (that is, with a round chambered and ready to fire). On firing, the two move backwards together about a quarter of an inch; then the link under the barrel pulls the breech end of the barrel downwards. This unlocks the two parts, so that the slide can complete the cycle in the same way as does a blowback pistol.

Browning's Colt M1911, with a magazine of seven .45 ACP cartridges, was such a success-ful design that it remained in front-line service with the US armed forces until 1985. Many firearms have to be reassessed and go through several marks or variants before a debugged weapon (or one that is easier to manufacture) finally emerges. The M1911 did not need to: Browning got it right the first time. There was only one minor re-work in 1926, mostly to help the pistol fit the hand better. The mainspring housing on the rear of the grip was reprofiled to a convex shape and the frame was relieved behind the trigger.

Children of the Colt .45

One measure of a successful design is the number of copyists its principles attract. Norway simply adopted the post-1926 version, manufacturing it under licence. FN in Belgium, initially with Browning on the team, and continuing after his death in 1926, developed the 9mm Browning GP35A along the same lines. Soviet Russia used the swinging-link lock for its TT30 and TT33 Tokarev pistols, the Poles cribbed it for their Radom model VIS 35 and Charles Petter used it for the MAS M1935A adopted by France, and subsequently in pis-

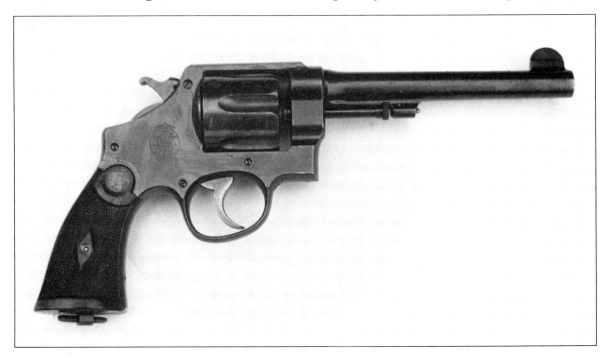

tols he designed for SIG. Other copyists from Spain to Argentina have made them, and today a good 'no-frills' copy of the M1911A1 comes from Norinco in Communist China.

The .45 ACP cartridge fires a 230-grain bullet at subsonic speeds—typically 870ft/sec—and delivered sufficient knock-down power over the performance of 9mm ammunition in tests on live animals to impress the US Army in 1904. With the calibre decided, various pistols competed for the Army contract, and it was Browning's Colt-made entry that won the pistol trials.

Military service along the Mexican border and in the Great War led to the pistol being revamped, and the new design, first issued in 1926, was designated the M1911A1. Mechanically, the M1911A1 and the M1911 are the same, and all the parts are interchangeable. Because of this interchangeability, older M1911s continued in service beside the newer model through the Second World War, Korea and Vietnam, until the GI .45 finally gave way in 1985 to a 9mm pistol by Beretta.

The M1911 is justifiably one of the most famous firearms in the world, and one of the longest-serving front-line weapons of this century. Nearly five million were made by Colt alone, who produced both military and commercial models. During the Second World War they were also made by Remington Rand (a typewriter company), Singer (a sewing machine company), Union Switch & Signal (a railway company) and Ithaca (a shotgun company). This massive wartime production led to surpluses: returning GIs inevitably took them home as souvenirs and many were released from government stock over the years.

Those kept for military service were refurbished between wars and consigned to stores against future use. Large numbers were left in Korea and Vietnam. The most recent batches of unmodified military-specification M1911A1 pistols sold in Britain have come from Vietnam, where dealers have gradually penetrated in search of firearms.

The M1911 Rises Again
In the United States the Colt .45 is probably the most popular pistol ever among amateur and professional gunsmiths. More alternative parts and add-on accessories have been pro-

Left: Smith & Wesson Mk 2 hand ejector in .455, one of many American firearms ordered in a British calibre for use in the First World War.
Right: Smith & Wesson hand ejector with service flap holster and commercial .455 ammunition. The S&W is a solid-frame revolver with a swing-out cylinder, from which the cases are ejected by pushing a rod mounted on the central axis of the cylinder. This is visible beneath the barrel.

duced for the M1911 than for any other fire-arm, and later versions have been stripped to become little more than a chassis around which build elaborate 'race guns' for 'action pistol' target-shooters. The American propensity to modify guns has meant that original, military-specification M1911A1s are now getting hard to find and are becoming sought after by collectors.

The basic modifications to which these pistols have been subjected can be illustrated by one example, made by Remington Rand in 1943. The original military finish has been removed and the metal blued, the pistol has been fitted with new sights and Pachmayr grips, and the mainspring housing has been replaced with a grooved one, so that a shoulder stock can be fitted. This example has not been altered mechanically. Others can be found with the ejector port enlarged, or various accessories fitted. Longer barrels, Magna-ports, compensators, heavier recoil springs, optical sights—there is no limit to the ingenuity of people who think that they know more than John Moses Browning did.

As a classic design, the M1911 has never really gone off the market. Colt continued to make commercial variants and developed the Series 70 and 80 pistols built on the same chassis. Then they came up with the M1991A1. But what was missing was a straightforward, no-nonsense, faithful reproduction of the military classic. Auto Ordnance had a go, making some commercially blued-finished reproductions of the M1911A1 with plain, hardwood grips allen-bolted on. They also made some garish commemoratives such as the D-Day Invasion model. But the quality of these never seemed to live up to the war-time originals. That was a pity, because Auto Ordnance have an excellent reputation for most of their products.

Then along came Norinco, the Chinese arms company, with just the beast—a faithful M1911A1 copy. It was robust and well made, and had a military parkerised finish. Anyone

who has handled original nineteenth-century Colt cap-and-ball revolvers alongside their modern Uberti reproductions will know that there are small differences between the two. Comparing an original Colt .45 and the Norinco M1911A1, the only obvious concessions to the passage of time are the sights. There is a slightly deepened rear-sight notch on the Norinco, and the Chinese have added white dots to the front and rear sights, which seems to be standard practice on pistols these days. This makes sense: the sights on a pistol are much more important today than they were 50 years ago, when men were taught to point and shoot the pistol one-handed. Adapting the sights is the commonest adulteration on wartime pistols, as those on the originals are so basic. Otherwise, Norinco's product looks, feels, handles and shoots like an original early model M1911A1.

When we looked at the two guns in more detail, we noted that the Norinco trigger and hammer spur are grooved vertically, while on earlier models Colt delicately checkered theirs. Later models and those by other manufacturers had grooves, as they are easier to work into the metal. There are small machining differences in the Norinco's slide, such as a flat surface around the front sight, but otherwise the design is completely faithful.

Right: The M1911A1is much cloned. This variant was made in Brazil.

Below left: Close up of the Smith & Wesson Mk 2 cylinder, loaded with .455 Mk 2 cartridges.

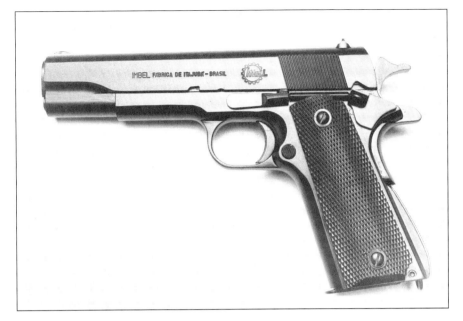

On Second World War examples we noticed that the small parts—slide stop, safety catch, muzzle bush, hammer, trigger and grip safety—were blued, while the frame and slide were parkerised. This military finish is a phosphate that gives the pistol a greenish tinge like cement before it dries. The finish retains oil, so a pistol that is liberally wiped over has a double protection against rust. Norinco have parkerised all the small parts, giving a more uniform appearance to the weapon.

We found that every part of the Norinco was interchangeable with the originals, which could come in handy: Norinco have gone to the trouble of making their parts look original as well as fitting original guns.

On the range, the Norinco outperformed the original Colt on accuracy, but not by much. The action was crisp and sure; the pistol worked exactly as one would expect, and felt just like an original. We interchanged parts with the Colt several different ways—Colt barrel and frame with Norinco slide, Norinco barrel and frame with Colt slide and so forth. The pistols both worked obediently throughout these trials and continued to give presentable groups with Samson ammunition, the tighter group going each time to the Norinco barrel.

That was only to be expected: the Colt we fired is more than half a century old.

Reborn in the USA

Reproductions sell for two reasons. First, they provide a safe, shootable alternative to wearing out a valuable collector's piece, and secondly they are often much cheaper than the originals. Aimco Inc., of Houston, Texas, have come up with a reproduction of another twentieth-century classic, the Luger. But it does not readily fit our preconceptions of what a reproduction is.

Aimco's 'American Eagle', which is marketed by Stoeger Industries, is ostensibly a reproduction Luger PO8 pistol. Made of excellent-quality stainless steel, it is available with 4in or 6in barrels. The American Eagle is expensive. It is very well made of fine materials, but while it follows the original Luger mechanically it is not a faithful reproduction. We thought of it more as a development of the original—like an Mk 1* or an M1A1—showing the way the Germans might have eventually gone if production had continued.

First, although it is a 9mm pistol, it is not to the same scale as the originals. Nothing on the American Eagle Luger can be used on an original German Luger, not even the magazine. Many original Luger owners would have liked a source of spare magazines.

We first noticed, in comparisons with a DWM Luger made in 1913, that the bolts were not interchangeable. We then checked every part and found that every dimension has been altered; not even the grips are interchangeable, and the grip retaining screws have different threads. We naturally asked Aimco why. They explained that old German Lugers were made to metric specifications, while modern American CNC machine centres operate to Imperial measurement scales, which the Americans charmingly call 'English'.

Aimco had set out to build a modern pistol on the PO8 Luger principle. They tried for two years to get the dimensions right, but the translated sizes, although in inches, were not exactly to standard sizes for which tools were readily available. They simply could not make the parts of the new Luger to the original dimensions. This is why the pistol is a development rather than a reproduction.

Although very well made, the American Eagle is a product of modern mass production techniques, so the quality of metal-to-metal fit is nothing like as close as on originals. Those were hand-finished by craftsmen, who did the job so well that complete interchangeability is quite normal in guns from the same production plant. The Aimco Lugers undoubtedly have complete interchangeability, but only with other Aimco Lugers.

As is customary in the gun trade, later models are a development of the earlier ones, with most modifications being intended to speed up or simplify production. The American Eagle is no exception. The machining of the toggle grip is much simpler than the complex original. The magazine-release button and the take-down lever have simple lattice patterns cast in, instead of the delicate cross-checkering cut into the original German products.

The take-down procedure is exactly the same as on an original Luger. The barrel is pushed back a quarter of an inch to release the take-down lever, then the side plate is removed. The barrel and breech now roll forwards off the rails. A cross pin at the rear of the breech block pulls out to the left to facilitate withdrawal of the block. This is generally as far as take-down needs to go for cleaning and maintenance. It gives full access to every place likely to be reached by fall-out from fired ammunition.

Reassembly is the reverse, but the coupling link has to be correctly located in the frame to catch on the recoil spring lever, otherwise the mechanism will not work. The sights on the American Eagle are quite faithful to original Lugers, but the 6in-barrelled model we tested did not have the long-range Navy rear sight, being fitted instead with sights that one would expect on a 4in model.

The Eagle Flies

On the range this pistol performed very well, once we had blacked the front sight to help acquire it in the rear sight notch. The sights remain faithful to the original—too small and not easy to acquire—but once blacked gave a reasonable sight picture and excellent groups on the targets. The performance of this pistol was faultless with all the ammunition tested in it, with the exception of some lead-bulleted rounds that would not feed at all. The round has to climb at quite a steep angle to jump from the magazine into the breech under pressure from the breech block. The lead bullets were simply too soft to bounce into the chamber, and got stuck against the chamber mouth each time. Light loads with jacketed bullets worked fine: we did not have time to test this product with hollow-pointed ammunition, but suspect that large hollow-points would probably not feed in it.

As a firearm to shoot it is fun, and it presumably qualifies for some competitions. Whether it is worth paying the money asked for a good stainless copy of an original that can currently be bought for half the price is a matter for the individual to consider. The excellent materials and stainless finish are definite 'plusses' for a pistol that would be used extensively in the British climate, and the ready availability of spares and springs (not the case with the originals) must also be a consideration. Aimco picked a hard number to copy, and have made a good job of it. The American Eagle certainly is in the spirit of the original, for the modifications have been made mainly with an eye to simplifying production. Ultimately, one's money is buying a new pistol, rather than a weapon that will be over 60 years old and in that time will have been used or abused by all sorts of other people.

These rebirths of early twentieth-century designs, and the enormous popularity of the British .455 revolvers in target-shooting in the United Kingdom, go to show how advanced the fighting handgun had become in only 40 years. But the Great War taught many lessons. Fine pistols had been made, and used effectively, but there was still some dross about—much of it hurriedly acquired from sometimes less than perfectly reliable sources. Experience of large-scale warfare, in which citizens had to be turned into soldiers at great speed, made many nations reconsider their approach to the fighting handgun in the aftermath of the conflict.

SIX

From Peace to War Again

The guns of the Great War in Europe fell silent at 11 a.m. on 11 November 1918, although fighting went on elsewhere in the world into the New Year before word got around that the war was over. The old powers of Europe—Britain, France, Germany, Italy, Austria-Hungary and Russia—had suffered terrible losses on the battlefields. It was not surprising that the war was referred to afterwards, for a short while at least, as 'the war to end all wars'.

On 11 November 1920 the British unveiled the Cenotaph—a memorial to the war dead—in the middle of London's Whitehall, at the heart of the government bureaucracy and a stone's throw from Parliament. An 'unknown warrior' was disinterred from the battlefields of France to be buried in Westminster Abbey, where King George V led the nation in mourning. The mood did not last long. The same year the government introduced a strict firearms

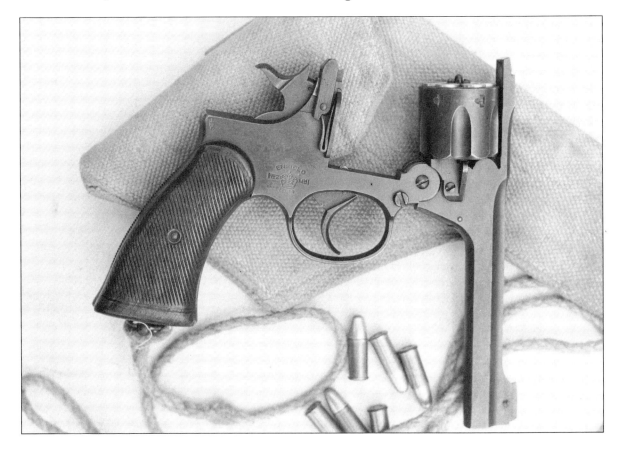

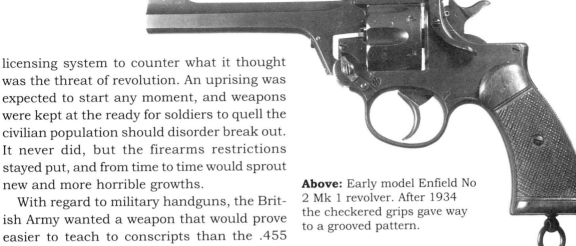

Above: Early model Enfield No 2 Mk 1 revolver. After 1934 the checkered grips gave way to a grooved pattern.

licensing system to counter what it thought was the threat of revolution. An uprising was expected to start any moment, and weapons were kept at the ready for soldiers to quell the civilian population should disorder break out. It never did, but the firearms restrictions stayed put, and from time to time would sprout new and more horrible growths.

With regard to military handguns, the British Army wanted a weapon that would prove easier to teach to conscripts than the .455 revolver. They did not consider replacing their revolvers with autopistol designs.

The firm of P. Webley & Son, who had designed Britain's front-line service sidearms since 1887, set to work scaling their pistol down for the .380in cartridge (a version of the .38 Smith & Wesson, not the .380 also known as the 9mm Short). When Webley came up with their .380in Mk IV revolver in 1923, the government did not adopt it. Instead, they took it as a basis for further development.

The design was re-worked at the Royal Smallarms Factory at Enfield Lock, Middlesex. The changes included making the trigger guard integral to the frame rather than as a bolt-on accessory, and the new pistol was unveiled in 1927. Manufacture began at Enfield that year, with no discernible benefit to Webley for their original contribution to the design. The Enfield No 2 Mk 1 revolver was officially adopted in 1932. The grips were simplified from cross-checkered to grooved walnut in 1934.

Two kinds of holster were issued: a flap holster for general use; and, for vehicle crews, one with an open top, with six loops for spare

Left: British .38in Enfield No 2 Mk 1 revolver, dated 1939, displayed with lanyard, canvas holster and 1941 ammunition. Note grooved post-1934 grips.

ammunition, designed to ride on the thigh. In 1938, allegedly after complaints about the hammer spur catching on parts of the vehicle, the Enfield design was modified to double-action-only. Some revolvers were converted, while others were built without hammer spurs. Production of spurred revolvers appears to have continued into 1939, but by the time the war started for Britain on 3 September that year it seems that no further spurred revolvers were produced.

This standard explanation of the adaptation of these British revolvers has always intrigued us, for the vehicle crew holster, despite being open-topped, fully protects the hammer spur, as it has the cleaning rod in front of it. Besides, the retaining strap on the vehicle holster relies entirely on the hammer spur to keep the revolver in, so removing the spur made no sense to us. We thought that possibly the lanyard caused the problems, or in some way the design of the holster—which in 1941 was modified to ride much higher. We suspect that removing hammer spurs was a little drastic in the circumstances and was not a properly thought-out decision. It would have been simpler to issue flap holsters to vehicle crews and solve the problem that way, but, instead, the revolver was made inherently less useful and

Left: Close-up of No 2 Mk 1** revolver, showing the Albion logo and year of manufacture (1942). The first star denotes double action only, as seen from the absence on the hammer of a cocking spur, and the second star denotes a safety stop, left out of later production models to speed manufacture. Double star models can go off if dropped on the muzzle! Note black bakelite grips with finger extensions: we have also seen this pattern of grip made in walnut and white metal.

undoubtedly compromised the safety of some British troops in the process.

The accuracy of the revolver on single action was quite acceptable, while double-action shooting was not taught systematically in the British Army at the time. The Army's pamphlet dealing with revolver shooting issued in 1941 merely suggests supporting the strong hand with the weak at the wrist. The real problem with the Enfield is pulling through its 10lb trigger.

Accuracy was not assisted by another change in 1938 in the ammunition—from a 200-grain lead bullet to a 178-grain jacketed bullet and a slight increase in the powder charge. This modification was said to make no difference to accuracy, but in our tests the lighter bullets shoot lower than the 200-grain lead ones that we obtained from the Imperial Bullet Company in Worcester.

Other brands of .38S&W, which are interchangeable with, but not identical to, the British .380in revolver, tend to have still lighter bullets—for example Geco, which have 146-grain lead. One needs to try 200-grain lead

bullets to duplicate the prewar performance of these military revolvers. With the right ammunition they shoot accurately and with good effect.

The grip was enlarged to the top on the post-1938 double-action-only revolvers in an effort to make shooting easier. These grips were walnut, but were soon replaced by hard black bakelite grips. These frequently have a brass disc, for unit identification marks, on the right grip.

Once the decision on a double-action-only revolver for the war period had been made, production was increased in 1941 by getting the motor company Albion to make some of them. They made a few hundred in 1941, and several thousand in both 1942 and 1943. The Singer Sewing Machine Company made parts—springs and the like—for the Albion production revolvers.

One Albion revolver turned up with white metal grips, sand-cast to duplicate the bakelite type. We do not know where these grips came from, and wonder whether they had been introduced by Albion (or Singer) in order to speed

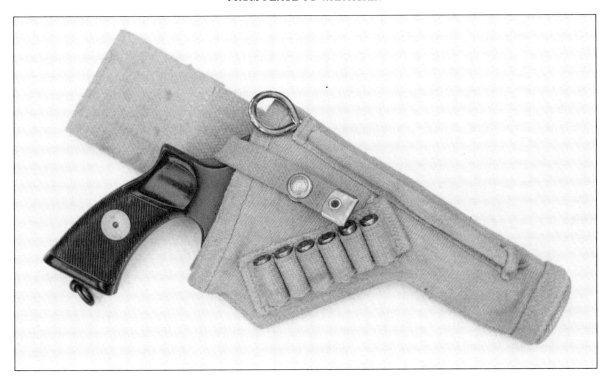

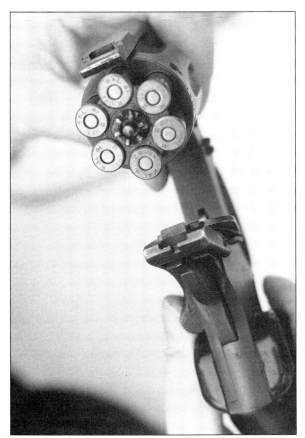

Above: The tank crew holster that caused the problem that was solved by making these revolvers double action only. This long strap version has been converted to short strap by folding the long strap over and sewing it down to make a belt loop. All open-top tank holsters have the six external cartridge loops and cleaning rod pocket.

Left: WD41 headstamped revolver ammunition, made in 1941 at the Woolwich Arsenal in London. The star extractor lifts all the rounds together.

up production at some point. But, if that were the case, we should have seen more of them. Other British weapons have turned up with similar grips: our collection includes a .455 Mk IV Webley and a .32 Webley automatic with such grips, and we have heard, but cannot yet confirm, that white metal grips were specified for pistols issued to the Shanghai police. Perhaps they are simply replacements, made where it was not practical to get wooden or bakelite grips. The Albion came to us from Israel and the .32 Webley has Egyptian police markings on it. Possibly someone in the Middle East can provide the answer.

new 9mm pistol, but he died in 1926. Dieu-donne Saive completed the project, which became known as the GP35A in military guise, or the Browning Hi-Power on the civilian market.

This pistol presented a new feature—a high-capacity magazine contained entirely within the butt. Browning was so concerned to keep the grip as neat as possible, and small enough for one hand, that he relegated the trigger transfer bar to the inside of the slide instead of in the frame. The pistol unveiled by FN in the 1930s was relatively small and compact—and, fully loaded with a magazine of thirteen rounds of 9mm ammunition plus one up the spout, weighed about the same as the Colt M1911A1 empty.

The first models were supplied with a tangent rear sight graduated to 500 metres, and a wooden shoulder-stock holster copied from that supplied with C96 Mauser pistols. The pistol enjoyed commercial success, while military purchasers included Belgium, Lithuania, Romania, Holland and Denmark. The last-named contract was interrupted in 1940 by German occupation and was not completed until 1946.

The pistol was made for the Germans during their occupation of Belgium, and issued as the 9mm P 640(b). There have been ru-

The Lessons of War

The rest of the world also took stock, and most countries set about rationalising their inventories of handguns. The Americans modified their M1911 Colt in 1926, the new variant being the M1911A1. John Moses Browning was working closely with FN in Belgium for a

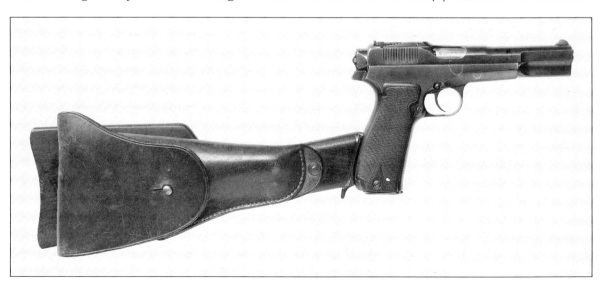

Far left: Enfield (left) and Webley revolvers in .38in calibre. The Enfield was derived from the Webley, which was developed in 1923.
Right: 1928 FN prototype, made two years after John Moses Browning had died.

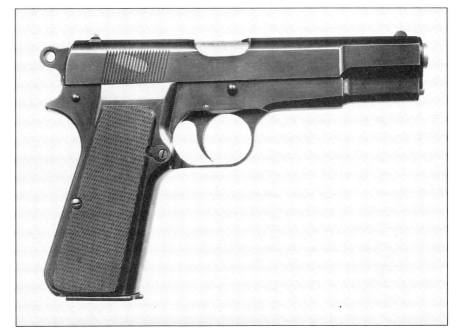

mours ever since that Belgian workers at FN sabotaged some of these weapons, or at least did not strive too officiously to maintain pre-war production standards, but no one shooting these pistols, as far as we know, has ever become their victim. The plans for the GP35A, meanwhile, had been taken to Britain in 1940, and the pistol was also manufactured in Canada by John Inglis & Co. The business was then in receivership, and it was brought out of limbo and got up and running by the Cana-dian government specifically as a weapons manufacturer.

Inglis's first Browning pistols were sent to China to assist in the war against the occupying Japanese, and were supplied with the long-range rear sight and wooden shoulder stock. Later variants were produced without these frills, and were used by British and Canadian commando and parachute units.

The two years from 1934 to 1935 were interesting for handgun development. Nearly

Left: John Browning's prototype of what would become the Hi-Power. The shoulder stock, holster and tangent sight were made necessary on a pistol by the popularity of Mauser's C96 Broomhandle, which boasted the same features.
Right: Another variant Browning prototype with a more permanent collapsible stock.

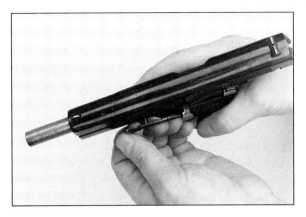

Above left: Browning take-down (1). Lock the slide open by putting the safety catch into the take-down notch, remove the magazine and remove the slide stop, which pushes out to the left.
Above right: Browning take-down (2). The slide then rolls off the frame forward, revealing the short slide rails on the frame and the recoil spring under the barrel.

every major design adopted after the Great War and in anticipation of the Second World War was unveiled during that short time. The Italians adopted the Beretta M1934 pistol—a small, simple blowback weapon in 9mm Short that was also manufactured in 7.65mm and used for military and police purposes.

In Finland, the Lahti model L35 was unveiled—a heavy, clever design that protected most of the working parts from dirt getting in or oil getting out. This made it complicated to strip for cleaning, albeit not as complicated as the Mauser C/96, which is the firearms equivalent of a monkey puzzle. The Lahti was also adopted by Sweden, whose pistols were locally made under licence.

The French adopted a design by Charles Petter as the Model 1935A. Petter worked for the Société Alsacienne de Constructions Méchaniques and patented his designs in 1934. The

Right: Finnish L35 pistol, later adopted by Sweden and manufactured under licence.
Far right: Swedish Lahti L35 pistol, made by Husqvarna.

pistol owed much to Browning's M1911 design for Colt, but had innovative features of its own, including the lock work. The French military arsenal slightly redesigned the pistol to speed production in 1938, and produced a less graceful weapon known as the M1935S. A licence to use Petter's designs was acquired by Switzerland's Schweizerische Industrie Gesellschaft (SIG) in 1939. They ultimately developed their excellent SIG P210 pistol as a derivative of the M1935A.

From the Czar to the Workers
Russia's M1895 Nagant revolver served in the Soviet forces throughout the Second World War, and production continued well into the 1950s. An automatic pistol was thought necessary, however, and the Soviets adopted their first one in 1930. The Tokarev TT30 was based very much on Browning's M1911 design—it was a conventional, locked-breech, recoil-operated pistol—but with some innovations of

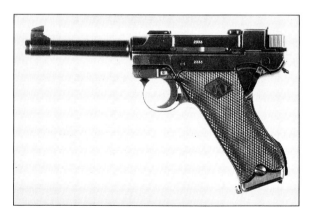

Right: Two 9mm Browning GP35A pistols of Second World War vintage. The pistol at top is of Inglis (Canadian) manufacture and has been subsequently adapted—note the replacement front sight, enlarged slide release and hammer spur, and also that the lanyard ring is missing. The pistol at bottom was made in occupied Belgium and was issued to German troops as the P640(b).

its own. It can be field-stripped entirely without tools—even the grips are held on by internal plates, which can be manipulated with the nose of a round.

Internally, the hammer group is a detachable sub-unit that also incorporates feed lips to direct the cartridge into the breech. The pistol lacks a safety catch, the nearest equivalent being a half-cock notch on the hammer. The 7.62 x 25mm ammunition for which it is chambered is close enough in size to 7.63mm Mauser—the Broomhandle cartridge—to be interchangeable, although the Soviet ammunition cases tend to split from the case mouth down past the shoulder when fired in a Mauser pistol.

The Tokarev pistol was slightly redesigned as the TT33 for easier production. In the rear edge of the grip the 1930 model had a unit that contained the trigger extension bar operating spring and the disconnector spring. On the TT33, this was assembled directly into the grip frame. On the later models the locking lugs on the barrel run all the way round it, instead of having the unnecessary bottom part ground off. The Tokarev's handle is small to grip, and the whole pistol is quite slim. This makes it a reasonable option for concealed carriage, particularly as the cartridge can defeat some soft body armour. It pumps out a slim .30in bullet at 1,450ft/sec, and concealed armour manufacturers cannot always guarantee that their products will stop it.

The Tokarev does not have a safety catch, so the alternatives are to carry it either with a loaded chamber at half-cock or at full cock with the chamber empty. The latter is worth pondering when carrying any auto pistol with an external hammer: racking the slide otherwise involves compressing two springs at once—the recoil spring and the hammer or striker spring. In pistols with an external hammer, there is less resistance to working the slide if the hammer is already cocked.

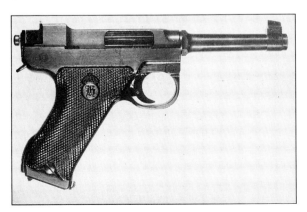

Left: Early model Inglis Browning 9mm Hi-Power pistol, sometimes called the Chinese Contract model. Later production had a fixed rear sight and no slot for a shoulder stock.
Below: Walther P38, stripped. One screw holds on both grips, which are not normally removed when the pistol is field stripped for cleaning.
Right: Tokarev TT33 pistol, right side view. This pistol is chambered for the 7.62 x 25mm cartridge, which is dimensionally similar to the earlier Mauser C96 round and was also used for the Russian PPSH sub-machine gun.

It can be argued that the noise made by working the slide can act like a rattlesnake's tail—nature's way of telling other people to leave well alone. There is also a school of thought that regards such a warning as inflammatory and more likely to escalate a potentially nasty situation into a really nasty one. As with most problems, when there is a choice of two ways to go, it is possible to try only one of them.

No one knows how many Tokarevs saw action in the Second World War. Only one published Soviet photograph shows a Tokarev in action, and virtually all those weapons we have seen have had postwar dates. There is no doubt that plenty of them were in front-line fighting, for there had been a steady production from 1930 onwards (one of Hitler's fundamental mistakes in invading the Soviet Union in 1941 was to overlook the nation's vast industrial capacity). What is not clear is what proportion of pistol-armed troops had auto pistols and how many had revolvers. But in a country that lost some 20 million people in what Russians call the Great Patriotic War, the chances are that more had revolvers.

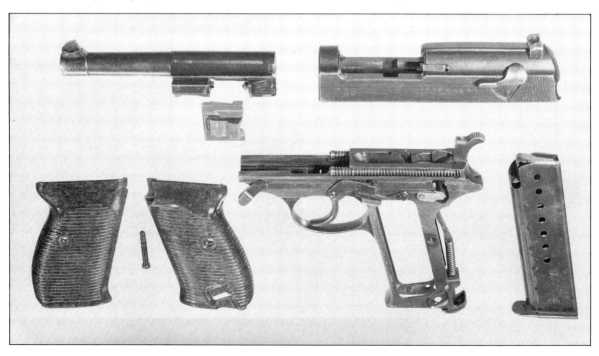

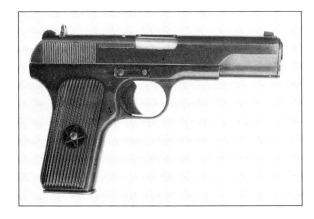

German proof marks are more common, just because most of these pistols were made under German control between 1939 and 1944.

Italy's Second World War pistol was the M1934, a .380in or 9mm Short blowback semi-auto that was a direct successor to Beretta's first blowback military pistol of 1915. The characteristic open-top slide first used by Beretta on their 1919 Model 15/19 continued right through to the 92F model. The only Beretta battle pistol without an open top slide since the Model 1915 has been the Model 8000 Cougar, unveiled at the USA's SHOT show in 1994.

The .380 cartridge is about as hot as a simple blowback can handle, and in a compact pistol it does represent a handful. The M1934 has pieces sticking out all over the place that diminish its potential usefulness as a pocket gun, but then it was not intended as such. As a holster weapon, it is relatively heavy for its size, and comfortable to grip. But it is a bit hot to shoot, leaving the webs of our hands red after 25 rounds.

The M1935 variant in .32 auto is exactly the same size, and the smaller round in the bulky pistol is comparatively pleasant to shoot.

Arms for the Axis

Poland also adopted a new pistol in 1935—the VIS-35, built at Radom. This again was a locked-breech pistol that owed a great deal to Browning's M1911. It was a hefty, eight-shot, single-action 9mm pistol with a de-cock lever instead of a safety catch. Production at Radom had not satisfied the armed forces' requirements by the time the Nazis invaded Poland in 1939, and pre-war models with the Polish eagle and proof marks are comparatively rare. Production continued for the Germans, who adopted it as the P35(p). Examples with

Right: 7.62mm Tokarev TT33 pistol field stripped. The takedown is achieved by sliding the slide-stop retaining claw on the right of the frame rearwards. The stop can then be withdrawn to the left and the slide assembly run forward off the frame. Reassembly is achieved as with a Colt .45 automatic in that the barrel, recoil spring and slide assembly are fitted to the frame, the slide stop is replaced, then finally the recoil spring is compressed and the slide bush refitted to retain it.

Both examples we tried, and an earlier Model 1931 in .32 auto, fed hollow-pointed ammunition with ease. That cannot be said for every military self-loading pistol.

In 1938 Germany adopted a Walther design as the P38, to augment the Luger already in military service. Many Lugers had survived the First World War, and production had resumed of the pistols in Germany. The P38 was a military development of the commercial HP (Heeres-Pistole). An eight-shot, locked-breech 9mm pistol, it achieved its lock by a wedge arrangement. The barrel and slide recoil together a short distance before the wedge drops and allows the slide to continue its travel. It also featured a safety catch that dropped the hammer, and a double-action mechanism for the first shot. The double action could also usefully give a second strike to a reluctant primer, and was an alternative to thumb-cocking the hammer. We found the safety catch unreliable. One P38 we tested fired the chambered round every time the hammer was allowed to drop—an experience that tends to sharpen one's awareness that basic safety rules, like 'Keep the gun pointed down-range at all times', are not just quaint old saws. Others have commented about this failing as well, and have also mentioned it in connection with smaller pistols such as the Walther PP.

The P38 grip is rather chunky and fits nobody's hand very well, but is actually quite comfortable to grip and shoot. Built with an eye to mass production, the P38 proved to be a reliable weapon to the extent that the West German Army (Bundeswehr), formed in 1957, adopted it as the P1.

With the P38 on the scene, all the major battle pistols used in the Second World War were in place.

Far left, upper: Hungarian-made FEG 9mm pistol, a straight copy of the Browning Hi-Power. Some were made with double-action trigger groups and some without the ventilated rib.

Left, upper: 9mm VIS35 Radom, Poland's adopted locked breech Browning type pistol. The slide mounted catch is a de-cock lever rather than a safety. The catch in the usual Browning safety catch position is only for locking the slide open. The weapon is heavier than similar 9mm pistols and the recoil seems less because of its weight.

Far left, lower: Beretta's model 1915 pistol. The weapon is a direct ancestor of the successful Second World War M1934 design and the later model 92F adopted by the US Army in 1985. This model is in 9mm short (380)

Left, lower: Mauser HSC, a modestly sized pistol in .32 or 380 produced in competition to Walther's PP and PPK models. Both Mauser and Walther pistols saw service in the war as holster weapons.

Below: A later Beretta M1915/19/23. Shoulder stocks were an essential sales point on pistols between the wars.

The Second World War

The precise date for the opening of the Second World War depends on one's nationality. In a sense, the conflict started as a series of regional wars that eventually became inextricably entangled. Germany, Italy and Japan had been seizing or reclaiming territory in the 1930s. The Japanese were expanding their influence across continental Asia by force of arms: they had set up a puppet regime in

Manchuria in 1932 and invaded China in 1937. In 1935 Italy invaded Abyssinia (now Ethiopia) to gain a toehold in Africa. Germany was more subtle: the Third Reich re-occupied the Ruhr in 1936, took over Austria in the Anschluss ('locking together') in 1938, and early in 1939 annexed the Sudetenland (old Bohemian lands, occupied by ethnic Germans and attached to Czechoslovakia after the Great War) before moving in to annex Czechoslovakia. Then, on 1 September 1939, Germany invaded Poland.

Britain and France both had treaties with Poland, and consequently gave Germany ultimatums to withdraw. They were not met, so both countries declared war on Germany on 3 September 1939. Germany completed the occupation of Poland, then rested for the winter before launching the *blitzkrieg* attack on western Europe in the spring of 1940, occupying Norway, Holland, Belgium and northern France.

The battle for air superiority over Britain began in July 1940, but by September Germany's mounting losses and Hitler's desire to finish fighting in the west and get on with attacking the Soviet Union caused the cancellation of Operation 'Sealion'—the invasion of Britain. The air and sea wars continued—British regional cities were bombed in succession, and shipping convoys were attacked, but the major land battles were fought in North Af-

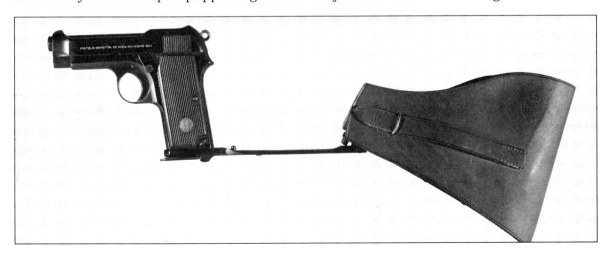

rica, where British and Commonwealth troops based in Egypt fought German and Italian troops based in Libya.

The position of France has to be understood in order to follow many of the shifting patterns of the Second World War. As a colonial power, France had troops and administrators all over the world—in North Africa, in the Middle East, in Indo-China and on Pacific Islands. In 1940 northern France, including the capital, Paris, was occupied by the Germans. The rest of France was not occupied, but arranged a truce with the Germans and was ruled by a provisional government formed under Marshal Pétain, sitting at Vichy.

The French government had evacuated to London ahead of the fall of Paris, so colonial administrations had, in effect, two governments commanding their attention and loyalty—the exiled government in London, and the quisling Vichy government in France. There were Free French armed forces in Britain, garrisons throughout the French overseas empire, and armed forces in southern France, including the French Navy based at Toulon.

French troops were very much in the hands of their commanders, who were faced with conflicting loyalties and immense difficulties in discussing their respective predicaments with either French government or other military units. There was pressure from Germany for French units and possessions to join the

Reich, and conflicting pressure from the exiled government in London. The British sank the French fleet in Toulon harbour to stop the Germans using it, and British soldiers found themselves fighting French troops in the Lebanon.

Germany annexed France's North African possessions, and the battle for North Africa began with the Germans and their Italian allies trying to advance east to capture Egypt and the Suez Canal. The British managed to stop them at El Alamein, and eventually pushed them back towards Tunisia before American troops landed at Casablanca in Morocco on 8 November 1942. Free French troops then pushed up from the south to end the campaign on 12 May 1943 near Carthage—where the Romans had stopped Hannibal more than 2,000 years earlier.

The main European battles of the war took place in the Soviet Union, which Germany invaded on 22 June 1941, breaking a non-aggression pact in the process. Three German

Below left: The Beretta M1931 is to the M1934 what the Colt M1911 was to the M1911A1. Mechanically it was right, but the grip profile needed changing.
Below right: The Beretta M1934 was made in both .32 auto and 9mm short (380). This model was made in 1937. The crowned 'RE' mark below the hammer is a government (Italian) acceptance stamp.

Above left: Detail of wartime Belgian Browning 9mm GP35A pistol, showing Nazi proof marks on the frame above the trigger and on the slide near the take-down notch.

Above right: Webley Mk IV .38in revolver, with 4in barrel and commercial finish. These were made by the company from 1923 onwards. Later (mid century) models have an integral trigger guard, but Webley & Scott did not change the designation to Mk V.

army groups drove east as far as Stalingrad in the south, Moscow in the centre and the Baltic port of Leningrad in the north, before the huge human and industrial reserves of the Soviet Union gradually turned them back. At Stalingrad, the German Sixth Army was destroyed, and more than half its quarter of a million men were killed.

The United States officially joined the war on 7 December 1941, when Japanese aircraft attacked the US Pacific Fleet in Pearl Harbor, on Oahu in the Hawaiian Islands. That was Japan's declaration of war. Germany and Italy made the fatal mistake of declaring war on the United States a week later. Japan followed up the attack by driving down the Asian coast to Hong Kong, French Indo-China, Malaya and Singapore, and by invading every Pacific island in reach from Sumatra to Tarawa Atoll in the Marshall Islands.

The Americans started fighting back just eight months after Pearl Harbor, and at enormous cost in lives on both sides took every island and atoll from the Japanese in turn.

British and Commonwealth troops fought the Japanese on mainland Asia, preventing the invasion of India by stopping the Japanese in Burma.

The tide turned in 1943 with the Allies on the offensive in every theatre of operations. The European war ended when Allied troops reached Germany and entered Berlin, the Russians fighting from the east in a series of merciless campaigns, involving gigantic tank battles, and the Allies coming up through Italy in the south and from Normandy in the west. Allied forces gradually pushed the Japanese back to Japan itself, where the war ended in August 1945 after two atomic bombs were dropped on Japanese cities.

Handguns Under Fire

Virtually every type of fighting handgun developed since the advent of smokeless powder had seen action somewhere in the world during that war. Older service models were in the hands of the police, local defence forces and rear-echelon troops, while the more modern designs served with front-line troops everywhere. A lot of handguns that we might regard today as too small for military service also saw action, issued to transport officers, drivers, military police, civilian support staff, special operations personnel and citizens of participating countries.

The reputations of some firearms fared better than others: the British short .38 ('.380in') revolver ammunition, for example, was widely

Right: .38S&W Webley 'War Finish' Mark IV revolver with 5in barrel. The 'War Finish' mark was Webley's apology for the poor quality finish, and denotes 1939–45 manufacture. Although widely used by the British, this pattern was not officially adopted for service until 1945.

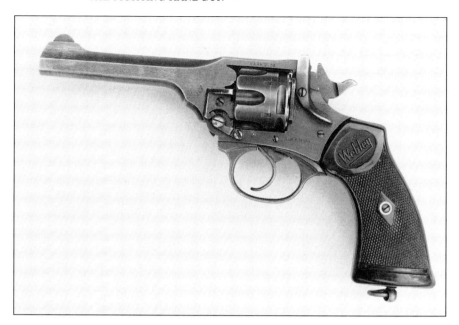

regarded as underpowered and incapable of penetrating a wet blanket. Front-line soldiers grabbed alternatives wherever possible, ranging from captured German kit to borrowed, scrounged or stolen American Colt .45s to the previous generation's .455in revolvers.

The Luger was probably one of the war's most popular souvenirs, despite not having a tremendous reputation for reliability; it was a highly distinctive piece and seemed quintessentially 'Nazi'. The Walther P38 showed up well in all theatres of war, even in the Russian winter, which posed as severe a test as any weapon could face. Small calibres were shown to be underpowered in many circumstances, but even the .45in Colt M1911A1 suffered from concerns about the effectiveness of its ammunition.

Retired American police officer Jim Andrews told us that he had tried to arrest a Nazi in 1945, only to be shot at for his non-lethal initial approach. The German had a .25 auto and managed to shoot Jim despite being shot twice by Jim's Colt .45. The mark where the .25 bullet bounced off Jim's forehead can still be seen. We thought that he might have had some reservations about the .25 as a result. But he had never carried one before then and would

not afterwards, so he reserved his pithy remarks for the .45in hardball.

All military ammunition is jacketed hardball, and the knockdown power of such ammunition is suspect. The reputation of the .455in Webley revolver ammunition was earned on the Western Front in the Great War with lead bullets, including the hollow-pointed manstopper. This was so effective that the Germans let it be known they would shoot out of hand anyone they found carrying it. In the Second World War issue .455in ammunition was jacketed, and the Webley's reputation may have suffered as a result.

The MAB.32 Model D

The French Manufacture d'Armes de Bayonne (MAB) continued to make pistols throughout the war, as their plant was in unoccupied France, administered by the Vichy regime. Founded in 1921, MAB supplied pistols to the French armed forces until closing in the mid-1980s. Throughout that time they produced a .25-calibre blowback based on Browning's 1906 model.

We tested the MAB .32 Model D, which was issued to the French military and *gendarmerie*, and to Germans too between 1940 and

Right: French MAB Model D pistol in 7.65mm (.32 auto), in the issue flap holster with spare magazine and ammunition.
Below: .32 Auto MAB Model D on the range— a tidy group from this oversized .32 pistol, shot from 25 metres' range.

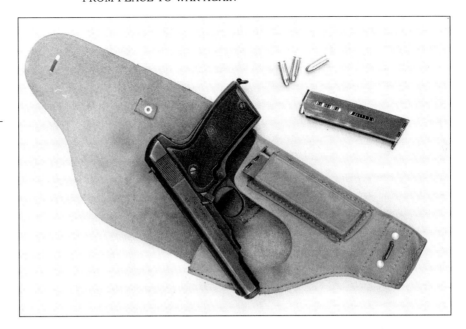

1944. Blued to a good standard (rather than parkerised) and marked 'Made in France', our example was a commercial model, quite possibly made for export to the United States—

hence the legend in English. Based on Browning's 1910 blowback self-loader, the Model D was first produced in 1933 and showed several improvements over the original. On the left of the frame, above the trigger, it has a side-mounted safety lever that locks both slide and trigger bar, and will also act as a hold-open catch for the slide if needed. The magazine release, which on the Browning is a catch at the base of the butt, is a more conventional button placed where the trigger guard meets the butt.

The Model D is large for a .32, no doubt because it was also produced to take the meatier 9mm Short cartridge. Its size makes it better suited to a holster than a pocket or purse, but also makes it comfortable to hold and shoot. Double taps were easy, as the relatively slow-moving slide soaked up much of the recoil. Once we had got used to the long and creepy, but reasonably light, trigger pull we managed some good groups firing off-hand at 25 metres: the best was a little under 1.75in and the rest were 2–2.5in.

It did shoot low—but only because, we found on inspection, someone had reduced the height of the rear sight to suit his own style. Careful, sparing work with a file on the fore sight would soon correct that bias. Other than that, the Model D's sights gave a better picture than we have come to expect from military pistols. The magazine was slick, and so was its release; the general quality of the moving parts was altogether higher than one would find on a production-run pistol today. The Model D does not hold the breech open once the nine-round magazine is empty, but the safety-cum-hold-open lever on the frame was easy to use. And our example digested every brand of ammunition we fed it without problems.

The Model D was issued in some numbers to the German police and military, as noted, and it is possible to find examples with Nazi acceptance marks. These are of some value to collectors.

A .32 for Assassins

The .32 was by far the most popular round with British Special Operations Executive (SOE) personnel. These clandestine soldiers were by and large using their weapons indoors at close range, where the lower power is less relevant than the fact that a .32 fired indoors may not sound like gunshots by people next door. That, combined with the weapons' small frames and the ease with which they can be carried concealed, may have been a significant influence on their popularity. The .32 auto pistol cartridge was also the commonest and most widely distributed in home defence and policing in Europe at the time, and it makes a lot of sense for those carrying weapons covertly to choose one for which ammunition can be had easily, if not necessarily legally.

Although the .32 is often regarded as underpowered, there seem to have been few complaints about it. At close range, which is where the SOE used it, the ammunition is generally up to the job. Gunfight anecdotes collected by Marshal and Sanow for their book *Handgun*

Below: A tighter group from the MAB Model D, shot from 15 metres' range.

Above: The French SACM Model 1935A, a graceful but underpowered pistol adopted by France for the Second World War. This pistol is distinguished as being one of the putative 'fathers' of the SIG P210.

Stopping Power included several police successes with .32 firearms and Winchester Silvertip ammunition. This round was the only one to expand on impact in tests we conducted for a murder trial at London's Old Bailey in 1994. Everything else was simply too hard to give any expansion at the velocities developed.

With so many military second-line personnel also armed with .32 calibre pistols, ammunition was indeed relatively easy to get for those operating undercover in occupied Europe. British boffins developed a silent pistol in .32in for special ops—the Welrod. Part of its name refers to Welwyn Garden City, where SOE had its workshops. This locked-breech pistol looks like an auto, but it is easier to think of it as a bolt-action firearm. The sequence of unlocking the breech, pulling it open to expel the empty case and closing it to reload the chamber is all done manually instead of automatically once a round is fired. This means that the pistol breech is locked when firing, which keeps the noise down. The series of baffles in the silencer have oversized holes in them, and on the inside of each metal baffle is an oiled leather one that is cross-cut rather than having a hole in it. When the pistol is fired, the bullet nose opens each leather washer through the enlarged hole in each baffle so it effectively slides down a leather barrel. Each leather washer is closed again by the back-pressure, ready for the next shot.

This system is as quiet as firearms get. The .32 is subsonic anyway, and, combined with the very clever silencer (and, if possible, muzzle contact with the intended victim), creates as quiet an assassination firearm as has ever been developed. We tested a reproduction made by Realm Defence Industries in the United Kingdom and can say that the buzz of conversation in a crowded room would prevent anybody noticing that the pistol was in use—unless the victim had the bad taste to scream!

The Virtues of .25 and .22

Smaller .25in auto pistols were carried and used, but they never developed any kind of reputation except for being convenient to carry. Browning's .25 cartridge had impressed enough people before the First World War as a pocket-gun cartridge for various manufacturers to offer pistols chambered for it, and to that extent nothing much has changed. The ammunition is arguably less effective than .22in rimfire (in Short or Long Rifle forms), although .25 is always jacketed whereas these .22 bullets never are.

The exception among .22 ammunition is the .22WMR (Winchester Magnum Rimfire) which is jacketed, can be hollow-pointed, and delivers more energy per unit of area than a .45ACP. We tested a 4in-barrel Smith & Wesson Model 48 revolver that, firing off-hand and single-action, delivered groups at 25 metres that would have done any centrefire pistol credit (around 2.25in). Perhaps not surprisingly, they

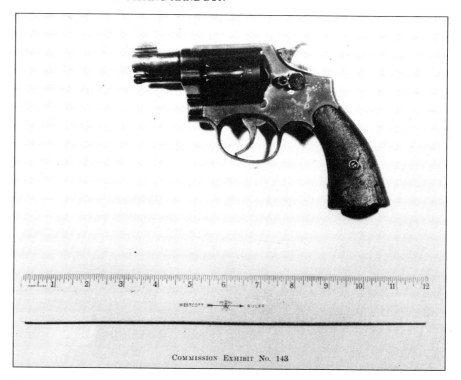

COMMISSION EXHIBIT No. 143

were less remarkable than groups (around 1.5in) achieved with the same gun using a .22LR cylinder and .22LR target ammunition.

The drawback with this particular pistol as a discreet carry piece was its size. Built on S&W's medium-size (K) frame, it could as well have been a .38 Special—and one wonders for just whom or just what purpose the Model 48 was really intended. But a .22WMR pistol in pocket size and at short range has the potential to be a more than adequate self-defence weapon. It also produces a loud bang and a suitably impressive flash (even from a 4in-barrelled handgun), which give it the same psychological advantages as a .25 pistol.

The advantage of the .22LR or Short rimfire lead bullet, or the .22 WMR hollowpoint, is that, unlike a fully jacketed .25 round, it can expand on striking its target. This gives a more effective energy dump and a disproportionately larger wound channel, but the .25in generally wins over the non-Magnum .22s on penetration—although it admittedly failed to make much of a dent in Jim Andrews's head, and may not make much impression on someone dressed for the dead of winter on the Great Lakes.

Despite concerns about its effectiveness, the .25 remains a popular option as a carry piece, mainly because of the small size of the pistols. If one has a choice, .22in firearms of the same size are at least as effective, given the practice that anyone carrying a firearm should have. And unless one decides in favour of the .22WMR, the ammunition is noticeably cheaper.

These points about small-calibre, soft-pointed ammunition are worth making, even in the context of the battlefield. Hardball is good for penetration, such as of skulls, but less likely to disable in torso shots because it does not expand—a fact that has probably given 9mm ammunition a worse press than it deserves. Jim Andrews found, when shooting a lightly armed opponent back in 1945, that even the .45in hardball failed to deliver a knock-down blow when he needed it. That said, wartime pistol ammunition that we have tested often seems to be underpowered as a class. Admittedly it was half a century old by the time we got to it, and that must have some effect. On the other hand, we have tested .303in rifle ammunition dating from between 1928 and 1944, and all of it performed near enough to specification.

America developed one clandestine pistol for the Second World War, although for an entirely different purpose than the British Welrod. The .45 ACP Guide Lamp Liberator was a single-shot pistol intended as a short-range assassination weapon for issue, with simple instructions, to civilians in occupied countries. We do not know to what extent these pistols were issued, let alone used—they were not that small—but we suspect that, of the Allies, neither the British nor the French would have favoured their uncontrolled distribution.

Trust the People

One of the more instructive episodes of the Second World War in Britain was the effect of local firearms laws on the nation's ability to defend itself when the crunch came in 1939.

The British government's attitude towards firearms in the aftermath of the Great War was at least as paranoid, if not worse, than it is today. The Firearms Act of 1920 was the first restriction of modern times on the free ownership of firearms in Britain, and was the first in a long, relentless series of moves toward civilian disarmament. It was passed in the panic-stricken belief that revolution was imminent, to ensure that only friends of the gov-

ernment had personal weapons. It also made sure that all those who had retained souvenirs of the war, or had been given captured German firearms in return for buying war bonds, could not keep them legally. Various amnesties, and further restrictions imposed by the Firearms (Amendment) Act of 1936, did much damage to the previously widespread civilian possession of firearms. Continued possession was actively discouraged. The upshot was that by 1939 Britain generally was very short of basic military firearms, and had no internal resources to draw on.

The Government had the Royal Small Arms factories, and some private companies made military weapons—the Birmingham Small Arms Company (BSA) made Short Lee Enfield .303 rifles (as well as airguns, bicycles and motorbikes), Vickers, Son and Maxim made machine guns, and the Sterling Cable and Wireless Company made Lanchester sub-machine guns. Beyond that, Britain had a small but world-class civilian gun trade that produced shotguns and some sporting rifles, and plenty of heavy industry that was perfectly capable of producing firearms should the need arise. However, when the need arose, industry could not change over or turn out firearms quickly enough for Britain's military needs.

Britain had to turn to the United States for military aid of the sort that Britain regularly denies other countries when they go to war. America's military firearms industry, unlike Britain's, was constantly being stimulated by demand—during the Great War, for example, it made P14 rifles for Britain and Mosin Nagant rifles for Imperial Russia as well as equipping its own expeditionary forces. And there was a sound, thriving home market for rifles, pistols and shotguns of all kinds.

Left: Japanese Nambu 8mm Type 14 pistol. This is the post-1938 variant with the enlarged trigger guard for use with gloves. Comfortable to hold and easy to point, the pistol suffered from various difficulties, including that of removing the magazine because the follower held the slide open.

Right: Japanese 8mm pistol Type 94, sometimes called the Baby Nambu. This pistol had a very poor reputation arising from several design defects.

As the Second World War became inevitable, America's firearms industry again began manufacturing firearms for British troops. Much of what they supplied initially was simply 'off the shelf' weaponry, such as the M1928 Thompson sub-machine gun and Smith & Wesson's .38 Military and Police (M&P) revolver. Many US citizens, too, responded to an appeal for arms and sent their own personal weapons to Britain to help in defending the country against a threatened invasion. These weapons were collected up again after the war and destroyed. So much for gratitude to a friend in one's hour of need.

The Victory Revolver

The M&P became known in Britain as the 'Victory' revolver, and was acquired in large quantities throughout the war in various versions that now provide much for the collector to seek. The earliest models came in a matt finish with walnut grips, complete with Smith & Wesson's silver logo on each side. As the war progressed, the finish deteriorated somewhat. The silver logo was the first thing to go, then the oil finish was replaced by sandblasting. Finally even the checkering was left off the grips, which were supplied smooth.

Smith & Wesson initially supplied the M&P Victory in 4in, 5in and 6in barrel lengths. Once their off-the-shelf stocks had been used up and they were manufacturing to order, only pistols with 5in barrels were supplied. This was the same as the Enfield revolver, and thus made the best fit in British webbing holsters. All Victory revolvers are chambered for the .38 S&W cartridge, which is much the same as the Enfield. Unlike the Enfield, however, the cylinder is long enough to accommodate the .38 Special cartridge, so that Victory revolvers can be rechambered for that round if required. The two rounds are hardly interchangeable though, as the .38 S&W has a larger diameter and cannot be chambered in a .38 Special revolver.

Although the chambering of Victory revolvers can be adapted to allow .38 Special ammunition to be used, the original chambers will actually be too wide, and this causes .38 Special cases to split. In any event, .38 S&W ammunition is still available, and can be hand-loaded with ordinary 158-grain round-nose or semi-wadcutter bullets.

All the Smith & Wesson revolvers supplied to Britain had hammer spurs, unlike the domestic Enfield pistols. The S&W revolvers, on

A VICTORY SNUBBY

Among a batch of Victory revolvers we sifted through when preparing this chapter was the illustrated snubby. It has the typical wartime finish and early pattern grips and is chambered for the .38in S&W cartridge. The short 2in barrel prevents the revolver from being equipped with a full length ejector, so on this model the ejector pushes only about half the cases' length clear of the chambers. This is not a problem if one points the barrel straight up and smacks the ejector rod firmly. It is slower than the automatic ejector on Webley and Enfield revolvers, but the advantages of a gun that shoots straight and has the single action facility undoubtedly made up for the slightly slower reload. The sights have a much lower profile than the Enfield's, so low, in fact, that the uncocked hammer obscures the line of sight altogether—a further reminder that this revolver dates from a period when single-action shooting prevailed except at extremely short distances when sights ceased to be relevant.

The snubby's lanyard ring is missing, and its serial number does not have a 'V' prefix, which it should if it was made as a Victory model. There are several candidates for this revolver's origin. It could be, for example, that the British Purchasing Commission ordered a few 2in-barrel models for special purposes; or, at the start of the war, when the Commission bought everything in sight, this revolver was still 'in the white' and was hastily finished for urgent delivery. It has a British inspector's stamp and British military proof marks on it, as well as civilian proof marks from Birmingham, making it an interesting and unusual collector's item.

the other hand, were accurate with the British 1938 ammunition and, having their single-action facility intact, were much easier to shoot straight.

Victory revolvers are still to be found in wartime condition, and generally quite cheap because of the finish. They are also very popular revolvers to refurbish. There are a fair number in circulation that have been refinished, sometimes with replacement grips, and sometimes converted to .38 Specials. Parker Hale, of Birmingham, converted a number of them into .22in rimfire trainers af-

ter the war by replacing the barrel and sleeving the cylinder down for the diminutive ammunition. Victory revolvers that have had such modifications are easy to spot, if only by the 'V' prefix on the serial number.

Once the war was over, stock was once again taken of combat experience throughout the world. The next generation of fighting handguns was developed in the light of what had happened on the battlefield, and also with an eye to the likely tasks that would face the armed forces of the victorious nations in the future.

Right: Smith & Wesson Victory revolver of Second World War vintage. This one has been converted by the English company Parker Hale to .22in rimfire. They replaced the barrel and sleeved the original cylinder for the smaller ammunition.

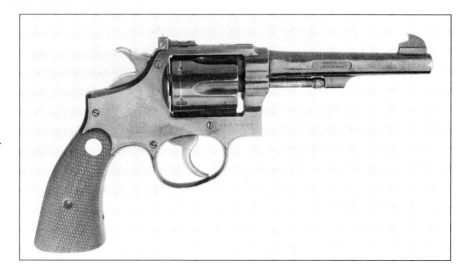

SEVEN

Sticking to Their Guns

The end of the Second World War was naturally a time for governments and manufacturers to take stock of the performance of all weapons and equipment that saw action in the conflict, whether officially issued or not. Some designs had demonstrated their effectiveness, such as Walther's P38, while other weapons had failed to make their mark, such as Britain's double-action-only revolvers. After each war the boffins get to work on the comments made on their brainchildren, and set about re-working the things that combat experience has shown need improving—or abandoning.

The French had reason to be less than pleased with their 7.65mm pistols and went for a 9mm Parabellum handgun in their post-war rearmament programme—in which they developed a new pistol, automatic rifle, submachine gun and section support weapon in succession. The Mac 50 pistol was adopted in 1950, the first post-war development of a fighting handgun.

French thinking must have been driven to some extent by national pride, which had taken a beating during the war. They finished the war on the winning side, allied to the British and the Americans. The former had destroyed their fleet in Toulon harbour, and to help defeat the Japanese the latter had equipped the Vietnamese leader Ho Chi Minh—who promptly became an enemy of France after the war, as he opened a guerrilla campaign to make his country independent.

Below left: French Unique Rr51 .32in Auto pistol typifies French production after the Second World War—a sturdy pocket pistol that could also be carried in a service holster. The short barrel contrasts with the full-length grip.
Below right: French MAC Model 1950, the post-war French pistol, a full 9mm design in which the prewar M1935A's influence can still be seen.

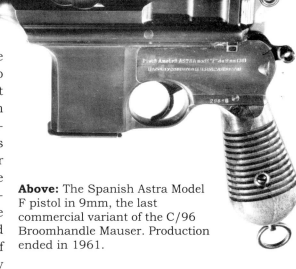

Above: The Spanish Astra Model F pistol in 9mm, the last commercial variant of the C/96 Broomhandle Mauser. Production ended in 1961.

The Swiss firm SIG, which had bought the rights to use Petter's patents that related to the French pistol, appeared in 1949 with what we now call the SIG P210. This 9mm Parabellum pistol incorporated Petter's locking mechanism, but the Swiss innovation was to place the slide rails inside the frame, rather than on the outside as was usually the case with automatic pistols. The SIG P210 is probably the most expensive and best-made battle pistol yet. It is very comfortable to shoot and accurate enough for the most demanding of competitions. It is probably the world's only 9mm combat pistol capable of routinely making possibles in UIT disciplines without demanding highly refined hand-loaded ammunition. Nevertheless the SIG P210 was made for military purposes, remained in Swiss military service for many years, and is still shot in military qualifying tests by Swiss reservists who live abroad.

In Italy, Beretta took their battle pistol ideas from the 9mm Short M1934 to create a 9mm Parabellum locked-breech pistol, which first made its appearance in 1951. This pistol enjoyed considerable success, being additionally adopted by Egypt which bought the tooling to make the weapon in their own country as the Helwan. It also saw wide service on the other side of the Suez Canal in the Israeli Defence Force.

This design has the open-topped slide that identifies a Beretta centrefire auto pistol, but is a locked-breech design. It uses a wedge, which is not unlike that used on the Walther P38 pistol, and that probably makes some homage to the Winchester rifle of 1873. The same lock-up can still be seen on the Beretta 92F, which as the M9 is also America's current service pistol.

Britain also went for a 9mm Parabellum pistol, but a tried and tested design rather than a new one. With so many weapons around that had been manufactured during the war, the British saw no point in developing anything new, and simply adopted the Inglis Browning Hi-Power, thousands of which were in store anyway. More than two dozen other countries adopted this successful design as well, making it the world's most popular combat sidearm. The next most popular was the M1911A1 (adopted by twelve or more nations), and the Walther P38 (six or more).

Below: Beretta Model 1951. This one was made under licence and supervision in Egypt and is known as the Helwan.

Above left: 9mm Makarov service pistol, right side—a straight derivative of the Walther PP. Note the small ejector port.
Above right: 9mm Makarov, left side. The safety catch, here in the 'off' position, also de-cocks the pistol when applied. Note the small slide release lever. Magazine release is at the heel of the butt, just visible below the lanyard attachment.

THE SILENT MAKAROV

One of the more interesting Makarov variants we came across was a silenced model made in Bulgaria. This is a standard military Makarov except that the barrel is 0.625in longer and left-hand threaded, and there is a slide lock fitted to the trigger guard.

The moderator is quite simple—a base unit, female-threaded to fit the barrel and male-threaded to fit the silencer body which is locked on by three screws. The body contains the primary expansion chamber, at the forward end of which is a rubber baffle, cross-cut to help the bullet through. A series of baffles beyond that terminates at the muzzle of the unit with another rubber baffle, cross-cut. The rubber baffles, like the leather ones in the Welrod pistol, are short-life and are intended to be replaced by the operative after a specified number of rounds. For the Welrod that was about 25. The Makarov silencer would probably manage more than twice that before the baffles needed replacing, although logic says that they would be renewed after each job.

When firing a simple blowback gun like the Makarov, there is a pulse of energy in each direction. The forward pulse projects the bullet out of the barrel and the rearward pulse uses the cartridge case as a piston to drive the slide backwards. The slide lock is intended to prevent the rearward drive of the slide, and so keep the noise in.

The slide lock was in the wrong place, in our view. The trouble with putting it on the trigger guard is that on the Makarov the trigger guard is also the take-down lever. We found that when we fired the pistol with the slide lock engaged, the pressure against the slide to travel rearwards simply unlocked the trigger guard—stage one of the take-down. In short, as a slide lock, it was a shambles. It also tended to work, or not work, in reverse. The spring below the slide lock on the front of the trigger guard is not strong enough to prevent the slide lock inadvertently engaging when not wanted, so we usually have the slide lock disabled with fuse wire for firing the piece.

With the sound moderator fitted the front sight was hard to locate, since the view through the sights was of the rear of the sound moderator. This would not matter normally, as one focuses on the front sight and can 'see through' the moderator to the target using the other eye. In clandestine assassinations, which is what the pistol is for, it should not matter either, since the final baffle for keeping the noise down is the victim's head.

Humane killers, by which we mean firearms adapted for slaughtering animals, sometimes have a kind of perforated flash eliminator on the muzzle to stop the bore being bulged by back pressure. With a sound moderator on the pistol, this is not necessary. The moderator is at its most effective when pressed against the target. We should perhaps just mention that we tested this on straw bales, which is our standard test for sound moderators.

Behind the Iron Curtain, the Tokarev TT33 saw a long service career, being in widespread use throughout the Soviet Union and its satellites for more than a generation after the war. The Tokarev pistol continued in production during the 1950s. Several variations were produced, all nearly identical to the original design. Yugoslavia went furthest away from the Soviet standard with their M57, which has a long recoil spring guide rod, a deeper grip and a nine-shot magazine. It was to be more than a decade after the war's end that the first Makarovs began to replace the TT33 in the USSR, and they had not superseded it in many communist nations even by the mid-1970s.

The Soviet Makarov Pistol

The Soviet Union inherited several traits from its Imperial Russian past, two of which can be mentioned in connection with the 9.2mm Makarov. The first is the old Russian tradition of encouraging the rest of the world to mind its own business. This is not so much secrecy, more a case of information starvation.

For this reason, historical information about much Russian and Soviet weaponry remains sketchy at best even today.

The other Russian habit inherited by the Soviets was that of discouraging interchangeability; their trains, for example, operate on a 6ft gauge as opposed to the rest of Europe's 4ft 8½in. This discouraged interaction in peacetime and stopped an invader running his trains on Russian tracks in time of war—a stratagem that paid off when Nazi Germany invaded the Soviet Union in 1941.

At that time, the Soviet Army was equipped with TT30 and TT33 Tokarev pistols—eight-shot, semi-automatic, recoil-operated weapons based on Browning's M1911 but without a grip safety or indeed any safety catch. The 7.62 x 25mm cartridge was interchangeable with the German Mauser Broomhandle's 7.63mm round, which presumably mattered little to the Soviets as the Broomhandle had never actually been adopted by any European army—despite being in common use in several.

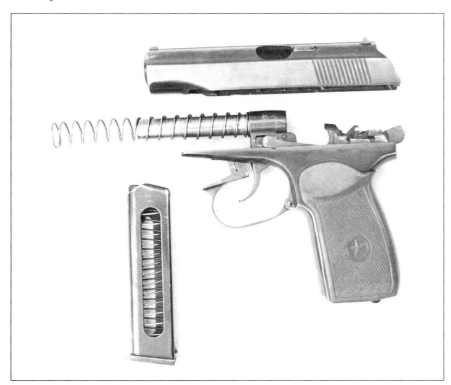

Left: The take-down of the Makarov is the same as a Walther PP: remove the magazine, pull the trigger guard down, pull the slide back to its fullest extent, lift it off the rails at the rear and take it off the fixed barrel forward. Note that the barrel is also the recoil spring guide.

Above left: Hungarian-made PA63 pistol in 9mm Makarov. This alloy-frame pistol is a derivative of the Walther PP of 1931, and was issued to the Hungarian armed forces in a traditional flap holster, with spare magazine and cleaning rod.
Top right: Czech VZ52 pistol, chambered for the 7.62 x 25mm sub-machine gun cartridge. It is a hefty, 'no frills' design, and take-down is achieved simply by pulling downwards on the threaded button at the front of the trigger guard.
Above right: Colt Police Positive Special revolver of 1951 manufacture. These weapons were made in both .38in special and the shorter cased .380in

The pistol's unique feature was its detachable ammunition feed lips, which guide the round into the chamber as it is stripped from the magazine. Instead of the feed lips forming part of the top of the magazine, they form part of the detachable hammer mechanism inside the pistol's frame. This gave the Red Army two

advantages: there were no feed lips on the pistol magazine to distort (which they invariably do after prolonged use); and, if the feed lips did get distorted, or if the mechanism failed, dropping in a replacement could be accomplished without tools in less than two minutes.

Keeping all the armed forces of the Soviet Union to a standard pistol design—which had to be simple—seems to have been the driving force behind the Makarov's development and adoption during the mid and late 1950s. The design is essentially a clone of Walther's PP design of 1931. The Walther pistol was introduced in .380in (9mm Short) calibre, with a safety catch that also de-cocked the hammer and a double-action option for the first shot.

The Walther PP is a small and comfortable pistol to carry, but as a defensive handgun it is probably overrated. The .380 cartridge is better than the .32 ACP chambering that Ian Fleming adopted for James Bond, but lags behind the 9mm Parabellum. However, in pre-war Europe, small .32 and .380 pistols were all the rage in law-enforcement and military circles. Designs contemporary with the Walther PP that were adopted for military service include the FN Browning Model 10 and Model 10/22, and the Italian Beretta M1934.

The Soviets were the first to issue their troops with a fully automatic rifle—the Kalashnikov—which was itself a much refined development of the German Sturmgewehr MP44 'assault rifle' experimented with by the Nazis. The Makarov accessories owe something to German thinking as well. The flap holster, with spare magazine and clearing rod within, are reminiscent of those issued with the P38. The ammunition, too, came, like German ammunition, in neat little boxes of sixteen rounds. One box will fill the two magazines.

The 9.2 x 18mm ammunition is about as powerful as a blowback pistol, particularly one this small, can handle. The slide velocity on the Makarov we tested was considerable—it

was almost a surprise to find the slide responding to the recoil spring and not burying itself in our foreheads. The empty cases finished up more than ten yards from the firer; compare that with a .45 Colt, which drops them tidily at the shooter's feet.

Despite being a light pistol, the Makarov shoots very well with its slightly hair-raising round. The collapse of the Soviet Union has put a large number of these pistols on the American market at budget prices, and this has persuaded the ammunition manufacturers to make cartridges for them. The standard Russian pistol is the most common one imported into the USA, along with those made in East Germany. We did not manage to get an East German example, and we are still looking for one made by Radom in Poland.

Small differences in manufacturing detail and quality can be seen among the differently sourced Makarovs, and one should take care to use the correct ammunition: some of these pistols have been made in .380 (9mm Short) for the US market. Ordinary .380 will usually work in pistols chambered for 9mm Makarov, but not vice versa. The .380 does not touch

Right: Ex London Metropolitan Police Smith & Wesson Model 10 revolver with 2in barrel and speedloader. Holster carry wears the blue off, particularly from the sides of the muzzle and high points on the cylinder.

RE-INVENTING THE WHEEL GUN

David Dardick's 1949 design for a 'revolver' was a new departure in firearms development. This cumbersome device has a rotary breech mechanism into which .38in ammunition is fed from an integral magazine in the grip. This has to be loaded through a flap on the left-hand side, after the ammunition has first been put in triangular carriers—dubbed 'trounds' by the designer—so that it fits in the chambers in the rotary breech.

Each of the three chambers is open-topped, and is loaded when at the left-hand side of its cycle. The cycle is purely mechanical, being either double-action (when the trigger is pulled) or single-action (when the external hammer is cocked). The ammunition is fired when at the top of the cycle, at which point the top of the receiver acts as the chamber wall. The third point on the cycle is the ejector port on the right side, where a small ejector boot in the rear of the receiver protrudes into the chamber via a slot, to catch the end of the triangular case carrier and dump it out.

The theory seems to have been to combine the positive aspects of a revolver with the ease of a self-loading pistol magazine, but the Model 1500 we examined seemed to us to offer neither advantage. The magazine is integral and has to be loaded from above, as on the M1912 Steyr. We think the magazine would hold ten or twelve 'trounds' but did not have any with which to test this opinion.

The line of the bore is very high over the hand, which is likely to accentuate felt recoil, and the sight base is high above the bore line. We did not test-fire this piece. Ammunition is about as scarce as the gun and equally collectable; even if the collector who lent us the Dardick revolver had been able to find a packet of ammunition for our photographs he would have counselled against test-firing the piece, because they have a reputation for metallurgy failures in the upper receiver.

The top of the receiver forms the chamber wall during firing, and apparently there has been some crystallising of the alloy compound as these guns have aged—which means that they are now possibly not safe to fire.

The example we examined, which has no serial number, also has no English proof marks. Under United Kingdom law all firearms and shotguns have to be proof-fired and marked before sale or export. In the case of a rare collector's item such as the Dardick, the Proofmasters would issue a proof exemption certificate to enable the firearm to be sold. In this instance it is unlikely that the collector would consider selling, so the matter remains academic.

No one seems to know how many Dardick revolvers were made. The patent is from 1949; the company went public in 1954, and bankrupt in 1960, so there could be several hundred of them out there and at least two models. The one we examined was a Model 1500, but we have seen photographs of a Model 1100, which has a shorter barrel and a proportionately shorter grip.

It was a bold innovation, leaving the chamber open-sided, but has so far proved to be a dead end. It might have a future in a fully automatic weapon.

---

the Makarov's rifling, however, as also happened when .38in S&W revolvers were re-chambered for .38 Special.

The essence of the Makarov design is simplicity. Made in just 22 parts, and easy to strip and clean, it has nothing to go wrong except springs, which are readily replaced.

The Choice Narrows

The trend among fighting handguns after the Second World War was to a smaller variety of calibres, with George Luger's 1902-vintage 9mm Parabellum in the lead, followed by John Browning's 1904-vintage .45ACP, Tokarev's 1896 type 7.62 x 25mm and with Browning's less powerful .32in auto still in the running. The Soviets developed the 9.2 x 18mm Makarov specifically for their new Makarov pistols, although one gun—the Czech VZ52—springs to mind as a post-war development using the 7.62 x 25mm cartridge.

Czechoslovakia emerged as a country in 1918 and disappeared in 1994. Despite having been a Soviet satellite from 1945 until the USSR collapsed in 1989, it maintained its own arms industry throughout. The VZ52 pistol was developed around the 7.62 x 25mm cartridge, which had been uprated during the Second World War for use as a sub-machine gun round. This pistol was intended to oper-

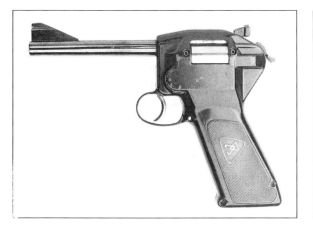

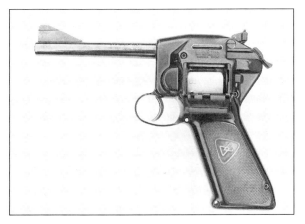

Top left: .38in Dardick rotary breech revolver of 1954 vintage, right side view.
Top right: .38in Dardick revolver, left side view.
Above left: .38 Dardick revolver with the loading port open, showing the polythene magazine follower. The ammunition had to be loaded in

through this port one 'round' at a time.
Above right: Hand held, two problems with the design of the Dardick revolver become obvious: the trigger is a long way forward in double action and the bore line is way high of the wrist, which would make for a nasty twist as the pistol recoils.

ate with sub-machine gun-rated ammunition, which is about 20 per cent higher than Soviet pistol ammunition and manages up to 1,600ft/ sec.

The VZ52 is a locked-breech design, using a roller-locking mechanism derived from the German MG42 machine gun. When fired, the barrel and slide recoil together the familiar quarter-inch before the wedge holding the roller locks in place, withdraws and allows the roller lugs to retract. The slide then continues its cycle in the usual way.

The safety catch works back to front, to a European or American shooter—'up' for safe, 'down' for fire. If pushed up past the safe po-

sition it also acts as a de-cock lever. The hammer can be thumb-cocked with the safety on. This pistol has a magazine release at the heel of the butt, as is often the case with military pistols, and lacks any kind of slide release. Bigger and chunkier than the TT33 pistol, it is less comfortable to shoot if only because the shape of the grip tends to push the hand down, away from the line of the bore.

The one we tested performed flawlessly on the range, and we fed it the most powerful sub-machine-gun ammunition we could lay our hands on; we could not help wondering where our 1953-dated example had been hiding all these years.

In the Land of the Free

After the war the United States flirted with a 9mm: Smith & Wesson's Model 39, a slim, eight-round Parabellum, came off the drawing board originally in response to a USAF request for an aircrew pistol, but attracted little further military interest in a country that still had plenty of .45s in store. The Model 39 enjoyed some success in the civilian market and as a police weapon, but its most interesting offshoot was not a fighting handgun at all. From the 39 was derived the Model 52, a self-loading .38 Special with a magazine of only five rounds, which would shoot only paper-punching wadcutter ammunition. It was carefully made, a superbly accurate target pistol, and very expensive, and, the last we heard, it is still in 'occasional production'. Meanwhile the Model 39 was re-worked into the Model 59, which was virtually the same pistol with a double-stacked fourteen-round magazine. The idea was to interest the US Navy, although in fact the USAF took up the 59. Derivatives of the Model 59 still feature in the company's product range, including the 10mm Model 1006 and the .45 ACP Model 645.

The trend after the war in the US military continued to be away from revolvers, although the revolver continued to flourish in the police and civilian markets. During the 1960s, police departments in the United States looked afresh at the traditional patrolman's .38 Special revolver, and began to re-equip uniformed officers with .357 Magnum revolvers. The move occurred in part at least because of the influence of Colonel Jeff Cooper in establishing the new, combat-based 'practical' pistol target-shooting discipline for civilians. The rules of the game called for heavy-calibre pistols, and Cooper powerfully promoted a two-handed shooting style. Both married up in the .357, which it would be daft to shoot single-handed with street loads. (We discuss these developments in greater detail in a later chapter.) The

---

LEE HARVEY OSWALD'S HANDGUN

Smith & Wesson's M1905/40 series of revolvers became the Victory model, supplied in .38S&W to Britain in the Lease-Lend programme. The earliest revolvers were blued finish, but later ones were sandblasted and supplied with smooth wooden grips. After the war, large numbers of them were sold off via the civilian trade, and one such finished up in Texas, in the pocket of one Lee Harvey Oswald. Oswald's revolver is pictured in this book in an official Warren Commission photograph.

Oswald's revolver bears a Birmingham, England, proof mark, which would have been impressed on the barrel after test-firing and is a legal requirement for firearms that are to be exported from the United Kingdom. The barrel would have been 5in long originally, but it was shortened and the original front sight refitted before sale by mail order in the United States.

The cylinder was also adapted to take the .38 Special cartridge instead of the .38S&W for which the revolver was originally chambered. The .38 Special round has a longer case and is slightly narrower than the .38S&W; extending the chamber to take the .38 Special means that the case is not properly supported for part of its length, where the chamber was originally cut wider for the .38S&W case. Barrels for the .38S&W cartridge are .359in in diameter, whereas barrels for the .38 Special are .357in. The modifications have two effects when .38 Special ammunition is fired in such a revolver: the bullets do not engage the rifling, and the case may bulge a little or even split.

Oswald was caught in possession of his revolver in a theatre shortly after the murder of Dallas Police Department officer J. D. Tippitt. Some of the fired cases were recovered at the scene by eyewitnesses, and in photographs do not appear to be distorted the way we would expect. The crime laboratory was unable to match the bullets recovered from the officer's body to the gun, which we would expect, because of the difference between the calibres of barrel and ammunition.

Oswald in turn was shot while in custody by Jack Ruby, using a .38 Special Colt Cobra. Ruby's gun had a hammer shroud fitted, for ease of drawing from the pocket, but which limits the user to double-action only. As noted elsewhere, and as Ruby's ambush graphically demonstrated, this matters little when firing at close quarters.

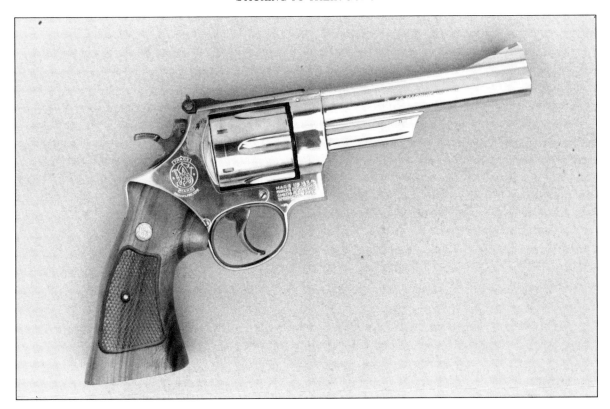

Above: Smith & Wesson Model 29 'Dirty Harry' revolver in .44in Magnum—nickel plated, with a 6in barrel.

grass-roots-level move to beefier revolvers became a positive fashion after 1971, when actor Clint Eastwood publicised the .44in Magnum revolver, his sidearm in the feature film *Dirty Harry*.

The movie (and the way Eastwood handled his pistol like a .22 target piece) was more gunfighting myth than reality, but, in a country that named its first space shuttle after the intergalactic ship in the TV series *Star Trek*, the distinction went largely unnoticed. Rumour has it that for *Dirty Harry* the studio props office could not get a real Smith & Wesson Model 29, as it was then an obscure hunting revolver of which only 500 a year had been made since its introduction in 1956. The film turned it into a runaway 50,000-a-year sales success, and now everybody seems to have one.

Opinions vary as to the virtues of .44 Magnum revolvers. If one can handle them, they are an excellent choice for shooting skittles, as in Richard Davis's Second Chance profes-

sionals' course of fire, and for certain kinds of hunting. One of us cordially dislikes it, for much the same reason he dislikes overpriced and overpowered Italian sports cars—they are more effort to handle than they are worth, despite the performance. Whether to wear on a daily basis or to shoot over a prolonged period, the .44 Magnum pistol is not a comfortable item, but for a one-shot stop in bear country one could carry a lot worse.

As noted, the .44 Magnum is the enlarged, mythical version of what is really carried on the street. The real thing, the .357 Magnum, emerged in 1935 as a hunting cartridge; developments after the Second World War had made handguns that could handle the round both possible and available. The Colt Python came out in 1953 as a target pistol—.357s happily digest .38 Special ammunition, and their extra weight makes them excellent pieces

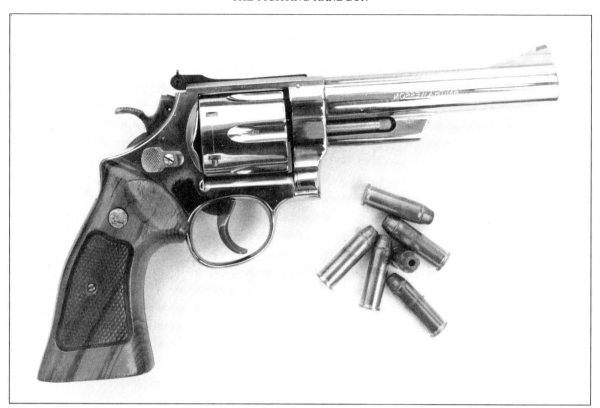

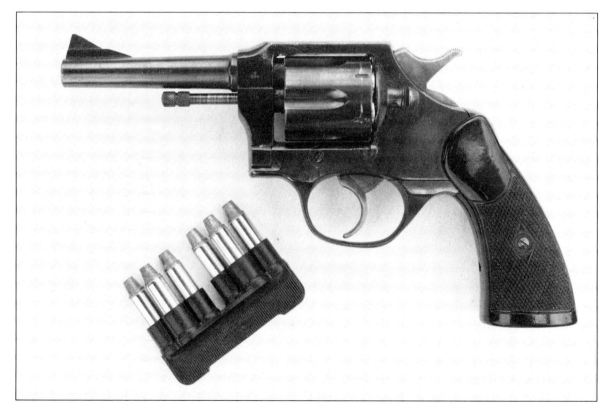

Left, upper: The .44 Magnum Model 29 Smith & Wesson revolver with jacketed hollow-point ammunition.

Left, lower: A revolver made by Miroku in Japan, perhaps for their own police. This weapon is loosely copied from the Colt Police Positive Special—note the cylinder latch and exposed ejector rod. The flat pack reloading clip is French. The authors picked up this revolver at auction. It is a double-action .38 Special 6-shot single- and double-action piece, marked on the barrel 'Special Police Model' and on the base of the grip strap 'Miroku, Japan'. Possibly it is a novelty, perhaps made for Japanese police to save importing guns—but then why put the words on the barrel in English? Usually, the native language is not used on products made for export, but who was the target of Japanese-made police revolvers? This curiosity shot well enough on the range, although the front sight is very large.

for deliberate, precision paper-punching with light target loads. Smith & Wesson's Highway Patrolman Model 28 followed in 1955. The S&W Model 13 was a .357 variation of the .38 Special Model 10. Originally specially made to an order from the New York State Police, it first appeared as a regular item in the S&W catalogue in 1974.

The divergence between the military preference for autos and the civilian and police adherence to revolvers stayed in place for a quarter of a century after the end of the Second World War. But in the 1970s and 1980s the fighting handgun evolved some more, and the lines began to blur. Perhaps even more to the point, styles of shooting evolved over that time too. And the handgun manufacturers took that into account as they sent their designers back to their drawing boards—not merely to find new ways to improve their products, but to make them more marketable and attractive as well.

EIGHT

By the People, For the People

The question that intrigued everyone interested in the fighting handgun in the early 1980s was, what the US Army was going to adopt as its new standard sidearm? The military had been looking for a 9mm alternative to the Colt M1911 since American ground troops withdrew from Vietnam in 1973. The veteran 1911A1 pistols, most of which dated from the Second World War or earlier, had been refurbished and stored in 1945, to be brought out again for the Korean War, and after a further period of refurbishment and storage, for Vietnam. Losses in those conflicts were considerable. Most pistols shipped overseas were not brought back to the United States, but were left in each country for the use of the local government.

A rapidly ageing and gradually diminishing stockpile of handguns provided the impetus for a new pistol to be sought out. Although both the .45in ACP and the 9mm Parabellum pre-dated the First World War, improvements in the loadings had improved the effectiveness of both—and of the 9mm in particular. There was, on paper, a difference of perhaps 8ft/lb energy in the power of the two rounds (the .45 being the more energetic), which was not reckoned to be critical in practice. Besides, newer 9mm pistol designs habitually featured double-stacked magazines, showing that a soldier could have up to sixteen rounds in his hand, as opposed to the seven or eight in the M1911. Twice the firepower and, in theory, only a slight difference in knock-down power made the 9mm Parabellum round a worthwhile consideration for the US military's next battle pistol.

That 9mm pistols and the Parabellum round had become so capacious and so powerful was not a product of military ingenuity or even experience. The specification of the new army pistol owed much to American civilian sports shooters and a few beady police officers. Indeed, it was, in effect, a collaboration between the American people and their armed forces, and shows what can be done when each respects and takes heed of the other.

The adoption of the new pistol was a tortuous business, but it stands in instructive contrast to the virtually simultaneous adoption by the British Army of its SA80 assault rifle. By then, however, the British Army no longer listened to what civilian shooters had to say, not least because the British National Rifle Association had long since ceased to take a direct interest in combat arms or shooting skills.

Right: Colonel Jeff Cooper developed and articulated the isometric Weaver stance in the late 1950s. The strong hand pushes forward and the weak hand pulls back; the resulting isometric tension snaps the pistol back to point of aim after each shot is fired. This was the first shooting stance that actively used two hands, and is a very strong position from which to fire. The disadvantages are a limited arc of fire unless the foot positions are changed, and the difficulty of maintaining the precise muscular adjustments under stress.
Far right: Ray Chapman modified the Weaver position to some extent—he favoured keeping the strong arm straight, using the weak arm to pull the strong arm hard back into the socket.

As a result, British civilian riflemen were not invited to test the new weapon. Nor did they strive to do so—there was little point, for it was a fully automatic weapon, and United Kingdom law put it beyond their reach. Consequently, the armchair-evolved SA80 was universally denounced as a pile of clanking rubbish, liable to disassemble itself at the slightest opportunity, by the fighting men on whom it was foisted. The section support weapon based on it is still limited to firing in semiautomatic mode only, because the barrel bends after a few magazines on full auto.

In the United States, the Army had watched developments in pistol design that were largely driven by the civilian market. They had also seen how the new pistols were actually being used—which in turn affected pistol designers'

approach to their wares. To see how this happened, we have to step back in time, for it was at the end of the 1950s that Colonel Jeff Cooper entered the story. Cooper was former US Marine, a combat veteran of the Pacific theatre, and an articulate and thoughtful man. After the war he stayed in close touch with fighting handgun techniques. His 'leather-slap' balloon shoots at Big Bear Lake, California, attracted various police and civilian competitors.

Grab it With Both Hands

Officiating in leather-slap matches, Cooper had seen one competitor cream the rest—Jack Weaver, then a deputy sheriff in Los Angeles. The leather-slap match was a fast-draw competition, shot at balloons at a modest seven

APPLEGATE, ROBERTS AND THE FBI

The Weaver stance advocated by Jeff Cooper in the 1960s contrasted distinctly with the style of shooting taught by the FBI at that time. The FBI method consisted of stepping forward and to the left while drawing, then thrusting the pistol forward at abdomen level to an instinctive point-and-shoot position. The FBI position was varied somewhat by Duke Roberts, who wrote on police matters in *Gun World* magazine. He brought his left arm across his chest in order to use the bicep and tricep muscles as additional protection for his heart. The FBI technique was influenced by the thinking of Rex Applegate, who had served in the Office of Strategic Services (the forerunner of the CIA) during the Second World War.

Applegate's system was to straighten the strong arm in a natural point-and-shoot position, while dropping to a crouch position at the same time, bending the knees and dropping the buttocks. He advocated that the strong arm be thrust forward until the elbow locked. With the pistol firmly gripped it becomes an extension of the index finger and should be pointed at the target. People who have trained on this tech-

nique reckon to get a better ratio of hits at short range than they could with the FBI technique even without using the sights. Yet Applegate's method does bring the sights very nearly into line, so that they can be used when they are needed, at longer ranges.

The Applegate and FBI techniques were designed for one-handed shooting. We have mentioned that virtually all pistol shooting was one-handed until two-handed stances began to be generally adopted in the 1970s, and that pistols were accordingly designed to be shot that way. The persistence of this tradition has been attributed to the cavalry needing one hand for the horse's reins, but it actually dates from much earlier, from the duel. Most people are right-handed and, by turning sideways on when extending their right hand to shoot, they also protect their heart to some extent by keeping it away from the other duellist. This was what Duke Roberts recognised, although he did not assume that his ideas would be practised on a field of honour.

---

yards' range. Competitors, in haste to get their shots off, made the old mistake of firing before the pistol was pointed in the right direction. Cooper recognised that, to hit something, the pistol's front sight had to be pointed at it. Jack Weaver was using his front sight, and any time he lost getting the pistol on line was made up when he hit the balloon first time.

Weaver was shooting two-handed, quickly, and winning. His technique was to draw and, as he brought the revolver up towards his line of sight, he dropped his head to meet it and caught his strong hand with his weak. Using the weak hand to pull the strong arm back, he resisted with his strong arm, so creating an isometric tension that locked the pistol on target and snapped the pistol back on line after each shot. Jeff Cooper worked out what Weaver was doing with his odd two-handed and almost off-balance stance and developed it, calling it, to his lasting credit, 'The Weaver'. Cooper was articulating and teaching the technique by about 1966.

To shoot two-handed one has to stand square to the target, which is not a natural position to adopt when incoming fire is whizzing about. There is a powerful tendency, under fire, to flatten oneself out against something solid—a wall, the floor, anything. If that means getting as low as possible, it means being flat on one's front or, more rarely, one's back. In the Great War, the British officer Captain Tracy identified a use for the weak hand when shooting from flat on the ground, and invented a cup-and-saucer technique. In the Second World War, the British Army's training pamphlet on pistol shooting suggested using the weak arm for support when aiming.

The same pamphlet also described an instinctive point-and-shoot technique with one's body squared to the target—and recommended firing two shots in quick succession. Applegate's point-and-shoot technique (see inset) picked up from here, and his name has been associated with police training in the United States. Shooters and policemen who

Right: Massad F. Ayoob propounds the isosceles position—a strong boxer stance with both arms straight and the torso thrust forward. This stance offers a wide arc of fire without the need to move the feet, and can be maintained without difficulty under stress. Ayoob also teaches the other two methods, as each has its relative strengths and weaknesses.

made original contributions to the craft of combat shooting in this period, and who spread the new wisdon, included Elmer Keith and Bill Jordan—both of whom committed their memoirs to print. Another man associated with firearms training and who also wrote about it was Ed McGivern.

Time marched on. Ray Chapman modified the technique and called his stance the modified Weaver, although most people prefer to call it the Chapman. What he did was lock the gun arm, straight out, with the weak hand wrapped around the gun hand and with the weak arm slightly bent and pulling back against the strong one.

Ayoob and the Isosceles

The isosceles position—both arms locked straight—was derided as the 'Angie Dickinson' position, after the actress who played the lead in the TV series *Police Woman.* Received wisdom is that the position was developed by Paul Weston, who after military service in the US Navy and police service in New York, retired to the Midwest to run a shooting school.

His position called for the shooter to lean backwards to counterbalance the handgun, leaving him in some difficulty during recoil. The position offers one interesting advantage over the Weaver, however. Beginners taught the Weaver have a tendency to anticipate the recoil and drive the muzzle downwards as they fire, which can result in bullets hitting the ground somewhere in front of the targets. That does not happen with the isosceles position, as the shooter is already off balance backwards. He has to shoot straight and then let the recoil push the gun upwards. This stance

attracted some followers; we saw it demonstrated by a Belgian army officer in 1989 and learned that he thought everyone shot pistols that way.

Massad F. Ayoob refined and adapted the isosceles position and made a case for its use. The essential difference is that Ayoob teaches the isosceles hand technique over what he decoratively calls the 'low vulture' stance—an aggressive boxer's position that provides a strong platform for any two-handed shooting technique. Ayoob argues that with this refined isosceles position the shooter gets a much wider arc of fire without changing his stance than is possible with the Weaver. He has also pointed out that the Weaver is a fairly complex and precise position, calling on the shooter to get everything meticulously correct for it to work. Under stress it tends to fall apart.

A simple technique that lines up as much of the tension in the body into a symmetrical posture is less likely to fail. Ayoob, however, continues to teach all three techniques on his courses, being of the opinion that each has its relative strengths and weaknesses according to the circumstances.

Two hands on the handgun and use of the sights as a fighting stance gradually had an effect on firearms development. Sights got bigger and better, while pistol grips started to bulge as the importance of making the grip fit one hand receded in the minds of designers.

Meanwhile, throughout this period, shooting for sport was taking off, and it was in the civilian clubs that new shooting techniques, such as the Weaver position, were developed and refined. Ayoob's refinement of the isosceles position has gradually crept into practical shooting, to the point in 1995 when every top competitor in the United Kingdom seemed to be using a variation on it. All this activity created a body of expertise in civilian clubs that gradually fed back to other firearms users such as the police.

Training is Experience

Ayoob studied police gunfights from about 1973, having succeeded Jan A. Stevenson as Guns Editor of *Police* magazine. Ayoob found that there were instances where police training conflicted with the needs of officers on the street and that, under stress, officers reverted to their training.

Bizarre as it seems, techniques used on the range appeared time and again in gunfights. One police department, before speedloaders were much used to reload revolvers, trained their officers to reload single rounds, then eject them into the weak hand and load them into the revolver again. This technique turned up on the street, when an officer fired six shots, ejected the empties into his hand, reloaded the cases into his revolver then tried to shoot the suspect with a revolver loaded with once-used brass.

This can happen even under the far milder pressure of range competitions. Jan Stevenson, who joined a police department in Alabama in 1961, and went on to be Guns Editor of *Police* magazine and a Pinkerton detective before pursuing an academic career in Europe, trained hard on Duke Roberts's version of the FBI technique in that period. He recalls using it once to shoot a snake, and did so on autopilot. His first recollection was of the smoking gun and bits of the snake falling around him.

In 1991 Stevenson was training with Massad F. Ayoob as a prelude to reviewing Ayoob's Stressfire training programme for *Handgunner* magazine. When put under enough pressure, trying to beat the clock in a draw-and-shoot stage, Stevenson reverted to the Duke Roberts method after years of shooting Weaver, proving Ayoob's point that in a crisis we revert to what we have been taught.

Below: One-handed positions are still taught and used. This technique from Massad F. Ayoob's Lethal Force Institute Stressfire training programme is derived from the reverse punch in karate: making a fist of the weak hand increases the grip of the strong one.

THE INFLUENCE OF IPSC

Colonel Jeff Cooper promoted his ideas for pistol shooting and saw the foundation of the International Practical Shooting Confederation (IPSC) in the 1970s, with himself as its first president. National practical shooting associations were formed—the British one soon after the American—and international shooting events followed. British practical pistol co-founder Steve Jahme-Smith was IPSC's second president, as practical combat shooting developed apace in civilian shooting clubs.

Ray Chapman, who modified the Weaver stance that Cooper had brought forward, was one of the original leather-slappers in the Californian shoots, and a founder of IPSC. His variation of the Weaver, in which the strong arm is straightened, Applegate-style, is still taught as a variation of the technique.

The United Kingdom Practical Shooting Association (UKPSA) was an all-civilian affair—Cooper's European visits to explain shooting techniques and his 'Bren Ten' pistol project had been largely ignored by the establishment. The UKPSA originated in two clubs, the Aintree Gun Club in Liverpool and the Milton Smallarms Club in Kent. Practical shooting was founded on the Weaver technique, which at the time was streets ahead of anything used by the police or military.

The FBI eventually adopted the Weaver stance, but quite late, in around 1980. Rumour has it that they sent undercover agents to train on Colonel Cooper's courses, and that those agents brought the technique back to the department. Somewhere along the way the isometric 'pull-push' of the Weaver was lost, and for years the FBI stance was essentially a cup-and-saucer affair. Its most noticeable characteristic was that the recoil of the pistol usually pulled the two hands apart.

Ayoob's patient analysis of police gunfight failures led him to rethink police firearms training. He began to crusade for improved techniques and training practices so that on the street officers were supported by what they had learned rather than being inhibited or even killed by it. As he put it, training should be 'authentically replicated experience'—tough, even daunting, but always positive. This trend in turn fuelled the demand for speedloaders and better holsters. What Massad Ayoob developed as his 'Stressfire' training programme was adopted by the US Army for their troops, but not before the Army finally made the switch from the Colt M1911 to a 9mm pistol.

It was against this background that the US Army was looking for a new battle pistol. Manufacturers were already working on new designs that would suit the two-handed shooting stances that were appearing.

The Search For a New Battle Pistol

In 1975 the Czech firm of BRNO launched their CZ75 pistol. This fifteen-round, double-stacked 9mm pistol owed much to Browning's GP35A but incorporated the internal full-length slide rails developed by SIG for the P210 and a double-action trigger mechanism. This last stayed faithful to the Browning in that it did not include the hammer dropping when the safety catch was applied. Take-down was copied from the French Petter/SACM pistol and involved easing the slide back to about the point where the barrel drops out of battery; then (and there) the cross pin could be withdrawn and the slide rolled forward off the frame.

The 'cocked and locked' option appealed to many shooters—in Europe the CZ75 was only offered commercially, and not at all in the United States. The grip was slightly longer and rather more bulbous than the Browning; the slide had a lower profile and was that bit harder to work with wet or greasy hands. The CZ75 was made to traditional specifications: all-steel, and with an excellent blued finish, it was much cheaper than most of its competitors when it reached the UK.

The British military took a sideways glance at the CZ75, coming as it did from the factory that developed the ZB26 light machine gun, which Britain had adopted in 1935 in .303 as the Bren Gun. It seemed to be a logical progression from the Second World War-vintage

Inglis Browning GP35A pistols that were still in front-line service with the British armed forces. The slight improvement in magazine capacity and the double-action mechanism would give a reluctant primer a quick second strike if necessary as immediate action number one.

The CZ75 was sufficiently similar to the Browning for retraining to be kept minimal, but political indecision left the Army with their Brownings for another generation. The stock of Inglis Browning No 2 Mk 1* pistols was supplemented with the commercial purchase of some 1965-pattern pistols from FN in Belgium, and occasional subsequent purchases of Mks 2 and 3 pattern Brownings, all 9mm and all known as the L9A1 in the stores lists.

Some Walther PP pistols in 9mm short were commercially bought for undercover use in Northern Ireland, and some similar purchases of SIG P226 and P228 pistols have been made for special forces use. With body armour now so common, 9mm is not expected in British

military circles to be the calibre choice of any future sidearm; the next British military individual weapon is more likely to be a compact sub-machine gun in a rifle calibre.

The CZ, meanwhile, enjoyed commercial success in Europe and the United Kingdom, but was not widely seen in the United States until after the collapse of the Soviet Union. Every one of these pistols we have tested has shot well, albeit with consistently wider groups than a match grade barrel would manage. The only problem we have encountered was that some had much stiffer trigger pulls than others, which was correctible by a gunsmith.

We Test the Beretta, Too

The Beretta 92F was the ultimate winner of the US army trials, being adopted for service in 1985. The only serious competitors to this were the SIG Sauer P226, which was a re-work of their P220 model specifically to compete in the trials, and Smith & Wesson's updated version of the Model 59.

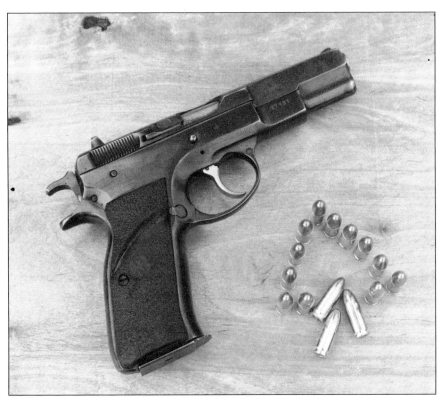

Left: 9mm CZ75, a 15-shot double-stacked auto pistol with features derived from both the Browning Hi-Power and the SIG P210 pistols. Introduced in 1975, it anticipated the trend towards high-capacity auto pistols. **Above right:** Beretta 92FS with the slide removed. The barrel does not tip towards the magazine as do Browning designs, but the magazine presents the next round high enough for virtually straight delivery into the chamber. **Above far right:** SIG P226 9mm pistol, the only serious rival to the Beretta 92F in the (some say fixed) US adoption race.

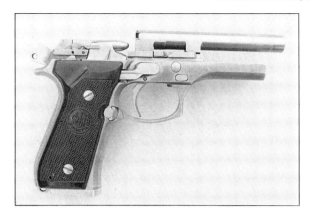

The Beretta we tested notched up mileage quite quickly and passed the 50,000-round mark after about eighteen months' service. We test-fired the pistol quite often, and allowed it to be used a great deal at our club, so that it was used a lot without our paying for the ammunition!

The working parts showed no signs of uneven wear, and we paid particular attention to the slide, as cracked slides and even slide separations have been mentioned in American military experience. The latest models for target-shooters have the slide beefed up a little in front of and around the wedge lock cutouts in response to the problems with some production firearms, but that 'improvement' was clearly not necessary for our test gun, which is still banging on cheerfully without any sign of wear in that department.

The Beretta does not have an ejector port because of the open-topped slide, so in recoil the whole of the top of the pistol opens and the empty case is released into fresh air with nothing for it to jam against. We never had a stovepipe jam or any other foul-up apart from the odd misfire which could be blamed wholly on the ammunition. Jams are a nuisance at any time, and with inexperienced shooters they cause the additional risk of the muzzle straying if they try to rectify the fault on the firing line themselves.

Not the least of the weapon's attractions was that the clear sight picture was easy to acquire, and the group printed where the sights pointed. There is probably nothing more irritating than fixed-sight pistols which shoot low left or otherwise off-centre. Aiming-off is an unsatisfactory way of getting a decent score, so any pistol which is not true should be adjusted if possible.

One is entitled to expect a decent performance from a pistol which, out-of-the-box, is one of the most expensive of its type, but in this case at least one gets what one pays for— a reliable tool which purrs on and on. The Beretta has a wedge lock to hold barrel and slide together, reminiscent of that on the old Winchester 1873 rifle. When fired, the barrel and slide recoil together a short way before the wedge drops and the slide carries on to the rear.

Unlike the Browning designs, the barrel does not tip during cycling, nor need to: the magazine presents the next round so high that the slide scoops it straight into the chamber without any problem. The hefty trigger transfer bar is mounted on the outside of the frame on the right. Also on the right is the extractor claw, which is red painted on top and is intended to act as a loaded-condition indicator. Unfortunately it does not protrude as proudly as does the Luger extractor, which could easily be felt standing proud as a warning that the chamber was loaded.

With the Beretta, the extractor stands out a little when held there by the cartridge rim, but when empty it is still rather proud, so feeling it in the dark is not a reliable way of as-

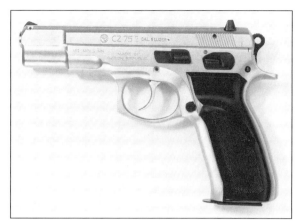 

Above left: CZ75 9mm pistol, a nickel plated version but otherwise unchanged from the 1975 model. The large slide release is seen over the trigger and the large safety catch to the rear of the slide release.
Above right: CZ85 takes the design forward—a Mk 2 CZ75!

sessing the pistol's condition. With the safety on, the slide can be eased back about half way and any round in the chamber will be partly withdrawn to where it can easily be felt, but when the pistol returns to battery the hammer will drop noisily unless it is eased down with the thumb.

The fifteen-shot magazines can have sixteen rounds squeezed in, especially if one needs to be chambered right away. Ease of dismantling is an attractive feature of this pistol, given that nothing springs out or drops on the floor. It is almost *too* cool: Highway Patrolmen in California found that they could snap the slides off one another's guns in a quick, one-handed movement. Although it is unlikely that any suspect could get close enough to a policeman to do that, the thought was there. Outside real policing, the Beretta 92F made it as Mel Gibson's piece in the *Lethal Weapon* series of films, and likewise in the hands of Bruce Willis in the *Die Hard* series.

The US Army adopted the pistol as the M9 at the close of a hard-fought competition that has done much to stimulate firearms development in recent times.

Outside the Race: Ruger P85

Ruger had their P85 under development at the time but did not put it forward for the trials, partly because it was not really ready and partly because the trials seemed to be politically rigged anyway. The P85 was eventually

put on the market and attracted a following, as have all Ruger's products. The P85 complies with all the requirements of the Army specification—a fifteen-shot, double-stacked magazine, a safety catch that also de-cocks the pistol and so forth.

In the hand, we found that although the grip allows a high hand position at the back, the trigger guard forces the hand downwards at the front. The position where the middle finger should be against the front grip is actually occupied by the trigger guard and the magazine release. Forcing the hand down the grip that way denies an ideal hand position on the grip.

Using the pistol two-handed compensates for that and does afford sufficient control. But it is little difficulties like this that detract from what is otherwise a good, strong design, improved on dramatically by the P90, which is still in production. Perhaps Ruger were influenced by the two-handed stances into not worrying as much about the pistol's performance in one-handed positions. However, the fact that two-handed shooting is currently the norm should not obscure the fact that a lot of gunfights still involve only one hand on the gun.

Another major development during the 1980s was the appearance of the Israeli Desert Eagle and its smaller relative, the Jericho (known in the United States as the Baby Eagle). These guns reflected the particular circumstances in which they were intended to work, but they showed an original approach to the fighting handgun and had features just as useful in mud and rain as they were meant to be in desert terrain.

The Desert Eagle

The Desert Eagle concept was that of an automatic pistol chambered for a rimmed revolver cartridge. American writers have created a legend that it was developed as a target or hunting pistol. The war-torn truth is that Israeli Military Industries had more pressing concerns than weekend leisure activities, and created it as a high-capacity, self-loading combat pistol that could handle the most powerful handgun ammunition around and still remain manageable. The Desert Eagle has been

Below left: John Slough's 9mm Spitfire, a compact, stainless steel derivative of the of the CZ75 made in Hereford, England. This is one of the prototypes, serial number 2.
Below right: Czech-made compact variant of the 1975 design follows John Slough's work on reducing the size of the basic model.

produced in four calibres, three of which are traditional heavy-duty revolver rounds—.357 Magnum, .41 Action Express and .44 Magnum. The pistol is large and heavy. The .357 version weighs 3lb 5oz and the monster .50 Action Express edition weighs over 4lb—unloaded in each case. The gun is gas-operated, which takes some of the shock out of these stiff rounds without compromising striking power much; and the breech is locked by rotation of the bolt head. These are features more usually seen in rifles, such as the M1 Garand, the Kalashnikov AK47 and the later M16 series.

The hefty slide recoils against twin recoil springs—another feature more usually seen in rifles. Accuracy has been excellent in all the pistols we have tried. We should say that the .41AE has never been offered in the United Kingdom, so we have not seen that one. It is a heavy pistol to shoot, and it is debatable whether such a large pistol falls within our ambit as a fighting handgun. That said, it is fashionable among gangsters in movies, and in the Middle East is issued to Israeli special forces. The ammunition will defeat most materials of which houses are made, and the pistol is an effective weapons for clearing buildings of unwanted inhabitants.

IMI developed their .50 Action Express round as an auto pistol cartridge. Although slightly bigger in calibre than the .44 Magnum,

Above: IMI Desert Eagle pistol. Available in .357, .41 Action Express, .44 Magnum and .50 Action Express versions, this model has the dual purpose .41/44 frame and a .44 barrel/slide assembly.

it is actually ballistically very slightly inferior. Never mind which is inferior though—the .50AE makes an almighty bang (and an impressive flash in the dark), which means that some of the powder is being wasted, but it leaves impressive holes in the target that conventional patches do not cover properly. In the Middle East the .50AE has found a niche for itself in policing as a one-handed road-blocker for punching out vehicles that fail to stop. In the old days a 10-bore Ithaca shotgun was used for that: now the necessary firepower is more portable.

From our armchairs, we tend to think of the Desert Eagles as recreational guns since neither of us has manned a road block or has had to clear any buildings for a long time. Reloaders can certainly have fun with them, as calculating the load to the pistol is part of the art of home-loading. They do not make the grade as fighting handguns in our view, on bulk. We appreciate that the difference between a 2lb .45 automatic and a 3–4lb Desert Eagle may sound insignificant, but it does make some difference when it has to be carried around all day.

But then perhaps we men are just feeble, for this argument fell flat for us when discussing the weight of different military firearms with a group of young mothers. We were discussing the difference between carrying a 9lb Lee Enfield rifle about as opposed to a 22lb Bren gun. This did not impress women to whom a 9lb new baby has to be carried about all day, and to whom 22 pounds simply represents an older baby that has to be carried about too. Nonetheless, the weight and bulk of a handgun do make a difference to the person—all right, man—carrying it. Heavy guns need a robust duty belt to carry them—steel braced for preference, and possibly a Sam Browne strap to stop the rig sagging on the gun side.

Baby Eagle at the Battle of Jericho

IMI also produce smaller pistols that fit into the category of fighting handguns very well. Marketed in the United Kingdom as the Jericho and in the USA as the Baby Eagle, their first 9mm locked-breech sixteen-shot pistol sample reached one of the authors in 1991 and almost immediately became police evidence in a court case against him. When that collapsed, importation went ahead. The first pistols were delivered as dual-calibre guns—they came as 9mm pistols complete with a .41AE conversion kit, consisting of a replacement barrel, a recoil spring and a magazine.

The pistol functioned much the same as the Beretta 92F—the slide mounted safety also acts as a de-cock lever. The full-length interior slide rails are copied from SIG and the lock-up and take-down is the same as in a CZ75. The innovation was that, like the Desert Eagle, these pistols were polygonally bored instead of rifled. Rifling is a number of grooves—usually four or five—cut in a spiral inside the barrel. The twist ranges from quite sharp, such as around one turn in 14in, to quite gentle, around one in 72in.

Virtually all pistol and revolver barrels thus have less than a full twist in them, although some rifles could have more than one full twist in their length. The polygonal bore does exactly the same job of making the bullet spin around its own axis, but instead of having rifling grooves the barrel is five sided (or five cornered) and the grooves created by the corners provide the twist. The advantage is that with no sharp corners for dirt, sand or debris to lurk in, it is easier to clean and is definitely more forgiving of bad conditions.

Sand has always been a problem for firearms. Metal guns are usually oiled, and the sand sticks to the oil. Together the sand and oil become a sort of grinding paste that in time can make a mess of the best weapon. Weapons that will work dry—without being oiled—have an advantage in the desert. Britain's current service rifle, the L85A1 (SA80) bullpup, failed the sand test before being adopted anyway. In the Gulf War troops had to clean the weapon and leave it dry, then lubricate it as they went into action. Some squaddies said that merely reflected what the bureaucrats who dumped them with the gun did every day of the week.

Caught in the Calibre Jungle

The dual-barrel Jericho model did not sell well in Britain, partly because of the complicated bureaucracy surrounding firearms licensing and partly because .41AE was in its infancy at the time and looked likely to be eclipsed by the .40S&W. The .41AE concept was a 10mm bullet and case mounted on a 9mm rim. The idea was that 9mm pistols could be converted to .41AE by means of a new magazine, recoil spring and barrel because the existing breech face and extractor claw would still work with the 9mm base of the cartridge.

We tested a Browning Hi-Power so converted in 1988 by Guy Savage. The slide velocity was tremendous, cases being thrown around 25 yards from the weapon on firing. Accuracy was impressive, which could not be said for the early .40 calibre guns we tried, but shooters had two misgivings about it. One was the concern about whether the slide could take that kind of battering, and the other was a concern about the thickness of the barrel walls.

To make a 10mm barrel fit inside a 9mm slide, the external diameter of the barrel had to remain the same with a bigger hole through the middle. This gave rise to barrel walls which were both proportionately and actually thinner than on a 9mm. Service pressures were about the same though, and the potential advantage of .41AE was that it made major for practical pistol shooting.

IPSC President Jean-Pierre Denis hosted a shoot for us in Belgium in 1989 at which we used his .41AE Tanfoglio pistol. He reckoned the combination of major ammunition in a large-capacity, gas-operated auto pistol was the way to go, but ultimately the .41 was eclipsed by .40S&W, and the American market was back in the driving seat.

Colonel Jeff Cooper's doctrine of combat pistolcraft was geared to the notion that the large, slow .45 was king. Subjectively, he was right. The 'housebrick' approach of a .45 did knock down more people more quickly than the 9mm, despite its similar capabilities on paper. Practical shooting developed a scale calculation for determining which ammunition was 'major' and which was 'minor'. The difference in scoring is that the targets have various score zones, but the bigger score zones count as centre hits for major calibres.

The basis of all practical shoots is to put two hits on each target, or more, but the best two score. Shooters using major-calibre guns thus have more leeway on accuracy than those with minor. The early .41AE conversions were intended to make a minor league pistol like the 9mm Browning Hi-Power into a major league one, while keeping the extra magazine capacity. Guy Savage's conversion took ten in the magazine, which beat the .45 Colt's seven.

Time seems to have sidelined the .41AE somewhat, although the ammunition is still made by IMI and kits to convert the 9mm Jericho—Baby Eagle—to .41AE are also still available. There is also a conversion kit, which includes a new slide, to make it into .40S&W—which seems to be the most accurate .40 on the market so far—and another kit for .45ACP, although we have not tested that.

The Jericho was bigger and chunkier than the Beretta and although a faultless performer could have been improved with a frame-mounted safety like the Colt/Browning types. IMI brought out a version with a frame-mounted safety, which cocks and locks—they must be mindreaders—then came up with a compact version, which is the equal of anything on the market for quality and functional reliability. The choice of finishes—a gimmick for American sales—does help sell more pistols. We prefer stainless-steel guns or nickel plate for ease of cleaning, as our guns see a lot of use at the shooting club, but it is a consideration, too, for those carrying a self-defence piece who want to be seen to be armed if the need arises.

Blue finishes seem less able to protect the metal from rusting, although the quality of blue finishes varies enormously. The CZ75 is excellent, the Kahr K9 poor. The Jericho compact is still a 13 + 1 capacity pistol in 9mm, and the base extensions sold add two rounds to the capacity of any Jericho magazine. The .40 only drops one round to 12 + 1 and the .45 compact is 7 + 1.

And Back to Browning Again

In the early 1980s FN in Belgium took stock of these developments and came up with the Browning Double Action (BDA). A decade later they looked up again and produced the Browning Double Mode (BDM). Both were direct descendants of the legendary GP35A, but the BDM put the shade of its inventor squarely back in the vanguard of modern pistol design.

The Browning Hi-Power (GP35A) has long been our choice of pistol. Old John Moses never completed the project, but Dieudonne Saive did and the result in 1935 was a diminutively framed, high-capacity, 9mm locked-breech pistol. The grip was designed for a one-handed hold, as that was how everybody shot in those days. Browning had taken such care to keep the grip slim that he had in the end put the trigger linkage up into the slide instead of having a conventional trigger bar. The BDM's grip is actually slimmer than the Hi-Power's, even though the magazine capacity has been increased from thirteen to fifteen 9mm Parabellum rounds. The narrower grip is mainly a result of thinner compound grip plates, and the extra magazine capacity seems to be down to the quality of the spring, since it is still a conventional coil type in there.

The coin-operated single- or double-action-only principle struck us as a sales gimmick. A screw head on the left side of the slide adapts the pistol to double-action-only if the single-

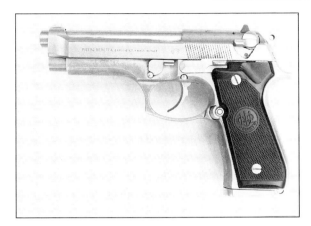

Left, upper: 9mm Beretta 92FS pistol, left hand side. All the controls are in easy reach for the firer: the magazine release button where the trigger guard meets the grip; the slide-mounted safety catch, shown here in the 'off' position; the chunky slide release at the top of the grip; and the take-down catch above the trigger guard on the frame.

Left, lower: Beretta 92FS 9mm pistol, right side, with the slide locked open against an empty magazine. The take-down button is where the trigger guard meets the frame in front of the trigger.

when officers almost always carry flashlights. The immediate problem then is that only one hand is free to draw and fire the pistol. There are techniques for using a pistol in conjunction with a flashlight of course, but they are slower than a single-handed response. Since action beats reaction, any learned technique which slows the officer's response down increases his jeopardy. These are among the factors to be borne in mind when choosing a police firearm, and the BDM comes fascinatingly close to ideal in many respects.

The grip is slim enough to shoot one-handed without any compromise over the magazine capacity. Fifteen in the clip equals the capacity of the Beretta 92F, which is considerably bulkier; the BDM and eight rounds of ammunition weigh the same as the 92F empty.

The magazine drops clear when the release is pressed, unlike the many Hi-Powers that have a magazine safety fitted in homage to military thinking. The magazine safety has the same effect as a magazine release at the heel of the butt—one has physically to pull the magazine clear. The logic of this is that soldiers are trained not to discard the magazine, as it is an expensive component, and if all are lost the pistol will not work. It is irrelevant to policing except in one respect: if the magazine is dumped in a gunfight the Scenes of Crimes Officer will find it later. The removal of a safety feature, however, could compromise a police officer's defence if charges result from a shooting in which he or she is involved.

action option after the first shot is not required. The longer, harder trigger pull of double action has been marketed to police forces as a way of preventing accidental discharges because it makes firing the pistol harder. It is also harder to hit anything without more training and practice, and a pistol that is designed to make effective self-defence harder in a life-threatening encounter does not impress us as good tactical thinking.

American police officers who get into gunfights know the score: for some of them who are killed, the murder weapon is their own service sidearm. Officers' lives have been saved in many instances where the suspect got control of the weapon but was unable to make it fire. The implication is that any safety catch or other inhibition to firing which has first to be overcome may help the officer in an emergency, provided it does not inhibit him also.

Another relevant factor in American police gunfights is that the majority are at night,

The coin-operated switch gimmick means that the pistol can be switched to double-action-only if required: this is a fad in police circles to save training time. But in single-action mode it is not completely a single-action Browning: it is still a double-action first shot, as the safety catch does not allow cocked-and-locked carriage. The safety catch is the really fascinating aspect of this pistol. It is ambidextrous as standard, which is handy as it saves having an after-market accessory fitted, which police departments might not bother with. When pushed down, it drops the hammer and disconnects the trigger, as on a Third-generation S&W auto. When pushed back up, the pistol is ready for a double-action first shot.

The interesting thing is that the safety catch also works the slide release. There is a separate slide release catch just forward of the safety which can be worked with the left thumb after some practice, but pressing the safety catch down is quicker; it also puts the pistol on safe. We can imagine that causing problems under stress.

Auto pistols universally can be brought back into action, having run dry and once a fresh magazine is inserted, by pulling back on the slide and letting go. This works on everything we have tried it on, after it was suggested to us that teaching students to pull on the slide makes the transition to an unfamiliar pistol easier. It also eliminates the possibility of hitting the slide release before the fresh magazine is properly home.

Massad Ayoob points out that, on the other hand, it takes longer to do, and anyway if one sweeps down with both thumbs one will catch whatever slide release there is. That is true, but on the BDM one has to remember to put the catch up again to get into action, and if one practises sweeping with both thumbs confusion when shooting one-handed of necessity may result. Moreover, some firearms do not have any kind of slide release catch—such as the Heckler & Koch P7 or the VZ52 of a generation ago.

A training challenge is in store for anyone who adopts the BDM pistol. We think that Heckler & Koch have pointed the way forward with the USP—one catch, which is safe in the 'up' position and de-cocks in the 'down'. If Browning tried that on the BDM, the design's only problem would disappear. Up for safe cocked-and-locked carriage and down to de-cock without locking down—that would really make this pistol worth having.

Smaller, lighter pistols come into their own for smaller shooters, but to call the BDM a ladies' gun would not do it (or the ladies) justice. The BDM's grip lends itself to one-handed and particularly to weak-handed shooting. It is said that the average American police gunfight starts in the dark without warning, and if the officer involved does not successfully shoot his attacker or cause him to flee in the first few seconds he or she will almost certainly take a hit in the strong arm, hand or shoulder and will have to finish the gunfight weak-handed or as the loser.

That is a powerful argument for being able to shoot weak-handed effectively with the handgun of one's choice (or departmental issue). If the pistol's controls are in the wrong place for weak-handed operation, this may be nature's way of saying that the pistol is unsuitable. Most 'practical' shooting competitions include a weak-handed stage, and doing well in that obviously gives one a better placing overall.

When choosing a pistol, single-handed and weak-handed shooting should be considered, and if the pistol does not measure up to one's tests it might not be the right choice. In our tests, the Browning BDM consistently came up to scratch firing it two-handed, one-handed and weak-handed only.

There were two initial irritations with the BDM: one is that the safety catch engages when used as a slide release, and the other is that the slight reprofiling of the slide and trigger guard mean that it cannot be used in conjunction with leather, boned-to-fit, standard

Browning holsters. Two other problems developed as the pistol saw more service. First, the finish seemed to deteriorate, giving it an almost greyish hue, rather like a pot metal replica. Secondly, around the 20,000-round mark the recoil spring appeared to relax, and we occasionally had to push the slide into battery. On enquiry, we were told that Browning UK recommend that recoil springs are replaced every 3,000 rounds. That was a well-kept secret, but we also subsequently heard the same from Kahr—and their springs are very strong.

Those criticisms aside, the BDM puts Browning in the market with a truly modern

Below: Gun manufacturers also have a sense of humour. This .44 Magnum version of the Desert Eagle is tricked out with an Aimpoint sight and a laser—not really a fighting handgun option, but good fun for posing, as long as one can suffer other people giggling behind one's back.

pistol that has the potential to succeed to the GP35A's throne—a piece equally at home on the battlefield, on the street with the police, or in civilian hands for home or self-defence. Not bad going!

The Trend to Double-Action Autos

Self-loading pistols started with single-action only, as did revolvers in 1836. Then the auto moved to a double-action first shot, found on pistols like the CZ75, Beretta 92 series, Smith & Wesson 59 and so forth, before moving towards double-action only. The idea of a double-action first shot was that pistols could be carried ready to fire with the safety off; the harder double-action stroke reduced the chances of a pistol being fired inadvertently.

Of the three main groups of pistol users—military, police and civilian—this thinking is mostly relevant to the police, as it is they who

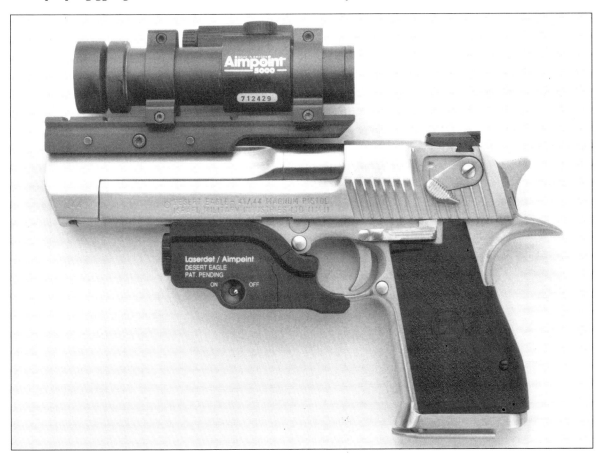

CUSTOMISING COSTS MORE THAN MONEY

Like adaptations of motor vehicles, the customising of firearms is a popular professional and amateur gunsmithing activity. The problem is that the alterations are to suit one individual and may make the piece worth less later on. The example we have is a military M1911 pistol. The slide is marked 'Remington Rand' and 'M1911 US Army'. The frame bears the legend 'Government Model' and the serial number, and also bears British military acceptance and proof marks.

The pistol has been customised, probably in the early days of 'practical' pistol shooting, when adapting 1911 and A1 type pistols was all the rage. It has new, higher-profile sights with a fully adjustable rear unit, which overhangs the hammer. The trigger is a replacement and the trigger guard has been squared off and checkered on the front, in homage to the two-handed grip in which the spare index finger sits loose on the front of the guard.

The frame has been groove-cut on the front edge and checkered on the back. The magazine has an added bumper pad. The trigger weight has been modified to around 2lb of pull, or about half that of a normal military pistol.

As older military pistols have become scarcer, their value has increased, but what is sought by collectors is military pistols in original condition. The 'improvements' to this pistol actually make very little difference to it in terms of performance. Trigger lightening is usually a substitute for learning how to grip and shoot a pistol properly, as is the modification to the front and rear edges of the grips.

The adaptation of the trigger guard similarly reflects a two-handed grip that in practice is not help-ful. The index finger of the weak hand wants to reciprocate with the strong index finger as the trigger is manipulated. Leaving it loose on the front of the trigger guard allows it to do so, which can have an adverse effect on aim. The weak-hand index finger is best wedged in under the trigger guard to help keep the line of the bore up. In that position it helps guard against the tendency to jerk the muzzle downwards in anticipation of the recoil.

The 'improved' sights would undoubtedly assist at longer ranges, but are not relevant to combat shooting, which 'practical' competitions were born to emulate, even if they rarely do any more. The problem with the old military sights is that the front sight is hard to see through the back sight. The solution is to shoot with the front sight proud of the rear sight, and to aim lower than usual on the target; then one can also see more of the target while shooting.

Adapting the gun to one's own shooting defects has been fashionable in the past and continues to be popular, but it is to the detriment of older military pistols like this M1911, which is worth less than half what it would be in original military condition.

Everyone would like a handgun that fits perfectly. There are two ways to get one that do not involve vandalising a fine original. One is to find the pistol that is best suited out-of-the-box, and work on what is there to bring it up to its full potential—more a tuning job than a matter of customising. The other is to have a gun built. This is expensive, but it need not result in one of those non-fighting poser's pieces that action shooters call 'race guns'. Either way, the result will be something that keeps its value.

most often aim their pistols at a suspect they do not intend to shoot unless they have to. Police officers in the larger conurbations in America expect to carry out the majority of routine arrests at gunpoint, but only rarely have to fire their weapons.

For this kind of work, a double-action first shot makes some sense—it reduces the risks of a nervous officer touching off a round when dealing with a nervous suspect. The notion of 'double-action-only' auto pistols takes the thinking a stage further. Since police revolvers are double-action every shot, even though most departments leave the hammer spur on (if only because most retaining straps on holsters rely on the revolver having a hammer spur), the makers' logic is that a double-action-only pistol would reduce retraining time for police departments wishing to switch from a revolver to a self-loader.

Pursuing this logic a little further, the edge the auto pistol offers to revolver-armed police departments is a higher-capacity firearm. What they are not being offered is the other advantage for which auto pistols are famous— single-action accuracy. This and auto pistol magazine capacity have sold a great many fire-arms to police departments. We cannot help thinking that the trend to double-action-only autos has been inspired by the manufacturers, who are trying to sell more guns, and that the trend will turn around in due course. And then the police will have to buy even more guns.

It makes perfect sense to have a comparatively heavy trigger pull on the first shot, as that shot will be taken only if the suspect starts potentially lethal resistance to arrest. Once that shot has been fired, it makes less sense to us to have officers armed with a pistol whose speed and accuracy is inhibited with every subsequent shot. However, the inhibition is not that great, if the shooter uses a two-handed grip. Colonel Sam Colt was rude about double-action revolvers, but single-handed shooting was the order of his day and, besides, Colt was a businessman whose main rival produced the objects of his scorn.

Later writers, such as the famous Englishman Walter Winans, also called double-action revolvers inaccurate and useful only at short range. Winans was at his zenith as a shooter in pre-First World War Edwardian England, and nowhere in any of his writings does he mention using a two-handed grip. In fact, the only time he commented on using his weak hand to hold a revolver was to note that he also had one in his strong hand.

Captain Tracy, whose small paperback pamphlet on revolver shooting was endorsed by Winans when published during the First World War, recommends a sort of cup-and-saucer grip on the revolver when shooting from a prone position, but otherwise follows the standard line of shooting one-handed and single-action except in very close encounters where double-action would do.

The British government's pamphlet on revolver shooting, which was given to servicemen to whom revolvers were issued, suggests that the firing arm could be supported by the weak arm to aid accuracy. British soldiers in the Second World War were issued with a variety of revolvers, some of which were double-action only. The combination of a revolver without a single-action facility and the lack of training for accurate double-action shooting left many veterans with a dislike of revolvers that still makes itself apparent when the subject comes up. It was Colonel Jeff Cooper who finally put it all together and recommended a strong grip with both hands on the gun.

With the adoption of two-handed stances and the slight increase in the size of pistol grips in recognition of the fact that most people now shoot with both hands on the gun—whether on the battlefield, in police work, or in 'action' or 'practical' competitions—the stage was set for double-action shooting to become a more accurate and reliable way of using a revolver. As double-action revolver shooting became the most usual way of shooting, so now the manufacturers are following this trend with double-action-only automatic pistols. We look at some of the key developments among these in the next chapter.

NINE

Into the Roaring Forties

John Moses Browning set the standard for a semi-automatic fighting handgun at the turn of the twentieth century. The Colt M1911 typifies his thinking—a steel slide, barrel and frame, wooden stocks, .45in calibre, and a magazine holding seven rounds of ammunition. A steel slide moving on a steel frame calls for metals of different hardnesses in the two parts. They have to be at least five places apart on the Rockwell 'C' scale, otherwise they tend to burr against each other as soon as the lubrication wears off.

In a semi-automatic pistol, all the pressure of firing is taken by the barrel and the breech face, which is usually part of the slide, which runs on rails against the frame. The barrel moves in recoil-operated weapons, but not very far—typically a quarter of an inch to the rear. In Browning's design and derivatives it also tips down at the breech on unlocking, to face the next round and make for smoother chambering.

The frame is not a pressure component, and in time manufacturers realised that it did not need to be made of steel. A lighter alternative would save weight overall and would not present the burring problem found with steel on steel. The weight saving could be translated into more ammunition—an increased magazine capacity in a lighter pistol would weigh the same as or less than a traditional steel design.

Using smaller ammunition also assisted this process. While the .45in ACP was the standard pistol round in the United States in 1911,

9mm became the standard in European pistols within a few decades, and eventually the US followed this example. The .45 ACP bullet typically weighs 230 grains, while a typical 9mm is half that at 115 grains. 9mm loads are available with bullets ranging from 95 to 147 grains, but 115 or 124 are probably the most usual. With the cases and powder added in, fifteen 9mm rounds will weigh the same as eight .45 ACP rounds.

After the Second World War, manufacturers tried using other materials in their pistols. The problem was to make the frame of a material that was sufficiently hard-wearing to tolerate the steel slide's movement without wearing away the slide rails. The two materials that eventually worked were alloys and polymer. Smith & Wesson used an alloy frame for their Model 39 pistol and continued the series with alloy slides—the double-stacked Model 59, the 459, the 469 and others in their Third Generation autos.

Beretta also went to alloy for the frame on their military pistol series, which reached the Model 92 in the 1980s. This was adopted by the US Army in 1985 and, loaded with fifteen rounds of ammunition, weighs the same as the old M1911A1 pistol and just two rounds of its ammunition. It may sound a small saving, and in ounces or grams that is true, but the weight of a pistol can have a significant effect on how it is carried.

Heavy or bulky pistols are harder to conceal under light clothing. When worn openly as part of a uniform, heavier guns have to be

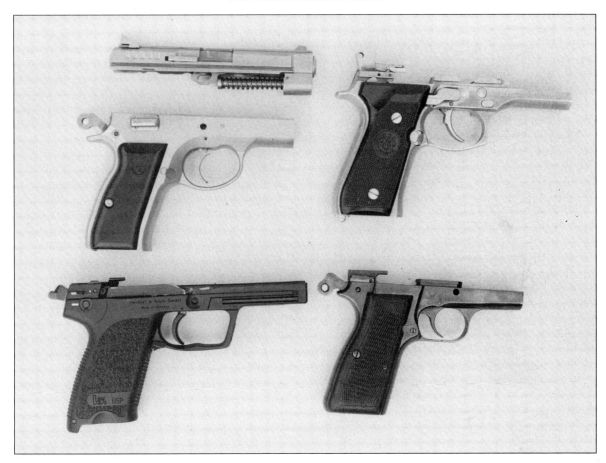

Above: Comparison of slide rails in pistol frames: (top left) the rails are inside the JSL Spitfire frame and run full length; (top right) the Beretta 92FS has short slide rails in front of and behind the magazine well (note also the chunky trigger transfer bar in this pistol); (bottom left) the Heckler & Koch USP has two small metal lugs set in the polymer frame, one right by the hammer and the other over the slide stop, for the full-length rails inside the slide to run on; (bottom right) the Browning GP35A has 2.125in of slide rail, divided by the magazine well (and it has not done that pistol's career any harm).

carried on a more rigid belt to prevent the belt being pulled down by the weight of the holster. The old solution was the Sam Browne strap over one shoulder to hold the weight of the pistol up; some police forces still use this technique to support the weight of the pistol, although nowadays the belt also carries a variety of other equipment essential to policing.

The other material to work successfully was polymer. This oil by-product is a dense, plastic-like substance that will withstand a wide temperature range, albeit not quite wide enough to cope with all the temperatures that can be encountered on our small planet. Despite its density, it weighs considerably less than alloys, giving yet another weight saving that is proportionately greater than that between steel and alloy.

Plastic Fantastic

The Austrian company Glock—previously unheard of in the world of firearms—were first in the field in 1984, with their polymer-framed Glock 17, which was adopted by the Austrian Army. This pistol came with a seventeen-round magazine as standard and was issued with a rigid polymer holster. The holster turned out to be one of the pistol's safety features—there

Top: Heckler & Koch USP (Universal Self-loading Pistol), 9mm double stacked pistol. The large catch at the rear is the safety catch when pushed up and the de-cock lever when pushed down— the sort of safety the Browning BDM should have!
Above: Heckler & Koch 9mm pistol with the slide locked open. Note that the barrel tips slightly, as invented for Colt by John Browning early in the twentieth century.

was no manual safety catch on the pistol, and no external hammer. The pistol itself has various safety features, intended primarily to prevent accidental discharges if the pistol is dropped.

The trigger is in two parts: the central part is like a small sheath trigger, the sheath being the main trigger lever. Both have to be pulled to fire the weapon. The absence of a manual safety catch is not relevant to holster carriage unless one tries the old speed-draw

trick of using the trigger to pull the weapon clear; then its absence becomes noticeable as the pistol will go off.

The weight saving between a Glock and the Beretta is worth mentioning. The Glock, fully loaded with seventeen rounds, still weighs less than an empty Beretta 92F. Glock's lead was followed by other manufacturers when the Austrian battle pistol found a following among US law enforcement agencies, despite public misgivings about the police having firearms with no safety catches and a steady stream of negligent discharges resulting in injuries to officers.

Smith & Wesson introduced their Sigma— on which, the trigger apart, one has to read the fine print to distinguish it from a Glock— and Heckler & Koch outmanoeuvred both firms with their Universal Self-loading Pistol (USP). Slightly heavier than the Glock 17 (by four rounds of 9mm), the USP features a safety catch that, when pushed down, is also the de-cock lever. The trigger mechanism offers the usual double-action first shot followed by single-action fire. A handy feature is that the locked-back slide releases automatically and chambers a round when a fresh magazine is slammed home. The USP offers familiarity to traditional pistoleers—the location and action of both the safety and the slide stop are the same as on a 1911 Colt—with the benefits of modern polymer construction, large magazine capacity and so on.

Not to be outdone, Walther came over the horizon in 1996 with the P99—another polymer-framed pistol intended for the same crowded market. The Walther company was formed in 1886 in Germany, and moved west to escape the Soviet-occupied zone that became East Germany after the Second World War. The firm had made compact pistols—the PP and PPK—as well as Germany's replacement for the Luger, the P38. This was re-adopted as the P1 by the West German forces in 1957, and served as the chassis for cosmetic successors such as the P5.

The P99 has been designed from scratch to comply with German police requirements and thus has no external safety catch. It is a traditional locked-breech design, utilising the Browning system for unlocking after firing, but it locks up on the ejector port instead of having locking lugs on the barrel to mate with grooves inside the slide. (The old Browning lugs work well if the gun is well made, although we have seen some weapons with lugs that did not engage properly when the firearm was in battery.)

Take-down is like a Glock, with a tab on each side of the frame, but unlike the Glock's they are of a good size. Internally the pistol offers no great surprises other than a flat-coil recoil spring. Mechanically this pistol owes a debt to Browning and Glock, with some flair from the German designers.

Colt's Premature Baby

For those used to buying by brand names it is a little disappointing not to see 'Browning' on a polymer pistol yet, but Colt had a go with their All American 2000. This pistol hit a disbelieving market. Aimed at the police service, it was a double-action-only pistol with an internal striker and a fifteen-round magazine. The innovation was that the barrel unlocked by rotating an eighth of a turn against a cam as the slide moved rearwards. Its main problem was the trigger, if one ignores the problems we had on trying to reassemble our test piece after field-stripping it, which resulted in the pistol jamming solid about half way through the process.

One of the interesting aspects of testing new pistols is the comments that we can elicit from other shooters about them. We are active members of more than one shooting club and try to make sure that our colleagues get to test new firearms—they are in turn a valuable source of comment about new weapons. Most are received quite well. After all, manufacturers work very hard to make their products ideal for the purpose for which they market them.

Right: The Glock 17 9 x 19mm Austrian battle pistol, here tricked out with adapted magazine base with adjustable flashlight holder, is the leader in polymer-framed pistols. The controls are all quite small—slide release catch on the frame just forward of the milled grip ridges, the magazine catch on the frame where the trigger guard joins it and the minuscule take-down lever on the frame under the '9 x 19mm' mark on the slide.

Exceptions to the rule are always interesting, and the most noticeable exception of recent years was this pistol. The All-American looked sleek when delivered. The two controls and the take-down catch were all on the left side, which naturally causes problems in a society where most people have two hands and some prefer one more than the other. There was a large slide release over the left grip and a large magazine release button on the grip at the rear of the trigger guard, both in the usual place.

When first handled, it felt like an anatomically correct grip on a top-heavy pistol. The slide being steel and the whole of the grip being polymer, the pistol does not balance correctly when empty, but it handles fine when loaded. It would take twelve rounds to bring the Colt's weight up to that of an empty Beretta 92. When the Colt is fully loaded the balance is fine, but as the magazine empties the imbalance returns, which can be disconcerting.

This minor irritation pales into insignificance, however, when one considers the trigger pull. The Colt 2000 is designed as double-action only, which is the current fad in the United States for trying to minimise accidental shootings. The theory is that a long, heavy trigger pull will prevent accidental discharges while not affecting the user's gunfighting ability under stress. It is a wonderful theory, but this pistol is not the perfection of that theory incarnate.

When dismantled, by way of a captive cross pin on the left side above the trigger, the trigger stroke was smooth enough. But when assembled so that the trigger had to cock the action, it became rough and awkward to pull. For most of its travel, the trigger did not appear to be doing anything except make firing harder. Towards the end of its movement, the trigger became more resistant. We found that we could consistently pull the trigger for nine-tenths of its travel and hold it there ready for a quick shot if necessary. This was the only way of using the pistol effectively for target practice, and if a street cop started doing that, sooner or later he would have an accidental discharge because it is not always possible to estimate nine-tenths of the trigger's travel accurately, especially under stress.

The alternative to an accidental discharge in the circumstances is a misfire; this happened several times to us. When the trigger was pulled its full extent, nothing happened. On one occasion the pistol actually fired when the trigger was released. The magazine was hard to load, and got harder as the spring became more compressed. The last three rounds were positively awkward to install, given that the top of the magazine and the feed lips are quite sharp.

The sights were easy to use, and the pistol shot as accurately and to point of aim as we would expect of a new handgun. Club members who tried the Colt 2000 were united in their desire never to have to try it again. Double-action-only triggers are a 'turn-off' in target shooting circles, where shooters are used to using them on revolvers (where there is a reason for them) but not on self-loading pistols (where for range work there is not). Condemnation of the 2000 from club members was universal, so we were unable to get the thing used as much as we would have liked for our standard endurance test.

Being Coy in Connecticut

We visited the Colt factory in Connecticut in September 1993 with Massad F. Ayoob. Staff who met us were reluctant to talk about the Colt 2000 and claimed first that the design had been debugged, then that there were none in stock because they had sold them all. Massad Ayoob's caustic views of the pistol were no secret by then, even though he had not at that time published an article on the product, and perhaps Colt were prickly because he was there. If so it was a pity, because we found the

tour to be the most comprehensive and open of the four factories we visited. We could not find any Colt 2000 pistols when going around, although we did see the boxes they were delivered in being finished. At the end of the factory tour is a large cage in which stock awaiting shipment is stored; they had fewer guns in it than we have at home. Colt's products do not stay on the shelves: the company fills eighteen-wheel semi-trailers with them and gets them on the road as soon as they are ready.

That means that there are quite a lot of Colt 2000s out there. Colt could not or would not tell us how many, and could not produce one of the 'debugged' specimens either. In theory, the design is exciting—innovative and right for this day and age when the competitor is a polymer framed pistol aimed at the same market—but unfortunately Colt's haste to get to the market made them release a considerably less than perfect product.

They could also be accused of not learning from their mistakes. Their 1893 slide-action

Opposite, top left: The 'no frills' Glock 17 pistol.

Opposite, top right: Walther P5, a derivative of the P38. The pistol is unusual in that the ejector port is on the left of the slide. P38 pistols eject left, but do not have an ejector port as such.

Right: Glock's baby concealed carry versions of the original Model 17—the Glock 26 in 9mm and the Model 27 in .40. Mechanically the same as the original, they feature shortened barrels and frames.

shotgun design had to be re-worked into the 1897—a superb design that stood the test of time and remained in production for 60 years. If this turkey gets redesigned into something half as good as the old 1897 shotgun, Colt will have a winner. Meanwhile, it is off the catalogued list.

Time will tell. Armchair critics have to re-mind themselves that their views of firearms may be confounded by practical experience. If we were writing in 1873 when the single-action revolver came out, we would probably have criticised the skinny, off-set trigger and the grip that does not fit anybody's hand. While both criticisms may be fair comment, the design worked well enough to be accepted and, nearly 125 years later, Colt are still producing them in homage to the original. Britain's 'Short, Magazine, Lee Enfield' (SMLE, soon dubbed the 'Smelly') was universally criticised in 1903 when it first appeared, and it went through five changes in four years to get to the Mk III in 1907. Criticism continued una-bated and the government was planning a re-placement along Mauser lines when the First World War started.

The front line quickly proved the Lee En-field to be a superb battle rifle. (At the first Battle of Mons in August 1914, the German opposition met such a withering fire that they thought they were being strafed with machine guns. The British Tommy also knew how to shoot straight in those days.) The Smelly's would-be successor, known as the P13 or P14, went into production in the USA as an addi-tional source of rifles, but never made the grade as a front-line weapon, despite being everything the armchair critics wanted the Lee Enfield to be. The P13/14s were good rifles, but they did not work sufficiently well on the battlefield to be an outstanding rifle. Ameri-can servicemen also had them in .30-'06, and this version is known as either the P17 or the 'Enfield', depending on whom you talk to.

Britain's most recent battle rifle, the SA80 bullpup, also met a barrage of criticism when

launched, and in less than ten years went through 39 modifications, a third of which called for factory refurbishment. When the Gulf War started in 1990, armchair critics were naturally keen to see how the rifle made out, and some perhaps hoped it would fail. In the event, the Iraqi Army did not stand long enough to make an infantry fight of it, so in-terest has turned to the Balkans where Brit-ish troops have been serving in both United Nations and NATO formations. Line infantry units in Bosnia in the early stages of the UN presence seemed to have dredged up a healthy supply of obsolete light machine guns to sup-port them, which may have eased the burden on their rifles, but subsequent troops into the fray have not brought back any stories of woe about their smallarms. Perhaps those 39 modi-fications have done the trick.

When it comes to pistols, we have rather more experience as shooters and trainers, and we can predict that the 2000 is not going to make it with such a quirky trigger. If it has to be double-action only, and the sooner that trend dies off the better, it must be a smooth double-action; and the stroke does not need to be as long as Colt made it. We hope that they will be far-sighted enough to go for a sin-gle-action option, as on Browning's BDM, which can be converted from single to double and vice-versa at the turn of a coin.

Big Italian Cat
The outstanding feature of the Colt 2000 was the rotary breech lock, so it came as no sur-prise to see that on another pistol soon after-wards. The Beretta 8000 Cougar is a bit of a pantomime horse. Its back half is Beretta 92F, and its front half is Colt All American 2000. The barrel is shorter than the 92F but the grip has been left full size, so it is not a true com-pact and to us it looks rather French, remi-niscent of the old Rr51 and other Unique de-signs. After examples from a batch of Beretta's 92 series split next to the wedge lock because of inadequate heat treatment of the slides,

Above left: Walther P88. The Browning-inspired successor to the Walther P5 did not achieve the desired impact in the market place, so Walther went polymer with the P99.

Above right: 9mm Colt All American 2000 pistol, left side. The large catch over the grip is a slide release only. The pistol has no safety catch. For this and many other reasons this piece was regarded as one of Colt's most comprehensive disasters—the company's equivalent of the famous Ford Edsel.

there was a clear incentive for the Italian company to come up with an alternative to sell alongside its well-known 92 series.

A comparatively heavy, well-made 9mm pistol, with a fifteen-shot magazine, a short barrel and a rotating breech lock, the Beretta Cougar is a handsome cat. The small ejector port reminded us of a Browning Hi-Power. The grip is slimmer than the 92F's, making it closer to the Browning grip, which was intended to be shot one-handed. As a result, the magazines are not interchangeable between the two Beretta designs. The action is conventional: the safety catch de-cocks the pistol so that the first shot is double-action, after which each subsequent shot is a short single-action pull.

We liked shooting with this pistol; being used to the 92F action meant that the trigger and safety catch were already familiar. On the range this pistol shot predictably well with a considerable variety of ammunition and was comfortable to work with in both one- and two-handed stances.

If the idea was to build a compact pistol, it would have made more sense to reduce the grip as well as the barrel length to compete with IMI's Baby Jericho. On balance, the reason for the short barrel is probably that it is as long as necessary for the rotary action. The hammer is external, so the cocked condition can be assessed by feel; the 8000 also has all the safety features of other current Beretta pistols. The departure is purely the solid slide

and rotary lock, and that seems to be a reaction to the criticism Beretta experienced over slide failures on some of their 92 series pistols. The 8000 was a pistol that we thought the club members would buy, and certainly one that a club should have in hand for members to train with.

Meanwhile, IMI's Jericho/Baby Eagle has started production with a polymer frame as an option to the steel framed versions. We have not had this on the scales, but can anticipate that there will be a weight saving. However, steel Jericho frames have a full 7in of rail inside them, whereas all the polymer-framed pistols we have seen have just four small metal tabs, front and rear each side, for the slide to run on. We anticipate testing the polymer frames thoroughly to see if there is any drawback in having so little holding frame and slide together.

History shows that Browning's 2.125in of slide rails was not detrimental to the pistol's performance, and that SIG's vaunted full-length slide rails can bind up occasionally if very dirty. But can pistols actually make do with virtually no slide rail at all? Glock has managed nicely enough, although we have now seen two Glock polymer frames blow to pieces when infiltrated by faulty ammunition. Conventional railed frames would probably have contained the blast and directed it downwards through the magazine well.

Israel's Beefy .45

The first high-capacity .45 with a polymer frame that we tried was the BUL M5. This amounted to a conventional .45 Colt type barrel and slide assembly mounted on a polymer frame. The barrel and slide look as if they may have been made by Norinco in China, while the frame probably originated in Israel, where the complete pistol came from. It would not surprise us if the frame turned out to be a stalking horse for the anticipated new IMI line of multi-calibre, high-capacity pistols.

We managed to get twelve rounds into the magazine, but it got progressively more difficult after seven. It may have held more—thirteen or fourteen—but we would need a loading tool to fill this magazine to capacity. The machining of the slide was identical to that on the Norinco—they could have come off the same machine. The Norinco and Bul M5 slide assemblies could actually be swapped over; we tested their interchangeability by firing the Norinco slide and barrel on the BUL frame, and had no problems at all. The sights were basically identical as well. But there it ends: the BUL M5 has a satin stainless finish to the slide and trigger, an extended beaver tail, a Colt Commander-style hammer and a bright stainless finish to the barrel to contrast with the black polymer frame, in which a steel liner holds the working parts rigid.

The BUL M5 performed flawlessly, as one would expect, and without any gunsmithing could become a major-calibre racegun. It was a peach to shoot, bowling pins diving for cover in rapid succession as the .45in Samson ammunition slammed into them. The wider grip made no difference and was comfortable in both one- and two-handed positions. The full potential for this pistol will be on the 'Toys 'R' Us' circuit, but as it stands, it is a good .45 ACP pistol with a magazine capacity advantage of at least five over standard .45 M1911 derivatives. And it still fits into standard M1911 holsters.

All the polymer-framed designs weigh less than equivalent pistols with metal frames. The choice of pistols nowadays for policing is wider than it has ever been, with traditional revolvers and auto pistols, auto pistols with double-action first shots and autos with double action only. Then there are steel, alloy and polymer frames to consider as well as 9mm, .40S&W or .45.

The Right Place, the Right Bullet

Marshall and Sanow, in their book *Handgun Stopping Power*, concluded that bullet placement was fundamental to shooting anyone—to stop them doing whatever it was that required lethal force to stop them doing. In a lethal encounter there is no second place winner; Bill Jordan made this observation in the title of his book about his days in the Texas Border Patrol.

Those whose responsibility includes arming others to go out and do battle, be it with the enemies of society or the enemies of one's country, have taken it upon themselves to search for a round of ammunition that will stop the enemy with one shot. The choice in the 1900s was between an American .45 cartridge that delivered a half-ounce bullet at subsonic speeds and a German 9mm bullet that weighed half what the .45 did and travelled a bit faster.

To use the formula for determining the magic ingredient of 'striking energy', the weight of the bullet and the speed of its flight in feet per second (ft/sec) have to be known. The calculation is to square the velocity—multiply it by itself—then multiply the result by the bul-

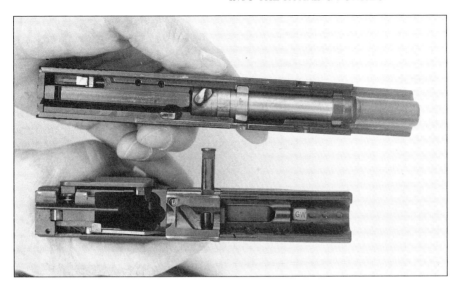

Left: Take-down of the Colt All American 2000. The slide rolls off the front; with the recoil spring removed, it is possible to see the cam that rotates the barrel to unlock it, and the locking lugs are visible too.

let weight in grains, then divide that total by 450,240 to get an answer in foot-pounds (ft/lb).

The speed of sound is 1,060ft/sec at sea level. Bullets travelling faster than this are supersonic, and those that go slower are subsonic. Pistol ammunition brackets the speed of sound, with some bullets travelling as sedately as 600ft/sec and others cracking along as fast as 1,600ft/sec.

The Second World War .30in M1 carbine round does 1,900ft/sec, placing it neatly between pistol ammunition and the highest-velocity rifle ammunition, which can really scorch the air at up to 4,200ft/sec. In the US Army trials that led to the adoption of the .45 cartridge and ultimately to the M1911 pistol, the choice was between an 870ft/sec, 230-grain bullet, and an 1,150 ft/sec, 125-grain bullet. These respectively calculate out to 386 and 367ft/lb of striking energy. All ammunition varies, so there would have been a spread of results and an average of, say, 375 on the .45 and 360 on the 9mm.

The difference between these two cartridges when expressed in foot-pounds may not sound much, but there are further considerations, some of them more subjective than others. 9mm ammunition weighs less than .45in, for example, so more can be carried for the same weight, at a ratio of about 150 to 85. The 9mm pistol would have weighed less, then as now, which may have some influence on choice in favour of the 9mm.

The Power of Life and Death

The US Army resisted that influence in the early 1900s, for what these figures do not indicate is the relative 'stopping power' of the two cartridges. While 9mm wins on weight without losing much energy, the .45 appeared to do more damage to tissue—it left both a wider bullet track and a bigger temporary wound cavity caused by shock displacement. The .45in ACP cartridge was much the same as the earlier .45in Long Colt cartridge, which US troops had cause to regret not having in the Philippines, where .38in ammunition simply did not have the stopping power to deal with juiced-up natives.

The smaller 9mm round, and indeed smaller .30in rounds like that from the C/96 Mauser, tend to pass through human bodies, causing less damage than slower bullets with a larger surface. The experience of the Philippines campaign was fresh in the minds of the US Army when the tests were conducted and this may well have influenced them in favour of .45in over the advantages that 9mm offers on paper.

The debate has raged for most of this century and is not one we seek to get into more than strictly necessary here. Suffice to say that lighter ammunition and smaller bullets tend to slip through human bodies without causing as much shock damage as larger, heavier bullets. This is particularly noticeable at longer ranges. The .30in M1 carbine round has a 110-grain bullet and shoots at 1,900ft/sec. This generates an awesome 880ft/lb of energy at the muzzle—virtually the same as a .44 Magnum—but it did not stop enemy troops the way a 375ft/lb .45 round would if fired at similar distances from an M1 Thompson.

The British found in the Boer War (1899–1902) that long-range sniping by the South African Boers, who had 7mm 1896 Model Mauser rifles, resulted in through-shoot wounds that were neither serious nor incapacitating. It seemed that, when the bullet flew below a certain velocity, probably around 1,500ft/sec, it simply did not create any shock displacement. There were examples of troops surviving bullets through the brain, which were unheard of in the days of large-bore lead bullets. Such incidents, however, were the exception rather than the rule: many troops in South Africa were killed by accurate sniper fire from long distances. In South Africa, rolling hills gave extensive views from their summits and the opportunity for very long range shooting. The British did not fight over such terrain again until the Falklands campaign in 1982.

On most battlefields the range is quite short. Veterans of South-East Asia will know that while from some positions there were long views—and there always are from helicopters—there were plenty of other locations, from barracks to trenches to tunnels, where the range will be short. Some long-range views can alter drastically once a serious fight develops. One can see a long way over some deserts from ground level until a tank battle gets into its stride, and then dust and smoke reduce supporting infantry's field of fire from miles to feet in minutes. The generalisation that battlefield ranges are usually quite short led NATO in the early 1980s to adopt the .223in cartridge. The theory was that in a jungle or in savanna (long grass) or European woodland, an infantryman's effective range was dictated by hitting the ground under fire and then looking up to find out how far he could see to shoot back.

In handguns, the bullets have low velocity to start with, and also slow up more quickly. One of the reasons why the .30in M1 carbine has such limited recognition as a combat round, despite having a paper striking energy akin to that of a .44in Magnum, is that it slows down rapidly, and was probably being used by many soldiers at too long a range. Used in a sub-machine gun at 50 yards' range or closer, it should have had the stopping power. But a lot of its striking energy was being lost, as the bullet went right through the people shot.

This brings us back to Marshall and Sanow's point—that bullet placement is more relevant than anything else in achieving a one-shot stop. A running man is most likely to be stopped by skeletal damage: break his hip bone with a bullet, and he stops running. He should also stop if shot where he lives—in the lower brain behind the nose. These are precise locations, and handgun fighting has never been that precise.

The FBI Learns the Hard Way
On 11 April 1986 FBI agents engaged two suspects in Miami, Florida, and found themselves outgunned. One suspect, Matthew Platte, was armed with a Ruger Mini 14 rifle in .223in. He put his accomplice, John Mattix, out of the gunfight by shooting across him: the muzzle blast blinded Mattix. Soon after this an FBI bullet hit Platte in the chest, after passing through his right arm. It was a fatal wound; the pulmonary artery was severed and at that point Platte had less than two minutes to live.

It was not a shot that stopped him, though. The 9mm, 115-grain Winchester Silvertip bullet lodged near Platte's heart but, as with so many chest cavity shots, it did not stop him continuing to take part in the gunfight. By the time he died he had fired about 70 rounds of ammunition, and seven of the eight FBI men involved had been shot, two of them fatally.

There are a number of ways of dissecting an incident of this kind and deciding where the blame should lie. In the United Kingdom, we would expect blame to fall on the availability of weapons for villains, and that law-abiding licensed shooters would become the scapegoats for someone else's crime. That happened to us after a lone gunman shot people at random in Hungerford, Berkshire, on 19 August 1987. We completed this book under the shadow of another such incident in Dunblane, Scotland, on 13 March 1996, expecting the licensed shooters of the UK once again to be the undeserving objects of any government action. In Florida, the blame seems to have fallen on the FBI's equipment rather than on their absurd tactics. Soon the search was on for a new round of ammunition to give the FBI a one-shot stop, regardless of the improbable circumstances they might create in order to open fire.

As experienced scapegoats and armchair observers, we wondered why the FBI would go looking for a fight with two men who were

Below: 9mm Colt All American 2000 double-action pistol, right side. The rotary locking lugs can be seen at the front of the ejector port.

known to be armed with at least one rifle, without first taking some basic precautions—such as wearing body armour, taking along shoulder weapons of their own, staggering their attack—which began with one FBI vehicle ramming the suspect vehicle, a manoeuvre the FBI driver had never attempted in training—and having agents armed with shoulder weapons far enough away to use those weapons effectively. And, most obviously, we wondered, why did the FBI attack Platte and Mattix in the street at all? Armed suspects are at their most dangerous at home, and potentially at their least dangerous at work. The suspects had jobs, and were least likely to be able to resist arrest at their place of work. The FBI could have walked up to them in the right circumstances and taken them without a fight.

Anyway, the thinking was that if the bullet that hit Matthew Platte had gone a bit deeper and actually penetrated the heart, it would have brought him down more quickly: a little more penetration and some more expansion would have done the trick. This is not necessarily true, however. A bullet through the heart can be virtually an instant stop, but is not guaranteed. It all depends on the bullet.

Judicious Enquiries

We were consulted by the defence lawyers in a murder trial at the Old Bailey in 1994 about the effectiveness of .32 auto ammunition and whether truncating the jacketed bullet to expose the lead core would make the bullet capable of more damage. The male victim in this double murder had been shot from behind at close range, probably twelve inches or slightly closer. The bullet had tracked from its entry upwards and to the right straight through his heart.

The physical evidence suggested that he had immediately slumped face down; there would have been a massive adrenal response from his body to this trauma wound, but nothing could have restarted his heart because of the bullet track through it, and he died within a minute. That is how a one-shot stop should work, but this victim was not in a state of extreme excitement when shot. Had he been in the process of attacking his killer, for example, his body could have kept going for a few seconds at least before the lack of blood supply to the brain closed him down.

The other issue raised in this case concerned the bullet. In this case the round was a home-loaded one using a factory jacketed bullet. The nose of the bullet had been filed down to expose the lead core. This actually made no difference to the bullet's performance as the .32 was travelling too slowly to expand the remaining metal jacket, which was too hard to be deformed at the velocity involved. The intention to maximise any wound channel was clearly there, but it was not a suitable round with which to do that.

Jacketed ammunition is made to preserve the life of the gun barrel. Lead bullets work well at velocities of up to around 1,400ft/sec—faster than that and they tend to strip in the bore and foul the rifling grooves with lead. For this reason, faster loads use jacketed ammunition. The jacket is usually bronze or nickel—soft enough to engage the rifling—with the jacket having a lead core to keep up the weight and maintain the bullet's knock-down power.

Faster pistol rounds, like .357, .44, hot 9mm, .30 carbine and all the rifle rounds, need a jacketed bullet. (Military ammunition, by international convention, is fully jacketed, so rounds in common military calibres are often found in this configuration.) Manufacturers have recognised for many years that a hollow-pointed or soft-pointed projectile will expand on impact, and they have given a lot of attention to developing loads in which the bullet will mushroom on impact and give a disproportionately greater wound channel than it would without expansion. Fully jacketed ammunition tends not to expand like this.

In handguns, the three main types of expanding ammunition are jacketed soft point (JSP), jacketed hollow point (JHP), and full metal jacket (FMJ). Purely lead bullets in factory ammunition seem to be almost exclusively .22 rimfires these days. Even then, the .22 Magnum is usually jacketed, while the hotter .22LR rounds have a thin copper coating to stop the bore fouling.

Thus, apart from striking the right place, the stopping power of a handgun bullet depends on a compromise between its jacket and the ability of the lead in it to expand, on its weight, and on its speed. In a sense the FBI's search for 'the round that would have killed Matthew Platte' was an attempt to re-invent the wheel. As it happened, a better wheel was already gestating in the wings.

The Birth of the Roaring .40

The choice between a supersonic 9mm and a subsonic .45 widened with the appearance of the 10mm Norma in 1983. This round, with a 170-grain jacketed, hollowpoint bullet travelling at 1,340ft/sec develops 680ft/lb, which makes it two-thirds as good as an M1 carbine, or nearly twice as good as a .45ACP. The FBI considered adopting the round, as their doctrine was now 'penetration driven', but opted for a downloaded version to make the round subsonic. This decision presumably was a reflection on their mutation of the Weaver stance, as no one else had a problem with full-house factory 10mm—it is excellent in the Glock pistol, and nicer to shoot than their 9mm. But no one has told us the official reasons for giving FBI men cadet loads.

The full-house 10mm did not perform as well as anticipated in gunfights. Despite its high performance on paper, actual street results were disappointing, probably because the bullet had been designed to hold together at high velocities and so on hitting a target did not open up as expected. To put it another way, a bullet made that hard and travelling that fast seemed to have been designed to expand fully in a rhinoceros rather than a hoodlum.

The FBI had their custom load for two years before Smith & Wesson unveiled their .40in

S&W at the Shot Show in 1990. With a 180-grain JHP bullet travelling at 950ft/sec, the paper value of this round was not promising. It was about the same as a 9mm, and that was the problem in the first place, according to the FBI.

However, the .40 was in the right place at the right time and was accepted by some law enforcement agencies and a lot of civilians for that reason. Glock rushed out a .40 version of their Model 17 and beat Smith & Wesson's own pistol on to the street. The first police force to test the .40 was the California Highway Patrol, and the first to adopt it was the South Carolina State Police. Then came the street results—gunfight reports. The .40 was knocking suspects down, although there were cases of over-penetration as well. Evan Marshall reckoned that the Federal Hydra-Shok .40 round was delivering 89 per cent one-shot stops, and that the later 155-grain Winchester Silvertip was outperforming Hydra-Shok. This puts the very best of the new .40 calibre ammunition on a par with the very best of the .357 ammunition around. As most people know, .357 is a revolver round while .40 is for auto pistols. The new ammunition's unprecedentedly rapid success was another factor that helped persuade police agencies to re-equip with self-loading pistols.

The FBI, meanwhile, went back to 9mm after all, and in 1996 were issuing their agents with SIG Sauer P228 pistols—a choice automatic, but not a .40. The SIG series are all locked-breech, recoil-operated pistols, and none of them has a safety catch. They come instead with a de-cock lever that is just as good, except that, if the firearm is lost in a fight, anyone picking it up can fire the pistol simply by pulling the trigger.

The Double-Action-Only Debate

This introduces another long-running argument in police circles. Revolvers can be fired simply by pulling the trigger through its double-action stroke, so a lot of auto pistols have followed that thinking by offering either a double-action first shot or a double-action-only trigger group that gives effectively the same feel to an auto pistol trigger as has a revolver trigger.

This simplifies retraining revolver officers to auto pistols, and gives them a higher-capacity carry gun than they had before, but with the same potential disadvantage that the one gun they can guarantee will be at the gunfight is the one they bring along. And it will not have a safety catch. Every year a number of American policemen are killed with their own firearms, wrested from them in a street fight. We have also heard a good number of anecdotes about officers whose lives were saved by the safety catch on their pistols—some weapons still have them. The typical anecdote has it that the 'scumbag' wrenches the pistol free from the officer's grasp or his holster, then cannot fire it because there is a pre-firing sequence to go through, and he does not have the time to work it out before the officer either takes it back or shoots him with a back-up piece.

Auto-pistols have to have the slide worked once to chamber a round before firing. Once that round is chambered—and some police and civilians carry their weapons with an empty chamber—there may be a safety catch to engage or a de-cock lever, or the safety catch may double as a de-cock lever. Confronted by a strange pistol, one has to check the chamber and the status of the safety catch before being able to fire it. That auto pistols have confounded some potential killers is a point worth bearing in mind when choosing a firearm.

One of the cleverest safety devices we came across was on the Heckler & Koch P7. This neat 9mm pistol is a delayed-blowback design and has virtually no levers or buttons on it. There is a take-down catch on the left side of the frame below the rear sight, and an ambidextrous magazine release catch. The front portion of the butt is a grip safety, which has to be squeezed to cock the pistol; working the slide does not cock the action.

Squeezing the grip safety also acts as a slide release. Once a new magazine has been slammed home, cocking the pistol on the grip safety also closes the slide into battery. When the pistol is released—holstered or dropped— it de-cocks at the same time. Most people who pick it up—and we have handed it to over 100 novices at shooting clubs—do not realise that the grip safety has to be squeezed to cock the piece. That impressed us as a particularly safe option. It is not obvious, and it does fool all of the people some of the time.

.40 Calibre—Punch versus Accuracy

When Israel Military Industries' .41AE round came on to the market in 1988, it put a major punch into minor pistols. Guns in 9mm, and thus in the 'minor' category in 'practical' pistol sports, could be converted to .41AE to make 'major' while retaining their magazine capacity, or at least more capacity than a traditional .45. The concept was good, but did not take off in the United States. Quite why not is anybody's guess, but Smith & Wesson unveiled their .40 calibre in 1990 and eclipsed the .41AE at that point.

The problem with all the early .40S&W pistols was accuracy. They were hard hitters, but lacked the pinpoint accuracy of 9mm and .45, which the .41AE had matched. Whether the rifling twist in the barrel was wrong, or the ratio of powder to ball weight in the ammunition was wrong, is not clear, but the problem with factory ammunition seems to be resolving itself. Before the polygonal-bored Jericho/ Baby Eagle hit the market, the only people to get good accuracy from .40S&W were patient hand-loaders who experimented until they found a combination that worked out of their particular barrels.

Above: Heckler & Koch P7 squeeze-cocker pistol. This clever design incorporates a grip safety on the front of the butt, which also doubles as a slide release. The pale blue bar markings signify that only plastic training ammunition must be used in this gun. The rounds are lethal at short ranges, and these weapons make ideal sidearms for sky marshals, who need to be able to deal comprehensively with hijackers and the like without the risk of shooting holes in an airliner.

We suspect that the problem with .40 lies in the rifling twist. H&K's USP performed better in our tests than earlier .40s, although our Springfield Armory M1911A1 Linkless always shot well enough for us—so that we did not realise there was an accuracy problem with .40 until we read about it in a magazine. Like all firearms, .40-calibre pistols are more than capable of outperforming the person holding them. But 9mm and .45 guns have the advantage of three generations of refinement by experts, and are that much tighter in their groups. The .40 will no doubt catch up. Meanwhile the 'lack of accuracy' commented on is not a major consideration at short gunfighting range.

TEN

Choosing a Fighting Handgun

Modern fighting handguns have three major groups of users: the military and the police carry them in the course of their work, while the ordinary citizen in civilised countries keeps them to defend his home and his person.

In the first part of this chapter we look at a neglected and sometimes derided class of pistol—the miniature defensive handgun and its slightly larger relations, the so-called 'Saturday night specials'. In the UK, these pistols have become curiosities, thanks to the aversion of officialdom to the notion that people have a right or duty to protect themselves, their families and their property from predators. While British politicians come out in hives at the prospect of an armed citizenry, in many European countries and in large parts of the USA governments recognise a greater degree of partnership between those in power and the law-abiding members of the populace who put them there. In the history of the fighting handgun there are more weapons made for the private individual's defence than for any other purpose, not least because in most societies there are more common folk than there are policemen, soldiers and government spies.

We end this historical survey of the fighting handgun with assessments of what we believe were the finest examples of military, police and people's pistols from the 'classic' period—that is, breech-loading handguns made before 1918—and in the inter-war years; and finally, from the comfort of our armchairs, we discuss the guns we would choose for the battlefield, police work, and personal and home defence.

Pistols for Pocket and Purse

History is stiff with tiny handguns—portable and easily concealed weapons for self defence, to be carried against the occasional need to remind others to mind their own business, to displace the problem and prevent crime. Muzzle-loaded versions were quite often supplied

Below: Pocket fighting handguns, all top break models (top) Webley Mk 3 in .38in; (centre) Smith & Wesson 'lemon squeezer' (so named because of its grip safety) 5-shot revolver; (bottom) .32in Harrington & Richardson pocket revolver.

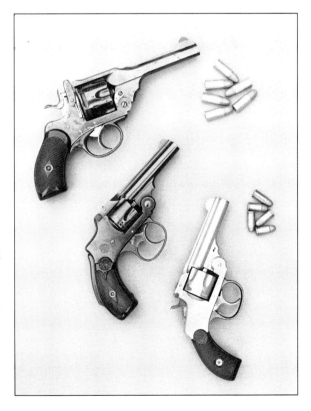

in pairs, and many have survived without being separated.

A pair of pistols is better for one's balance—one in each hand in the overcoat pockets or, for a lady, in the hands inside her muff. Louis Flobert's bulleted breech cap ammunition, developed in 1845, did not need a pistol much bigger than a matchbox to fire it, and the later nineteenth century saw many very small handguns made for close-range self-defence that emulated the dimensions Flobert achieved.

When semi-automatic pistols became a practical proposition after the development of smokeless powders in the 1890s, it was Browning's minuscule .25 ACP cartridge that worked best for pocket pistols, and it was adopted by other designers who developed pistols around it. Browning's baby was the standard to which others aspired. It was a simple blowback pistol, a small-scale version of his M1910, which was produced in both .32 ACP and .380.

Some pocket pistols did not even need disassembly. The .25 pistol by Manufacture Française d'Armes et Cycles de St-Etienne, which dates from 1926, had a tip-up barrel released by a lever on the right side of the frame that facilitated both cleaning and loading. This pistol has an awkward magazine release catch on the heel of the butt, which makes quick magazine changes out of the question. When the magazine is removed, the barrel pops up

automatically, so loading is a matter of inserting a full magazine, and a loose round in the barrel. There is no need to work the slide to bring the pistol to readiness as the mechanism is double-action only, and rather stiff to operate at more than 14lb pressure. The pistol was well made and was produced between 1926 and 1939, and it is a typical example of the small self-defence carry pistol of the period.

Competitors for this market included pocket centrefire, rimfire and pinfire revolvers as well as numerous other small pocket pistols. We have selected just a few to remark on as examples of the many types that can still be seen and acquired through specialist arms fairs and auctions, often at modest prices.

The .320in cartridge was a black-powder relative of the later .32in Smith & Wesson. It was a very popular cartridge for pocket revolvers, such as the charming miniature nickel-plated German bulldog revolver we photographed, which cost us £10 at a British auction in 1995. The .320in cartridge was available until the start of the Second World War, but always as a black powder load. We have not been able to determine when either the firearms or ammunition became obsolete, but the war probably ended production of both.

The bulldog design was around for seven decades up to the Second World War. It was a solid-frame, gate-loaded system, with the cyl-

Far left: The classic .25 auto Mauser WTP pocket pistol makes a small handful for an adult.
Left: The .25 auto Mauser WTP does not fill any hand but is sufficient to remind other people to mind their own business.
Right and below: .25 auto by Manufacture Française d'Armes et Cycles de Saint Etienne. A slightly larger handful and double action only. Seen when the magazine is dropped, the barrel flips up automatically so loading is a full magazine and one loose round straight into the chamber. The right side lever can be used to open the barrel when the magazine is loaded in.

inder held in place by an axis pin. In this was stored the ejector rod, held captive on a swivel rather like the ramrod of the muzzle loading era. Always available in both single and double action, this design appeared as the Royal Irish Constabulary model and the British Bulldog, and in all sizes from a full-scale military holster variant down to the miniature .320in.

The double action on the .320 we had was quite stiff, as one might expect from a weapon

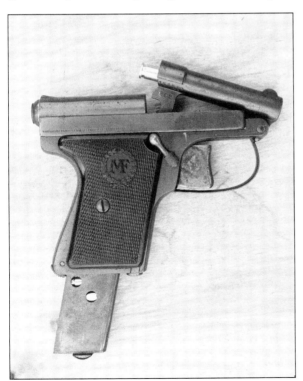

made when everybody thumb-cocked his revolver. It is difficult to reduce the tension of a double-action mechanism without also reducing the strike on the cartridge primer. Modern firearms have a finer balance in this regard, since double-action revolver shooting is what is most often taught now. But most of today's revolvers are bigger than the pocket models of Edwardian Europe and the hammer is proportionately heavier.

Walther's TPH pistol is essentially a scaled-down variant of the PPK, although being so small it has been simplified somewhat with a heel-of-butt magazine release rather than a button on the frame. Take-down was the same as a PPK: remove the magazine, check the chamber, then pull the trigger guard down at the front, withdraw the slide to the rear and lift the rear end off the rails, taking it forward again to clear the barrel. This charming little pistol performed the most reliably of all the .25 auto pistols we have tested over the years— six shots straight down-range without a hitch.

The .25 Auto Today

The .25 auto still has its place. We recently acquired a Sundance Industries Laser 25. This pistol is as small as any traditional .25 auto, but has an integral laser sight that projects a red dot on to the target to simplify the point-and-shoot techniques that used to be guesswork.

Laser sights have some advantages, but the disadvantages must be carefully considered as well. The dot is virtually invisible in sunlight, good daylight and at longer ranges. In the dark it comes into its own. If one cannot see the iron sights there are problems anyway, but if the red dot cannot be seen on the target, one is not aiming where one thinks. The dot could be illuminating a telephone box three blocks away. The bottom line is that a laser can assist an experienced shooter, particularly in the dark, but it should not be relied upon..

The Sundance laser fades if kept on too long at one time. The switch is the rear of the grip, which looks like a grip safety but is not one. We have found laser sights very useful for showing beginners how much they are wobbling, and they are a very useful training aid in other ways. They make a powerful psychological impact on a suspect who finds one on his shirt, too—as seen near the beginning of the feature film *Robocop 3*.

On the range the Sundance performed flawlessly—a nice group and a perfect action, provided the grip is held tightly enough for the slide to work against.

'Saturday Night Specials'
Having said that .22in rimfire is about as effective in combat terms as .25 auto, it should come as no surprise to see .22in firearms marketed for self-defence. The term 'Saturday Night Special' was coined the United States during debates on gun control (which we pre-

fer to call civilian disarmament) in 1968, to mean 'cheap imported handguns of no great value'.

This disparaging way of denying those of limited means a right to self-defence that they could afford was enshrined in American law. The gun about which the term was coined was the RG Industries Model 14, which, we understand, was made up in Florida from parts imported from Germany. American firms had their own variants, of course, such as the Hi-Standard Sentinel—a nine-shot revolver produced in both .22LR and .22WMR for the self-defence market. The Astra Model 250, made in Spain, was of the same ilk.

The North American Arms Mini Revolver is something of a curiosity. Extremely small, it is single-action only, and the cylinder has to be removed from the frame for loading. This is not quite as bad as the RG 14, on which the

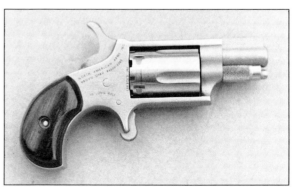

Right, upper: The 9-shot Astra .22 revolver—a typical 'Saturday night special' if ever there was one. Despite its diminutive proportions, this is a comfortable pistol to grip and is unexpectedly accurate on the range.
Right, lower: North American Arms Mini Revolver in .22in calibre—good quality single action 5-shot revolver. Is it a 'Saturday night special' or a novelty? Better than nothing on the street and virtually small enough to keep in your wallet.

axis pin had to be unscrewed to release the swing-out cylinder and then used manually as an ejector rod. On the Mini Revolver the axis pin is removed and the cylinder dropped out loose to the right. Five rounds of ammunition could then be loaded in—both .22in and .22 Magnum variants are made—and then the revolver is reassembled.

Being single-action only, and being so small that only the middle finger grips the handle, shooting it is a slow process and accuracy is a challenge. The revolver is, however, capable of much greater accuracy than most shooters. Whether this is a 'fun gun' or a serious fighting handgun is a matter for the owner. It is a well-made piece in stainless steel, nicely finished. We used to see similar guns on belt buckles in Europe; this is too big to have a pair of them as cuff links, but as a vest-pocket companion it is a possible carry option for people who do not think they are seriously at risk. (We regard personal defence as a sort of 9mm *versus* .45 debate. If the risk is in the .45 bracket, we try not to go there.)

The Astra Model 250 revolver was a more typical 'Saturday Night Special'. Small, but with nine chambers, it would sit in an ankle rig or a pocket unobtrusively, and might thus be a comfort to the person carrying it. The problem with very small guns is getting them to be taken seriously. In the United Kingdom, where firearms are not often seen by the general public, we found that really small guns are assumed to be toys, and really big, ugly ones are assumed to be air guns.

In any encounter, the gun has to be seen and be respected to be taken seriously, and those that are too small may simply not be seen. One remedy is the 'warning shot', but that uses up ammunition, may escalate the problem at hand and may land one in yet more trouble if the bullet lands in an embarrassing spot occupied by someone in a litigious frame of mind.

The smallest of the .25 auto handguns we tried for this book was Mauser's WTP. Fully

Above: North American Arms .22in Mini Revolver in the hand—virtually small enough to conceal in the palm.

loaded with six rounds of .25, it weighed the same as a Beretta 92F's clip loaded with fifteen rounds. The internal striker and gutter sight arrangement are familiar from Browning products, but the scale is slightly smaller than the Baby Browning. Webley made their .25 with both an internal striker and external hammer variations. We preferred the model with the external hammer, which is a scaled-down version of their .32.

The Best of the Classics

With all of handgun history to choose from, with the benefit of hindsight, and with the advice of some of the world's top gun writers to assist one, the choice of a fighting handgun is still not easy to make. It also depends on who one is and what one would use the pistol for. The authors are writers and target-shooters who take an active interest in firearms matters, and have read what the world's top gun writers have written. We differentiate between the needs of civilians, police and the military, but we also recognise that a firearm designed for one purpose may turn out to be better for another.

The .357 Magnum, for example, was developed as a long-range hunting handgun cartridge, but has been widely adopted for law enforcement. Prior to taking up the .357, police agencies used .38 or .45. In the period of 'classic' fighting handguns before 1919, the choice for policing was a revolver chambered for either .38 or .45. We liked the Smith & Wesson Mk 2 hand ejector in this regard, although with a 6in barrel and large frame it was rather bigger than the Model 1905, which would probably have been the policeman's choice for that period.

Although automatic (self-loading) pistols were around from the turn of the century, their take-up was slow in police circles. In Europe the .32 Auto eventually achieved dominance as a police and military cartridge for a time, and some British police forces, including London's Metropolitan Police, carried Webley .32 auto pistols. These are small enough to pocket, but would also look smart in a holster when used as part of a uniform. The .32 is currently not rated as much of a fighting round, but it held its own in Europe for fifty years and was the favourite of the clandestine SOE, so it must have had something going for it.

The choice of a classic military pistol in the pre-1919 era was really seen at the US Army trials—the P08 Luger versus the Colt M1911. The .45 comes out on top in our minds, even though the Luger is such a nice piece to own and shoot. In the ultimate encounter, seven rounds of .45 hardball beats eight rounds of 9mm, provided one has practised enough. The Luger is actually easier to point and shoot instinctively than the Colt, is a little lighter to carry and is instantly recognisable as a real gun. The Colt is reliable, a hard hitter and, with hindsight, the most distinguished combat veteran of the twentieth century.

Moving on almost a generation to military pistols for the Second World War, the Browning GP35A is head and shoulders above the rest. The .45 was still there, of course, but thirteen 9mm rounds make a persuasive argument against seven .45s. The pistol is small enough for concealed carriage as well as being a good choice for a battle pistol, and it is still seen in some armies.

Our choice of classic military revolver is the .455 Webley. The large, slow bullet has the knock-down power that the .38 lacked in the Philippines, and it stood up well to the muddy conditions of the Great War with enough of a reputation to be sought after by commandos in the Second World War.

In the post-classic period, no really good military revolver emerged. The American Smith & Wesson M1905/40, which became Britain's 'Victory' revolver, was underpowered, as was the contemporary British Enfield design. Both used short .38S&W ammunition. At this time the military were drifting away from revolvers; we feel that it is better to acknowledge that than to try to dignify a second-rate design by choosing a pistol we would really rather not have. If we had been about at the time and had to have a revolver, we would have been among those busy scrounging an old .455.

Classic Pistols for the People

The civilian market was wide open in the classic period. Before the Great War the Bulldog design, as exemplified by the Royal Irish Constabulary (RIC) model, would have been our choice of revolver. If Sherlock Holmes had really lived at 221B Baker Street and not just in the imagination, he would have had an RIC revolver in his pocket, while Dr Watson would probably have had the Webley No 1 Mk 1. We would probably not have wanted a C/96 Mauser for concealed carriage, but when Browning's M1910 pistol came out there was an ideal pocket automatic for the prewar generation. Although 'only' a .32, the round is good enough to defend one's bedroom, taxicab or telephone box.

In the period up to 1945, the Webley Mk III pocket revolver, though underpowered in military terms, would have been a good choice of carry gun, and Browning's 1910 model in .380 (9mm short) would have been suitable for the gentleman's pocket in that period.

If our choices seem broadly European, that is because these classics are easier to come by in the United Kingdom. Every one of them has an American equivalent; for example,

Smith & Wesson made top-break revolvers in .380 in the nineteenth century that may have been very good, although our experience of them from auctions is that the Webleys seem to have withstood the ravages of time better. And for the interwar period there were any number of .32 autos made and sold in the United States from which to pick a pocket gun. The Seecamp seems to be today's choice there.

Many of the firearms noted in this book are still in production. Those that are not are often still available through firearms dealers: a well-made piece that has been cleaned after use and stored with care will outlast several generations of owners. In the course of preparing this book we have handled and fired firearms approaching 200 years old that were still in excellent condition. We have also seen a lot of newer firearms that will not last nearly as long thanks to the neglect of their owners.

Military Handguns Today

The late twentieth-century trend in military handguns has been towards high-capacity 9mm pistols, such as Beretta's 92F adopted by the American military in 1985. This has a safety catch that also de-cocks the pistol, and

Above left: The sizes of the various service pistols, their weight when empty and their magazine capacity. (Top to bottom) 9mm Makarov, 1lb 10oz, 8rds; .45 Colt M1911, 2lb 5oz, 7rds; 9mm Kahr K9, 1lb 12oz, 7rds; 9mm Browning GP35A, 1lb 15^1/2oz, 13rds; and .32 MAB model D, 1lb 8oz, 8rds.
Right: Astra .357in police model. The spare cylinder and clip are for firing 9mm ammunition through the same weapon; the barrel is the same diameter for either.

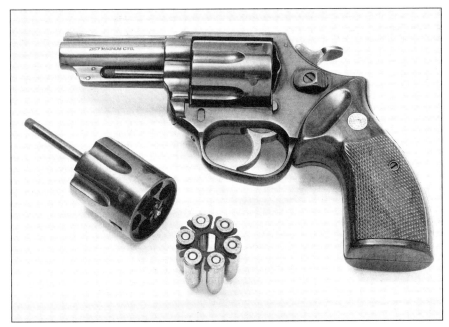

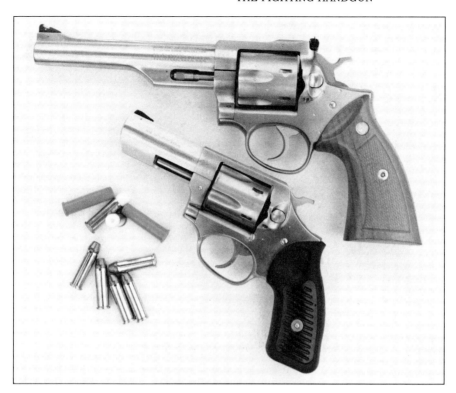

Left: A .357 Magnum Ruger Security Six revolver with 6in barrel, over a .357 Ruger SP101 five-shot revolver and some specialist ammunition. Both models have a choice of barrel lengths and some SP101s are .38 Special only.
Below right: .357in Magnum Ruger SP101 revolver. This 2in barrel, 5-shot piece is comfortable and discreet for daily wear, but it is not a gun one would want to shoot for a prolonged period.
Bottom right: Beretta Model 84, the 9mm short (380) version of Beretta's much-used design, compacted for concealed carry.

a trigger mechanism that provides a double-action first shot. These features, and the fifteen-shot, double-stacked magazine, were specified by the armed forces for their trials, so a number of other products have followed the same trend.

Exceptions include the Glock 17, developed in Austria and adopted by the Austrian Army. This weapon has various safety devices that prevent it firing without the trigger being pulled, but no manual safety catch to disable the weapon as such, except on one variant developed for Sweden. The Glock has no external hammer, so one cannot tell without physically checking whether there is a round in the chamber or not.

Heckler & Koch's USP remains traditional to the extent that the safety catch locks the mechanism without de-cocking the hammer. There tradition ends. The safety can be used to de-cock the hammer when pressed downwards, but there are umpteen variants of this pistol, including left-handed models—so *caveat emptor* when one is choosing which to buy.

If we were tasked with choosing a fighting handgun for military use, the Heckler & Koch USP (despite the company's association with David Mellor MP) would be the front runner at this, the armchair stage of consideration. It is considerably lighter than the Beretta 92F and can be carried cocked-and-locked, so teaching the double-action first shot can be left out of basic training, and on the range it delivers acceptable groups without uncomfortable recoil (the .40 we tested shot very straight indeed and was milder than many 9mm autos we have used). There are other tests that should be applied before a fighting handgun is chosen—how it stands up to sand, to mud, to soldiers cleaning it and so forth. But we would start with this model and see who could compete with it on equal terms.

The function of a handgun in the military is to arm those men who have other things to do with their hands, which includes anyone on a crew-served weapon or in a vehicle. Officers and military police need them, partly as a badge of office, partly to keep their hands free.

All those who carry handguns need training with them, in addition to the training they receive for their primary functions in the service.

Handgun training is often neglected in the circumstances, and there has been a tendency in some training regimes to keep it simple, to the extent that the training becomes inadequate. We reckon that sixteen hours of training will teach most people all they need to know about one handgun, how to use it and how to maintain it, although it will not make them confidently accurate shots: more time, more instruction and plenty of practice are the only answers to that. The initial sixteen-hour training does not need to be over two days. It could be eight lessons spread over a longer period, and followed up with occasional practices to maintain familiarity and preparedness for dealing with malfunctions.

Thorough familiarisation with one weapon makes retraining to others simpler. It is al-

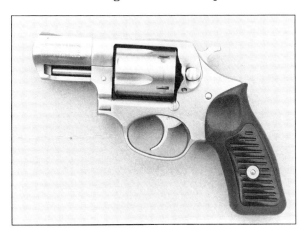

ways instructive to be familiar with the principal weapons one is likely to encounter in use by allies and potential enemies, if only for clearing them of ammunition after the enemy has surrendered. Once an autopistol is understood, there are few variants that present difficulties for long, although the take-down on a Mauser C/96 is best left to someone else!

Choosing a Modern Police Handgun

The police market is somewhat different. We cannot tell at this distance to what extent the double-action-only concept is a response to the possibilities of litigation after a shooting, and to what extent it is the gun manufacturers trying to sell more guns. Double-action-only has been marketed as a way of easing the transition from revolver to auto, and police departments are progressively falling for it; yet it does not offer the police the advantages of a semi-auto pistol other than that of a high-capacity magazine that can be changed quickly.

The police have tended to select military pistols such as the Glock, although their needs are somewhat different from those of the armed forces. They have to be able to shoot fast and shoot straight when the need arises, but more often than not they have only to threaten lethal force to secure compliance. With this in mind, the double-action *first* shot autopistol makes perfect sense. The safety catch can be released as the weapon is drawn, and the officer's finger is on a trigger that requires a long pull to fire.

This minimises the risk of a negligent discharge by an officer with a nervous twitch, but, if lethal force has to be deployed, after his first shot he has single-action accuracy. The trend to double-action only looks to us to have been inspired by gunmakers as a transitional tool for revolver-trained officers rather than a wholly appropriate, universal solution for policing the streets.

The issues of litigation in the United States are complex and not something we can ad-

Above: Ruger GP100—the .357in 6-shot general-purpose revolver. Note that the ejector rod shroud runs the full length of the 4in barrel.

dress with authority. From the perspective of the police, adapting firearms in any way can leave the department open to criticism. For example, Browning Hi-Power GP35A pistols made for the military have a magazine safety in them, which prevents the magazine dropping out after the button is pressed. The magazine has to be physically removed, the objective being to make soldiers retain the clip for reloading. Some shooters remove it, so that the magazine drops free. But imagine what a hostile lawyer could make of the removal of a 'safety device' from a police pistol. Police firearms should be issued out-of-the-box with-

out adaptation. If any modification is required, it should be carried out by the supplier, with an audit trail of explanatory letters between the department and the company that can be kept as a reference.

No firm favourite has emerged as our choice of a fighting handgun for policing. Among the latest self-loaders we liked Browning's BDM and thought that this was very close to ideal, especially if they could fit the same safety system to it as the Heckler & Koch USP's—down for de-cock and up for safe—instead of what they did, which is down for de-cock, safe and slide release all at once. With this one improvement, the BDM would be our first choice for policing.

As things stand, the H&K is probably going to be our first choice. The gimmick by which a flashlight can be added to the pistol will appeal to British police forces (who seem to have fallen for every gimmick on the market), although how long they will manage to keep the flashlights on the pistols without breaking them would exercise the minds of those with financial responsibility for replacing lost or broken equipment.

Below left: Heckler & Koch USP (Universal Self-loading Pistol), right side.
Below right: 9mm Browning BDM pistol. The large safety catch at the top of the grip doubles as a slide release, and the large screw head in the slide converts the pistol to double action only.

The Virtues of the Wheelgun
Revolvers still have a lot to offer policing, not least because they are instantly recognisable

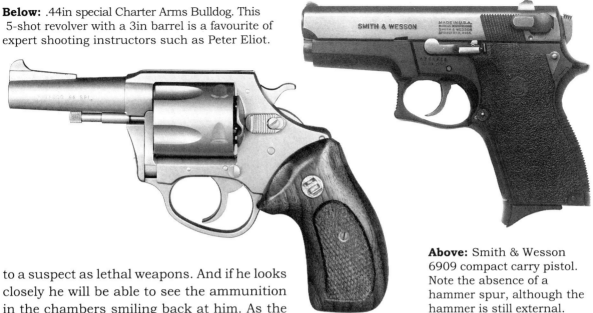

Below: .44in special Charter Arms Bulldog. This 5-shot revolver with a 3in barrel is a favourite of expert shooting instructors such as Peter Eliot.

Above: Smith & Wesson 6909 compact carry pistol. Note the absence of a hammer spur, although the hammer is still external.

to a suspect as lethal weapons. And if he looks closely he will be able to see the ammunition in the chambers smiling back at him. As the object of policing is to use only as much force as is necessary to secure compliance, the psychological effect of the revolver is no bad thing.

The basic choices lie in barrel length, in calibre, and whether to have a fixed or adjustable rear sight. We favour fixed sights on holster weapons and regard the .357 Magnum as the round for policing, albeit with a few caveats. The first is that training should *not* be on light loads throughout. It is acceptable to start students off on .38 Special ammunition, but one does them no favours by not training them hard with the ammunition they will carry in the street. There is a huge difference in the response of a revolver firing .38 and one firing .357. Officers need to be able to get used to and control the latter's recoil, and shoot confidently, quickly and accurately with it. They will not, if the first time they have to handle this beefy round is when their life is at risk. We know of one officer who had just that experience, and was so amazed at the roar his revolver made that he thought it had blown up—so he threw it at the suspect.

Likewise, on the street, under pressure, will they have ear protection? What will they be wearing? If they are going to wear body armour, then they must train in body armour.

Training needs to be as realistic as possible. It rains and snows outdoors, so training should not evade adverse conditions. It is also dark at night, and in unlit buildings in daylight. All these variations should appear in the training programme.

A 4in barrel is probably as long as it needs to be for policing. Longer barrels take longer to clear the holster, and, while they are relevant to target-shooting at longer ranges, policing is a close-up activity, not a long-range sniping match. Officers who engage at too great a distance may be misunderstood or not noticed.

We could not choose between Ruger's GP100, Colt's Python and Smith & Wesson's wide variety without some assistance, although S&W do have triggers that work beautifully, both single- and double-action, straight from the box. One of us prefers the ergonomics of their cylinder-release catch to the others', but admits that long familiarity may create a prejudice here. Anyone cramming seven rounds into the cylinder as the new line of S&Ws do would have an edge to begin with, but might (at the time of writing) have some difficulty finding a suitable speedloader for

Left: Aserma ADP 9mm pistol, in the delivery case from the manufacturers.
Below right: IMI Jericho pistol. This 15-shot, 9mm, locked-breech autopistol has a polygonal bore instead of rifling, and is a full-size quality pistol which is rather too big to carry in a concealment rig. Where concealment is not a requirement, it is a good choice service handgun for military or police purposes. This illustration shows one with a slide mounted safety, which decocks when safety is applied. The frame-mounted safety version cocks and locks.

drawn-out gunplay. The usual assistance given to police departments choosing a new weapon are sweeteners in the form of free holsters, speedloaders and other related accessories, so the final choice would rest with the company's ability to sell us their product. There is nothing like competition to keep business lean and fit. That said, a .357 for street work needs to be as heavy as possible to soak up recoil, and there is no point in issuing any gun without also being sure that the ammunition with which it performs best is issued with it.

Carry Guns for a Polite Society

The civilian usually needs a more compact weapon for convenience of carriage. In the USA, the trend of the 1990s has been towards States of the Union passing concealed-carry laws in recognition of the fact that the police cannot be everywhere to protect everyone all the time and that the citizen has to take some responsibility for his own safety both at home and on the street. Generally these laws make it mandatory for the police to issue a carry permit to any adult who has a clean criminal record. Some states require prior training for applicants; others do not.

Outside the United States the position is somewhat different. The British citizen's right to a firearm for self-defence was administratively terminated in 1954 by a change of government policy and, while the common law right to defend oneself still exists, various statutes currently make it an offence to carry any kind of weapon in anticipation of the need to exercise that right. By contrast, we hear that sub-machine guns are the Belgian housewife's weapon of choice for home defence, and may be legally bought for that purpose in that country.

In the United Kingdom, in most (but by no means all) cases in which somebody uses lethal force to defend himself, there is subsequently no police action against him for having been prepared, since *de facto* he was right to anticipate the attack. But there are numerous examples of victims of crime who suffered or were killed without having any chance to defend themselves. British government thinking seems to have been dominated by the police perception that some firearms incidents were unpremeditated, and thus the result of people being able to carry guns. Some incidents would indeed fall into that category, but the official thinking refuses to recognise that an enormous number of crimes have been prevented, and more would be prevented, when criminal predators find themselves facing an armed citizen instead of a helpless victim. Burglary is far more common in the UK than in US states that do not prevent citizens arming themselves against intruders.

Citizens have two areas to consider when choosing a weapon: defence of the home and street carriage. At home, concealment is not an issue, although keeping the weapon safe from children, visitors and burglars is. The dedicated combination-type gun safes seem to be the answer for that: the weapon can sit in it ready for use, yet unauthorised persons cannot get to it. One does not ever want to come home and find a burglar in possession of one's gun, nor should children use it in a game of cowboys.

Firearms safety has to be taken seriously as tragedy is only a trigger-pull away. On a ride along with local police in New Hampshire, we were called to an incident of accidental suicide. The victim had put the house defence gun to his head and pulled the trigger to demonstrate that the weapon was unloaded. According to the witnesses, it had been when he was being stupid with it earlier, but it had been reloaded and put away while he was out.

We think that a revolver probably has the necessary presence to impress unwanted visitors to one's home. If auto-pistols are preferred,

anything with a laser sight or flashlight attached would be very impressive when seen from its front, particularly at night. Since the object is to impress, nickel-plated or stainless steel firearms come into their own for home defence. Apart from being dishwasher proof (which saves cleaning time—provided the ammunition is taken out first), they show up better in low light, when they need to be seen.

Outside the home, the problem is that weapons that are too compact may simply not have the necessary presence to be noticed in a confrontation. So a balance has to be found between the extremely small and easy-to-carry handgun on the one hand and something that delivers the necessary non-verbal threat of lethal force on the other. Our comments about stainless steel or nickel plate hold good outdoors as well. Such finishes on guns are used in feature films to make them show up better: the armed citizen wants his firearm seen when he has need to draw it. And if it comes to the crunch they have to deliver, which is another reason not to go for too small a piece.

In auto-pistols we came out in favour of the Kahr K9, described below. This all-steel, seven-shot, 9mm, locked-breech, semi-automatic pistol is about as small as full-house 9mm pistols get. We tried it in an ankle rig, which is not necessarily the ideal way to carry it, but does conceal it effectively. In a dedicated inside-the-waistband rig, it will disappear under any jacket, baggy jumper or even a tee shirt. The Star Firestar, discussed in detail first, is not quite as small, but runs the K9 a close second as a personal defence weapon.

The 9mm Firestar

The Firestar emerged on the compact pistol market in 1992 and rapidly became the USA's best-selling auto pistol for back-up or off-duty. Star was one of only three gunmakers at Eibar in Spain to be allowed to continue making firearms after the Spanish Civil War, and the company has long been known for 'cheap and cheerful' target pistols, and to a more select audience for their military small-arms. If one asks older shooters what reputation Star pistols have, one is likely to be told that those that work actually work well, but that it is a matter of luck getting one that will. Feeding difficulties seem to be the one point on which Star owners and ex-owners agree. Attitudes may be changing, though, along with the company's products: its new products are so much more serious.

The Firestar is small, but heavy at 1lb 14oz empty; it is about the same size as a Soviet Makarov or a Smith & Wesson Model 6906—although the latter is fatter across the grips, because it has a double-column magazine. The Firestar takes a single-column, seven-shot magazine, against the 6906's twelve rounds. The Firestar looks much more traditional than the 6906, with a steel frame instead of alloy and rubber grips instead of plastic. Even the magazine follower is steel, so there is no hollow 'click' that the Smith makes when the slide is opened and the plastic magazine follower kicks the slide stop into position.

Mechanically, the Firestar holds no secrets for anyone familiar with the CZ75, having the same low-profile slide and similar full-length slide rails and lock-up arrangement. It has a frame-mounted, ambidextrous safety catch, so it can be carried 'cocked and locked' like the CZ, but there the similarity ends: the Firestar has a single-action trigger mechanism.

It also has a magazine safety. No pistol that has a magazine safety can be fired without the magazine in place. This offers the owner two advantages: first, there is less chance of an accident if he or she fails to clear the pistol properly; and secondly, storing magazines in a separate place from the pistol renders it useless to any unauthorised person who might gain access to it. The Firestar's magazine safety is overridden by the magazine before it is fully inserted; the hammer will fall in response to a trigger pull when the magazine is only about two-thirds the way in. Most other pistols with this feature will fire before the magazine is fully home, but not usually with the clip that far out. The magazine safety also prevents the magazine dropping cleanly when the release button is pressed: the empty magazine has to be pulled clear before a fresh one can be inserted.

The Firestar benefits from having an automatic firing pin safety, which prevents the firing pin touching the primer cap of a chambered round until the trigger is pulled fully rearwards. This stops the pistol firing itself after being dropped or otherwise mishandled. The manual safety catch can be applied regardless of the hammer position—fully down,

Left: .380 (above) and .32 auto (below) versions of the Italian Sites Resolver—'no frills', stainless steel, double-action-only pocket pistols, slimline single stack models. The .32 will not feed with the magazine full, but will work when the load is reduced to five rounds. The .380 performs flawlessly. Note the take-down catch inside the trigger guard; the trigger passes either side of it. Once pushed, the slide just rolls off the SIG-type rails.

Above, left and right: Jericho/Baby Eagles come in a choice of finishes.

half-cock or fully cocked—which is not the case with other designs.

The manufacturing quality of the Firestar is good—there are no grind marks or other indications of short cuts in production. The slide and frame are finished part matt and part bright, giving a tidy, two-tone appearance described as 'starvel' in trade literature. The sights are black with white dot inserts. The barrel is black at the muzzle, but bright where it shows through the ejector port. This pistol has been made to a price. The slide stop, for example, is made from five pieces, as opposed to the one-piece Browning's, but overall it is a very nice job for the money.

On the range, the Firestar's accuracy was quite acceptable at 20 yards. We fed it everything in 9mm we had lying about, without any feed failures at all. Even when gripped like a bunch of flowers, it still cycled perfectly. Perhaps Star can finally lay the ghost of past problems with this one, as long as owners keep their guns clean. Being soundly made and well-finished, this pistol is dishwasher-proof, so there is no reason to have a dirty gun. Dirty guns will jam from time to time, and such faults are the responsibility of the owner, not the manufacturer.

The Firestar is available in 9mm, .40 S&W, and .45 ACP. It made a name for itself in the United States when .40 became all the rage in law enforcement circles, and where a small pistol that packs a full-size round inevitably attracts attention as a possible off-duty or back-up pistol for police officers. Detonics used to make a minuscule seven-shot pistol in .45 ACP for the purpose, and it is that gap in the market that Star are exploiting.

The sights are adjustable enough for most people to get on target. But if this pistol has one drawback for ladies, it is the strength of the recoil spring. Although it measured around 12lb on the draw weight—the same as a Browning Hi-Power—this pistol seemed much harder to cock, because of the low profile of the slide. A little practice should resolve that for most people. The trick is to pull the slide back with one hand and drive the frame forward with the other.

First Choice: The Kahr K9

Advertised in the US with the slogan 'The only smaller 9mms are .380s', the Kahr K9 has made an impact on everyone who has tried it. There has long been a gap in the market for a full-power 9mm Parabellum pistol for concealed carriage. There are lots of .32 and .380

SHOOTING WITH ONE HAND

Any firearm that not ideally suited to a one-handed grip puts the person carrying it at a disadvantage.

In a gunfight, there is a powerful tendency to shoot at one's opponent's firearm, as that is where the immediate threat comes from. When shooting two-handed under stress, there is also a tendency to drive the shots high and towards one's weak side. Two right-handers in a gunfight may therefore find themselves shooting high and to the left at each other. This could put the first shot above the opponent's gun, and left where his shoulder is. Julio Santiago reckoned that if one cannot win a gunfight in the first two seconds, there is a reasonable chance of being hit in the gun hand, arm or shoulder, which means that the gunfight would have to be finished not only one-handed, but with the weak hand.

We have always considered this possibility and have always tested handguns in one-handed and weak-hand-only stances, to see what extra disadvantages some designs have for the weak-handed shooter. Most pistols have their magazine release catch on the left side, which is no great problem because it can be worked with the index finger, as can slide release catches. Some are easier than others to work, but unless we have commented adversely on any particular design the reader can assume that it worked fairly well in either hand.

The pistol design features that leave the weak-handed shooter at a particular disadvantage are things like magazine safeties, which mean that the magazine has to be physically withdrawn from the pistol, and heel-of-butt magazine catches, which are there for the same reason—to make soldiers keep the empty clip to refill in the future. To work these with just the weak hand takes practice, and means either holstering the weapon or clamping it somewhere such as behind the knee while kneeling. The absence of a slide release is less of a problem—just catch the rear sight on the belt and push down to release it. This works reliably on duty rigs but in mufti it creates the risk of catching clothing in the action as it closes.

pocket pistols, some of which have been around for decades. Nowadays, however, .32 and .380 are regarded as less powerful than what is needed for effective gunfighting.

With police thinking putting 9mm or .38 Special +P as the minimum for self defence, various companies have worked on suitable carry guns. In .38 Special it is less of a problem. Snubby revolvers like the Colt Detective Special or the 2in-barrelled Smith & Wesson Model 10 have been around for years. If one

wants a newer design there is the Ruger SP101 five-shot revolver, and numerous competitors vying for Ruger's 'pocket rocket' slot.

In 9mm Parabellum, however, there are fewer true pocket models to choose from, as the 9mm cartridge needs some sort of locked-breech mechanism that typical 380in pistols do not have. That is why the Kahr was so interesting. All-steel but hand-sized, the Kahr weighs just 1lb 11oz—so with a full chamber and both magazines fully loaded it still weighs less than an empty Beretta 92F.

Taken overall, the Kahr K9 is a well-made, superbly tough carry pistol. It has just two controls on the left of the frame (a magazine release and a slide release), a larger than usual trigger guard, comfortable rubber grip stocks and a square slide. It looks like a scaled-down Glock, made of steel. The trigger, like the Glock's, has to be reset after dry-firing as it is double-action only: the pistol does not sport a safety catch. The slide cannot be released with an empty magazine in place, and the recoil spring is amazingly stiff. The rear sight has a

Below left: Factory picture of Kahr K9 plated version.
Right: 9mm Aserma ADP pistol from South Africa—a 10-shot, double-stacked, gas-operated compact pistol which competes in size with the Kahr K9.

KAHR K9
New, Electroless Nickel
Ultra-Compact 9mm

bright white stripe below it to align with the white fore sight, which we found more intuitive to use than the seemingly ubiquitous 'three-dot' system.

The incredibly stiff recoil spring is not surprising, as the pistol is rated for the hottest 9mm loads: it was built around the premium CorBon Parabellum +P cartridge, which leaves the muzzle at 1,350ft/sec. The K9 is heavier than it looks, and shoots beautifully. Recoil was easily controlled and, unlike most 9mm pistols, it groups well with a wide range of ammunition and is capable of feeding hollow points without effort. But it is a better choice for a professional or experienced user than for a beginner, and anyone who has trouble working an auto slide will have trouble with this one.

For years, for self-defence in parts of the world where carry guns are legal, one of us has worn a Smith & Wesson 6906, loaded with CorBon, and swears by the combination; the other is deeply fond of his Browning GP35A, which he has packed with a similar load for

even longer. But even we are casting disloyal and covetous eyes upon the Kahr. As a choice for back-up or concealed carriage, we predict that the Kahr K9 will be up front among the fighting handguns of the twenty-first century.

Packing a Revolver

In revolvers, we found that the Colt Detective Special was easy to conceal, particularly under baggy clothing, and carries six rounds rather than the more usual five in snubbies. If .357 is preferred, the Ruger SP101 five-shot is the natural choice, but not on the ankle, where we would use a Smith & Wesson 640 Centennial airweight. One of us found the Ruger unforgiving and uncomfortable with hot loads and prefers his veteran, slick-triggered and discreet .38 S&W Model 10 snubby, loaded with 158-grain Federal hollow-points. That is not said to advertise the brand of ammunition, but to make the point that all pistols have individual idiosyncrasies. It really is worth spending time to track down the most suitable round for one's own piece. The military and the police do not have that luxury, but the private citizen does, and it is one's own life that one is defending.

Of course, any of these pistols or revolvers will slip easily into a fanny pack dedicated for the carriage of a firearm. Choose one that has the clip at the front next to the pack rather than at the back, where it is vulnerable to being undone by someone else. The last we heard from Arizona is that a fanny pack designed for a firearm amounts to open carry there and is thus legal.

When travelling, it is a good idea to think about where to keep one's firearm overnight. To have it accessible in a motel room it needs to be nearby, but it should not be put under the pillow—it is too easy to leave behind. Rhodesia (now Zimbabwe) passed a law making hotel guests check their firearms in on arrival, as so many were getting left behind under pillows during the terrorism era there.

The place to keep a pistol overnight is in one's shoe, next to the bed. We have left a few places in a hurry, and have both had to jump from ladies' bedroom windows on several occasions—once with the lady—but we have never been in such a hurry that we left anywhere without our shoes. When a warm foot touches the cold metal of a handgun, one remembers to take the weapon.

A Few Last Thoughts

The divergence in the market that we have addressed here, with the military going for auto pistols and the police using revolvers, has left civilians wondering whom to follow. In general, civilians want either smallish firearms for concealed portability, or reliable, impressive pieces to catch an intruder's attention. On the range they want reliability and accuracy as well as comfortable all-day shooting and out in the woods they want a guaranteed one-shot

stop on anything with teeth and an attitude that might want to spoil their day. And that, pretty much, is what the military and the police want as well. But they get one gun each, on issue. Civilians have something called 'disposable income', and gunmakers know that.

The gun trade considered various choices that would fill all the requirements of the civilian market before opting for the obvious, which was selling citizens as many guns as possible, one for each job. Gun buffs now find themselves with large collections of firearms and a good reason for having each one. In Britain one needs to give the police a good reason to keep each gun on a licence. In the rest of the world, a good reason for each one is still needed, especially if one is married: the reason for buying a gun may not have to be explained to the police, but it may be to one's spouse.

Whatever one's needs or interests, there is a greater choice in handguns today than ever before. Given the variety of the human frame and the range of available ammunition for most handgun calibres, there is a pistol out there for everyone—although, vivid as our imaginations are, we still cannot picture the person for whom the Dardick was ever a godsend. Such a wilfully eccentric piece shows how the best handgun designers have wrought astonishing changes and refinements within surprisingly narrow ergonomic and technological limits. And common to all modern handguns is one thing that has yet to be improved upon from basic principles—the centrefire cartridge. Centrefire-cartridge fighting handguns look as if they are here to stay for the foreseeable future. And even if someone comes up with an innovation to eclipse the current market completely, it would be five to ten decades before the current arsenal of fighting handguns was consigned to history.

Appendices

Appendix I. Proof Marks

Firearms manufacturers test their products at the factory to ensure that they are properly made, satisfactorily set up and ready for the customer to use before they release them for sale. Every manufacturer in the world does the same; nobody wants a firearm to be rejected by someone who has paid for it, and no manufacturer wants to have to re-work something that should have been done properly in the first place.

In the United Kingdom, firearms have to be submitted to a proof test before sale. That test originated in 1637, when the Gunmakers' Company of London was formed by Royal Charter. The purpose of the company was to provide the public with a guarantee that firearms were safe to use. Proof became compulsory in 1813, and an additional proof house was established in Birmingham by the gun trade, a large proportion of which was based there, in a much tighter space than the American gun trade spread along the Connecticut Valley.

In 1980 an international Proof Commission (the CIP) was set up. The United Kingdom recognizes the proof marks of all the other member nations, who in turn recognize British proof marks. America and Israel are two examples of countries that have never taken part in the proof-testing of firearms by somebody independent of the manufacturer, so guns made in those countries and imported into Europe have to be proofed before sale.

Proof marks can tell us a little about the route by which a firearm reaches us. For example, IMI rifles, pistols and sub-machine guns used to be imported from Israel by a London company and proofed on importation in London. A number of Uzis were acquired by an offshore dealer who had them proofed in Birmingham for sale in the UK. In the 1990s Israel set up its own distribution companies in Europe, with a headquarters in Belgium, after which Uzi and Desert Eagles were sent to Belgium first, proofed at Liége and then sent on to the UK. Since each proof house uses different marks, the marks visible on the gun can help with what the source was.

The proof test amounts to each barrel or cylinder being fired once with a load that is 30 per cent hotter than the standard service pressure load for which the firearm is intended. The firearm is then marked with the proof house stamp which shows which house conducted the test, but not in which year.

The British proof marks have changed occasionally (in 1904, 1925 and 1954, for example). By looking at the marks we can see within which period a gun was proofed—and find some surprises as a result! We had a Cape rifle in from South Africa, a double-barrelled side-by-side weapon, with one barrel rifled and chambered for a military rifle round and the other barrel smoothbored and chambered for a conventional shotgun cartridge. It is a sort of compromise gun: there is no need to have two guns, and one is always ready to deal with a lion or a Zulu with the left barrel and a snake or a bird with the right. The one we had was chambered in the left barrel for the .577/.450 round of the Martini Henry rifle, Britain's service rifle from 1872 to 1888. We speculated that the gun might be an antique, but the proof marks showed that it was nitro proofed and marked with the stamp used between 1925 and 1954. The South Africans were a conservative lot, and stuck to large, slow-moving ammunition long after the British Army had dropped it in favour of the .303in. The Boers knew what would stop a lion, a rhino or a hostile native and thought that the small, pointed, fast moving .303 was not it.

Firearms, once proofed, seem to stay in proof for ever unless the barrel bulges or splits. The rules for shotguns are more complicated, and reflect the fact that the gun trade tended to polish the bores when servicing shotguns. That removed small pits and blemishes but gradually wore the bores out, so the rules include a measurement inside the bore, 9in from the breech face.

When the bores become oversized, which is because of this polishing rather than from use, the gun is deemed to be out of proof and can only be sold after the barrels have been cut to show that it is not safe for use. Most worn-out shotguns belong to the black powder era. The barrels are usually still thick enough to shoot safely with black powder ammunition. When in doubt, they are still fun and safe to use with adaptors as .410 shotguns or .357 rifles.

Appendix II. Fully Automatic Pistols

Sir Hiram Maxim (1840–1916) developed a machine gun prototype in 1884, and went into production with a revised version the following year. We regard this as the first machine gun because it used the recoil from the cartridge detonating to cycle the action, unlike the earlier Gatling gun. That, in effect, was a series of single-shot weapons operating in harmony around a single axis. Maxim's weapon used a hinged breech block that worked quite like that on the Luger pistol, locked straight for firing and breaking at the elbow to cycle another round.

Once Maxim had established the principle of using recoil to reload the firearm automatically, others followed. Semi-automatic handguns came a decade later, when smokeless powders enabled the ammunition to be scaled down; and it was inevitable that, sooner or later, someone would want a miniature machine gun. Mauser gave their C/96 design a new lease of life with the *Schnellfeuer* variant— a fully automatic Broomhandle pistol with (on later models) a twenty-shot box magazine.

Fully automatic handguns are notoriously difficult to control, especially in short bursts. We tried a full-auto Browning Hi-Power with a twenty-shot magazine, and that was like controlling a full-pressure fire hose. Once you get over the initial shock it is possible to keep the rest of the string on target. That is no good in a gunfight, however, where short bursts are what is wanted.

John Thompson (1860–1940) addressed that issue simply by making the pistol big enough to be controllable. Having retired from the US Army, he was working on an automatic rifle when he was recalled to the colours for the Great War. He left a design team working on the problem, and they found that, while they could not get John Blish's patent retarded-blowback lock to operate with rifle ammunition, the system worked quite well with the .45 ACP.

The blowback principle used in fully automatic weapons is the same as that in small pistols, except that in most cases the sub-machine gun bolt locks open against the trigger. When fired the whole bolt slams forward, stripping a round from the magazine on the way, and chambers it and fires it as part of the same forward stroke. The blowback then sends the bolt back against its return spring, dumping the empty case on the way. If the trigger is still held back, there is nothing to hold the bolt so it flies forward again and continues the firing and extracting cycle until either the ammunition runs out or the trigger is released.

Sweeping Up Afterwards

Thompson went for a pistol design, which he waggishly called the Trench Broom—a two-handled, fully automatic pistol, which appeared as the Model 21—some three years after the Armistice had cleared the trenches. The weapon had arrived in time for the 1920s to roar with it. Thompson promoted it as a police weapon, but the majority of the take-up was by civilians, some of whom were engaged in bootlegging and other illicit activities.

Later models were fitted with a detachable shoulder stock, and other modifications to aid manufacture followed. The US Marine Corps bought some, but it was the Second World War that put this sub-machine gun on the military map with early models bought by Britain and the later M1 and M1A1 variants widely issued to US formations.

We tried a 1921 Thompson carried by the Police Chief in Grantham, New Hampshire—a man with good taste in firearms if a bit classic for some. The slow rate of fire was a novelty, but it made signing one's name in the targets that much easier!

In the 1960s a closed-bolt variant was developed and this is still manufactured by Auto Ordnance as a pistol. A carbine version is also made to comply with US law for sale as a rifle, having a 16in barrel and a fixed stock. These weapons became subject to British law in an interesting way while we were working on this book. Under British law, semi-automatic rifles, other than those chambered for .22 rimfire, cannot be possessed by civilians.

Quite a few civilians have the Auto Ordnance .45 pistol, which is manufactured and sold in the United States as a pistol; in the United

Right: Beretta Model 1950 full-auto variant. The problem is still the limited magazine capacity. Nothing full auto has really succeeded with less than 32 rounds in the clip

Kingdom, however, prosecutors are claiming that the Americans do not know their own product, and while they may think it is a pistol, it is, so the argument goes, actually a carbine—and in British law 'rifle includes carbine'. The fact that Auto Ordnance make a different weapon and call it a carbine is regarded as beside the point.

Although fun to shoot, the Auto Ordnance is large and, in semi-automatic only, much more enjoyable with a shoulder stock fitted. Other manufacturers have found ways of shortening their machine pistols, the first of which was designed by Major Uziel Galil in Israel. What he did was keep the bolt as long and heavy as in a conventional sub-machine gun, but set the breech face half way back along the length of the bolt, so the bolt effectively wraps around the barrel at the moment of firing. This shortened the overall length of the weapon, as much of the barrel is inside the receiver instead of protruding in front. The Uzi sub-machine gun had an overall length of

just 17in, and the later Micro brought the concept down to pistol size.

The Micro Uzi and associated pistols present themselves as squarish lumps, which are difficult to carry without the dedicated shoulder rig. But the pistol shoots quite well—accurately enough for combat/practical shooting, if lacking the precision of a UIT piece—and does it with 20- or 32-round magazines. The Micro was difficult to control, and not just because of its top-heavy balance, which makes it very hard to shoot predictably with one hand. We were taught to set selective-fire weapons to full auto, then practise working the trigger for single shots: that saves having to look for the selector in an emergency and deals with the

Below: Czech VZ63 Scorpion. It has been said that a camel is a horse designed by a committee. The Scorpion bears evidence of the same thinking: it has a shoulder stock so that it can be a carbine and full-auto capability so that it can be a machine gun, and it is small enough to be a pistol as well.

fact that a lot of sub-machine guns do not have a 'semi' option anyway.

The British Sten gun was one such—full auto or nothing—so we had to learn to control the trigger for aimed shots. Its successor, the Sterling, had a selector that was also the safety catch—one click forwards for semi, two clicks for full auto. In practice, setting it to full auto and squeezing off single shots was simple enough, but when we tried this on the Micro Uzi we found that we could not get singles off at all. Three to five at a touch seemed to be the best we could do.

The Micro has a very high rate of fire, in the region of 1,100 a minute. The Ingram Mac 10 had a similar reputation, but the British-made ones seemed much easier to control and to get single rounds out of than the Uzi. Perhaps it was just luck. We do not practice much now, as we do not have a benevolent employer buying the ammunition for us.

The SF Mac 10 9mm Pistol
The original Mac 10 became a Hollywood legend without ever being 'combat proven'. John Wayne picked one up in a gun store in his 1974 feature film *McQ*, squeezed off the 32 rounds in a second and a half and carried the gun off to beat the baddies and kiss the girl (or was it the horse?). Anyway, the Mac 10 quickly established itself in Hollywood feature-film fantasy as one of the most recognisable rapid-fire weapons to grace the hands of both goodies and baddies.

The Ingram company's first production Mac was their Model 6, which is essentially a 9mm clone of Auto Ordnance's Tommy gun, and as such was competing with the Spitfire (another 9mm Tommy gun) for American police sales at a time when the world was awash with military-surplus sub-machine guns from the Second World War. Ingram made both the 9mm 'Mac 10' and a 'Mac 11' in .380, the latter being available in semi-automatic versions only.

Unfortunately, in a world full of bureaucrats, the Ingram could not survive, as the market for full-auto weaponry is kept too small for much of a living to be made from their manufacture. However, its mark was made, and the sincerest form of flattery is imitation. Next on the scene was RPB of Georgia, who manufactured a semi-automatic Mac 10, a full-auto version, and a .380 model. This company's products achieved quite reasonable sales, and remained in production for most of the 1980s.

Firing From an Open Bolt
All the Mac 10s were blowback-operated. Blowback firearms are generally those with lower-powered ammunition—.22 rimfire (5.5mm), .25 ACP (6.35mm), .32 ACP (7.65mm) and .380 (9mm Short). The more powerful cartridges, such as 9mm Parabellum and .45 ACP, are usually chambered in recoil-operated firearms. However, the 'open bolt' system was devised to enable the more powerful cartridges to be married up to a simple blowback mechanism. Problems of safety did not arise, for two reasons: the bolt is much heavier than a pistol slide, and the cartridge is detonated before the case is fully chambered.

The firing sequence starts with the magazine loaded, and the bolt pulled back until it locks open against the trigger sear. When the trigger is pulled, the bolt flies forward, pushing a round from the magazine in front of it. As the round chambers, friction slows it down enough for the fixed firing pin to drive into the primer. The detonation cushions the bolt's forward travel, then the increased pressure drives the bolt back until it catches on to the trigger sear again. This system is not self-loading; it is really best described as self-cocking. As such, it does not appear to be subject to Section 5 (as amended) of the Firearms Act, 1968.

Most open-bolt blowbacks are sub-machine guns, and semi-automatic versions are simply downgraded full autos. However, the semi-automatic version of RPB's Mac 10 was manufactured as a dedicated, self-cocking, semi-automatic pistol and marketed as such. The British-made Mac 10 modified the lower re-

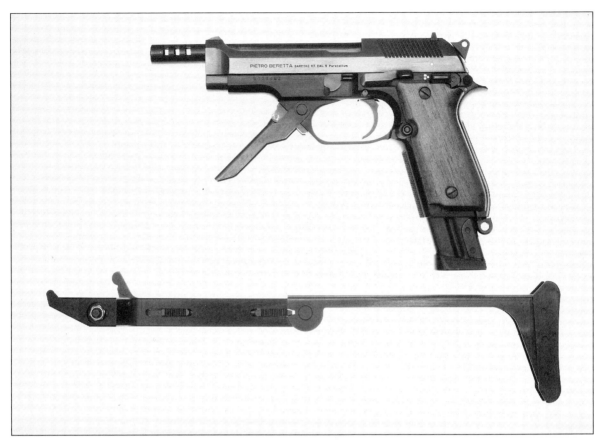

Above: Beretta 93R—not full auto, but with a three-shot burst facility. Magazine capacity is 20 rounds, enough for only seven bursts, but the weapon is controllable enough to use the bursts to good effect. Two-shot bursts would have made better use of the limited ammunition available.

ceiver configuration slightly, so that it could use standard Uzi magazines. The original Mac 10 had its own magazine, and the problem with having a unique design is that it makes it that much more difficult for customers to get spares.

Another concession was the stock: early models had a solid injection-moulded stock, while the more recent examples have a wire stock like the earlier American ones. The pre-production model we first tested was an open-bolt, self-cocking pistol. It operated with Uzi magazines and any old 9mm ammunition, and it had an optional shoulder stock fitted to the rear of the receiver via a dovetail bracket. The

barrel was threaded, faithful to the original, for a sound moderator. The cocking bolt could be turned through 90 degrees to lock the bolt shut (as a safety feature) and, when so locked, the bolt obstructed the line of view through the rudimentary sights. There was a safety catch on the lower receiver just forward of the trigger.

The height of the barrel within the receiver had to be modified, then the chambering was altered slightly, and finally the finish was changed, before production began in November 1991. The superior finish on the new pistol was immediately apparent, and survived our stringent septic tank storage and dishwasher gun-finish tests.

So, what does one do with a short, squarish, 9mm open-bolt self-cocking pistol and shoulder stock? The answer is have fun with it, unless one is in the bodyguarding or house-clearance trades. It is not a precision target pistol, and in professional hands it would be at best an area weapon for suppressive fire, not a piece for a one-shot stop; and then it would be fully automatic. The sights are basic, so one can expect to see Mac 10s in civilian hands with all manner of optical, laser, red dot and flashlight sights—anything but the originals, which are simply there to help the user work out which way round it is in the dark.

On initial accuracy tests we did not fare very well, even with the stock fitted. The problem was the trigger, which took 24lb of pressure to move it. After consulting the manufacturers, we touched the bolt up with a grinding wheel until the trigger pressure was down to a respectable 4lb; then the groups tightened up. Even then, it has to be said, our off-hand groups with a Beretta 92FS were usually better even when blindfolded.

Being a stocked pistol, the first thing one notices when shouldering it is the absence of a fore end. The spare arm really is spare, so one has to choose between wrapping it around the other hand, which is conventional for pistol shooting, or else clutching on to the front of the receiver, which puts the hand rather close to the muzzle. At this point, the sound moderator can come to the rescue, as it screws on to the front and makes a handy place to put the other hand. The moderator we had on test was heavy, and altered the balance of the pistol on the shoulder. With the moderator but not the stock fitted, it was too heavy to shoot off-hand, unless using a handy thumbstick or fence post as an accessory.

British-made Mac 10 pistols were essentially the prototypes for a selective fire production series. These performed much better in our tests than the semi-automatic models. We learned how to fire sensible bursts well before the first magazine was empty. The striking thing was the recoil—it came in a straight line back into the shoulder, without the rising muzzle or wave-form reaction of other such weapons we have fired. The weapon stayed

where we pointed it, and the result was a series of impressively tight, evenly spread groups. Truly 'machine pistols' instead of submachine guns, these portable automatic weapons started out as novelties but are now serious contenders for some markets in close protection.

Both the Mac 10 and the Uzi pistol are essentially semi-automatic versions of sub-machine guns. British law is clueless as to how to classify them. A Home Office minister once told us that they should be banned because they are ugly—which sums up the level of wherewithal that British politicians bring to firearms issues.

The Burst-Fire Beretta

Much more of a pistol was the Beretta 93R. This sturdy, twenty-shot, 9mm, locked-breech pistol came with a change lever that gave a three-shot burst fire option. It also had a cute folding stock and a folding fore end to help with the recoil control. We found these pistols a challenge to shoot well in the burst-fire mode and thought that a two-shot burst facility might be better.

The reason burst-fire weapons are usually set for three shots is a matter of ballistics. The first and second shot usually strike quite close together, with the third drifting off in the direction of the muzzle climb. This last 'random' shot might hit a target that has moved since it had a bead taken on it, or hit something else entirely, or nothing at all; it is rather like shooting one for luck. A two-shot burst configuration would give ten bursts per magazine from the Beretta and fewer wide shots.

The other three-shot, burst-fire pistol we used was the Heckler & Koch VP70. This otherwise ugly piece of work had a solid detachable stock on which the change lever was located, so the pistol without its stock was semi-only anyway. This probably makes more sense than was apparent at first, as these pistols were hard enough to control in burst-fire mode as it was, with the stock attached.

Our most effective groups with the Beretta 93R were achieved by locking the end of the shoulder stock in the holster, clamping the strut to our side and then turreting from target to target, in a sort of two-handed variant of the old FBI drill. It worked well enough, although we doubted whether the Beretta 93R was a serious contender for being truly a fighting handgun. It was a bit too big for concealed carriage; but for overt use, such as by personal bodyguards, it may well come into its own.

Reasons to Stay Single

In theory, any semi-automatic pistol can be converted to full automatic. This is because, to make a pistol semi-automatic at all, the mechanism requires a disconnector in it so that retaining a grip on the trigger does not automatically rack off the rest of the magazine. There is good reason to keep most single-shot pistols that way. Small-framed pistols make unsuitable machine guns on two grounds—they are difficult to control, and they lack the magazine capacity to give more than a couple of bursts. Beretta tried an adaptation of the P51 pistol by putting a fore end on it. The Czechs, ever innovative, developed their Scorpion pistol with a folding stock. Their solution to the recoil problem was to go for smaller ammunition, chambering the Scorpion for .32 auto. Beretta's final solution was the 93R. But, really, these are oddities, neither pistol nor sub-machine gun. If a compact full-auto weapon is required, a shrunken sub-machine gun is the best option. The best of those we have tried is definitely the British-made Mac 10.

Appendix III. A Note on Ammunition

All small-arms ammunition is made to be as regular in performance as possible, each manufacturer having his own particular standards of bullet weight and powder that he uses. The service pressure of each round varies little from one manufacturer to another for standard loads; those of higher pressure are advertised as such with codings such as '+P' or '+P+' to indicate that the pressures and velocities are higher than normal.

Manufacturers in the United States will tell the customer whether the pistol is rated for the higher-pressure rounds or not; elsewhere, proof test marks on the pistol will show what service pressure the weapon has been tested to.

Older firearms may well not be able to handle modern ammunition. Black powder has a lower peak pressure than nitro, and black powder firearms are thus unsuited to nitro ammunition. This also applies to modern reproduction black powder weapons—they are not built to withstand nitro peak pressures and should not be used with any kind of nitro powder compound.

Some firearms designs are transitional. The Webley revolvers of British Army service were black powder originally, but later models were nitro-proved once the test became standard in the early twentieth century. Black powder did not fade out quickly: ammunition was still being loaded with black powder up to the Second World War, and blank ammunition still uses black powder to this day.

The older nitro rounds were not as 'pokey' as modern ammunition—9mm today is a faster, more powerful load than it was in the early years of this century. Manufacturers of ammunition target a particular market with their products. CorBon, for example, primarily make self-defence and hunting cartridges. CorBon ammunition is expensive, and has high velocity ratings. It is meant for police and armed citizens who have an occasional need of a reliable stopper, and for hunters who know that every shot must count, and kill cleanly. Such ammunition would not be used to test older guns. We found that it is still possible to shoot veteran and antique pieces with modern ammunition, as long as a suitable load is selected. In the United Kingdom, Magtech (made in Brazil) was ideal for many of the older firearms we have tested.

A lot of target-shooters hand-load their ammunition for accuracy, as do hunters. We improved on the first batch of .41AE we had to test by reloading the cases and experimenting a little, and serious .40S&W users have had to do the same thing. Hand-loading calls for diligent research and the guidance of an experienced person to start with: there are so many pitfalls for the careless.

Handload With Care

Every firearm we have seen fail was loaded with hand-made ammunition at the time. The Smith & Wesson Model 10 illustrated blew because the round was double-charged with powder and the bullet was seated too deeply in the case. We have seen a Glock 17 blow too. Most 9mm pistols are quite picky about ammunition, to the point that one gun can behave quite differently from another of the same make and model when one is shooting rounds from the same box. In this instance the owner was 'hyping' his loads, trying to maximise velocity, and he neglected to seat the bullet deeply enough in the case.

When chambered, the bullet engaged the rifling grooves rather than having the customary short distance of free bore to get going in before hitting the rifling. This increased the pressure as the bullet was reluctant to get started. As the bullet flew out of the muzzle, the back blast unlocked the pistol and blew the magazine out. The polymer frame split

where the trigger bar sits inside it. A metal frame would have contained that blast, and the only damage would have been to the magazine retaining catch.

A week later a .45 Glock blew in similar style; in this case the bullet was not crimped properly into the case, and so was rammed back into it as the round chambered. This reduced the available space in the case for the gas to expand before the bullet needed to start moving, and again gave an excess pressure that blew the gun open and wrote off the frame.

These accidents were nature's way of saying that great care has to be taken when assembling rounds oneself. The advantages of hand-loading lie with developing accuracy for a specific purpose. Some money can be saved by reloading ammunition in bulk, but that saving is actually quite minimal if the value of one's time is taken into account.

We would not seek to discourage hand-loaders from making their own ammunition, but beg to point out that simple mistakes in loading and, even more often, a failure to check the results of one's handiwork, can have expensive consequences. Nobody was injured in the three examples we mentioned, but in the .45 blowout the range officer's safety glasses were badly damaged. Ponder for a moment the consequences for both him and the shooter if he had not been wearing them.

Factory quality control is usually good, but we have found variations of up to 300ft/sec in the velocity of factory ammunition that we have chronographed. That is the inconsistency hand-loaders are usually trying to do away with. Hand target-loaders also seem to go for the minimum amount of powder in each case, to stretch their pound of propellant over more reloads. The thinking is that all the bullet has to do is travel seven, ten or maybe 25 yards in a straight line before hitting a sheet of paper. Economy is one thing; stinginess can be dangerous. Very light loads can actually create higher pressures in a gun barrel than hot ones, so care has to be taken at this extreme too.

Right: A .38 Special Model 10 revolver with oversized grips. This revolver's cylinder has been ruptured by a double-charged handloader's cartridge. By good fortune, the blast went upwards and bent the top strap without injuring the shooter or the people standing around him.

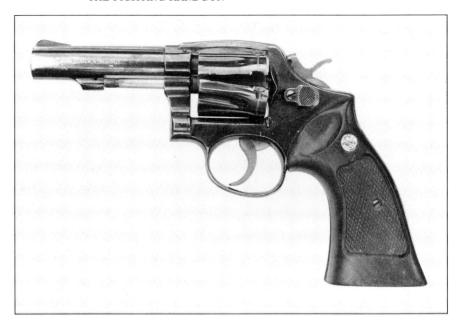

The twentieth century is full of cartridges that have been developed in unison with gun projects. Some were very successful, such as the .45 ACP; others have fallen by the wayside, such as the 9mm Browning Long, which John Moses developed to compete with the German 9mm Parabellum cartridge. Incidentally, Parabellum means 'prepare for war'; it was also the abbreviated telegraphic address of the DWM factory where Luger pistols were made.

Quite a lot of early pistols were chambered for 9mm Browning Long. They can still be used if one cares to make the ammunition oneself. In this instance it is also necessary to make the case by turning down the rim on a .38 special, cutting a groove for the extractor and shortening the case to length. Making up ammunition is worthwhile and necessary for testing the older weapons—British .455 has to be made from components made by specialists in the United Kingdom and in Italy.

Some ammunition has simply vanished. We would not care to try making 'trounds' for the Dardick, but we have made pinfire ammunition for testing the 1858 Lefaucheaux. It was fiddly, but well worth the effort, because to know what was good or bad about any particular fighting handgun we had to try it ourselves.

The Time and the Place

When one tries guns and ammunition out one can feel which would inspire confidence in men carrying them and which would be thought of as liabilities. Colt's Patterson failed partly because it was very complex to make and therefore expensive, not because it was no good. His simpler, cheaper Walker model is a milestone in history. Lefaucheaux's pinfire revolver, which gave the French Navy a six-shot, single-action, cartridge revolver fifteen years before Colt gave America the 1873 Single-Action Army, failed in the United States because of the logistical problems of getting ammunition for them and to them.

Various good firearms designs failed for the same reason. A frontiersman had to carry everything with him; but loose powder, lead and flint could work in any of his guns. He could recast lead bullets recovered after use, re-cut or sharpen his flint and, in certain circumstances, even make his own powder. Percussion caps did get accepted eventually on the frontier, as huge numbers of them took up less space than the equivalent in flints, but once they were used up, that was it—back to civilisation for more.

As civilisation crept westward across North America, cartridge weapons became more acceptable as they became available locally, which meant within a week or two's ride of where people lived or worked. In Britain and Europe, cartridges were accepted earlier because the infrastructure for making them readily available to users was in place earlier than it was in America. We cannot know, but we suspect, that cartridge weapons were probably in use earlier along the eastern seaboard of the United States than they were in the interior.

The development of self-contained ammunition continued apace through the remainder of the nineteenth century; some rounds succeeded in the market and some failed. People who used guns as tools made the final decision. This is true for all manner of products. The middle-aged reader may recall eight-track cartridges competing with audio cassettes in the pre-recorded market, or the battle between VHS and Betamax video recording systems. We all know which came out on top.

The cartridge market was the same: the cartridge always comes first, usually developed in conjunction with a firearm from the same inventor. If the gun is successful, other manufacturers wrap firearms designs around the cartridge it takes. The 9mm Parabellum made it courtesy of the Luger; the 9mm Browning Long and 9mm Glisenti did not. The Dardick tround failed to make it as well, because the first pistol designed around it failed in the market place.

Each new cartridge to hit the market has to make itself a niche to survive, or it goes the way of the Dardick 'tround'. Pinfire was successful, particularly in Europe, for more than eight decades, but is history now. The first pinfire shotguns were seen at the Great Exhibition in 1851, and Britain's cartridge company Eley finally stopped making pinfire 12-gauge cartridges in 1968.

The twentieth century has seen the development of Magnum loads, including the .22 Magnum, and new loads in 10mm and .40in for self-loading pistols, to mention just three. Some developments in firearms and ammunition have occurred for political reasons; Italians are not allowed firearms in military calibres, so they developed the 9 x 21mm round to use instead of the military 9 x 19mm Parabellum. Smith & Wesson developed that still further for their .356TS&W cartridge, so far used only for target-shooting. In Britain we have straight-pull, single-shot, centrefire rifles because we are not allowed to tap gas from the barrel and use that to cycle the action automatically, while Americans have a ten-shot limit on handgun magazines and a five-day waiting period before they can take possession of their pistols.

Index